If Ever You Go

First published in 2014 by
Dedalus Press
13 Moyclare Road
Baldoyle
Dublin 13
Ireland

www.dedaluspress.com

Introductions copyright © Pat Boran
and Gerard Smyth, respectively
Selection copyright © Dedalus Press

All poems and songs copyright their authors or other rights holders
as listed in the Acknowledgements (pages 355 to 360) which
constitute an extension of this copyright notice.

ISBN 978 1 906614 87 4 (paperback)
ISBN 978 1 906614 88 1 (casebound)

Dedalus Press titles are represented in the UK by
Central Books, 99 Wallis Road, London E9 5LN
and in North America by Syracuse University Press, Inc.,
621 Skytop Road, Suite 110, Syracuse, New York 13244.

Typeset and designed by Pat Boran
Photograph of the Ha'penny Bridge by Mariusz Tarapata
Printed in Dublin by Gemini International Ltd.

The Dedalus Press receives financial assistance from
The Arts Council / An Chomhairle Ealaíon

If Ever You Go
A Map of Dublin
in Poetry and Song

Edited by
Pat Boran
&
Gerard Smyth

DEDALUS PRESS
DUBLIN, IRELAND

Contents

CONTENTS

CONTENTS

3. SOUTHSIDE

CONTENTS

CONTENTS

❧

The Poetry of Place

PAT BORAN

PLACE, WHATEVER ELSE IT MIGHT BE, is where we live our lives. We are born, reared, educated, fall in love, marry, have children, die and are laid to rest — somewhere. And just as these interactions shape the places around us, so too do places leave their mark on us. The richness or monotony of our environment has an incalculable effect on everything from our present happiness to our future creativity, our general well-being to our ability to adapt to new experiences. A description of a place, therefore (especially one like this by many hands) is also a portrait of the people who live there.

We might also think of place as something like the doorway to memory. We have only to revisit the old haunts — the first school we attended, the corner where the old cinema used to stand, the road where we rented that grim first flat — to be transported back there again, back *then* again, to experience the physical, even dizzying, gravity of place.

Some places hold memories that are not even our own, or not ours alone: when I first moved to Dublin from Portlaoise in the early 1980s I found it impossible not to hear on the cobbled backstreets off Thomas Street the sound of factory workers heading off on the early shift, though those streets had long been without such scenes. Something similar is experienced by many of us when, through the names memorialised on church pews, we become aware of an earlier generation of worshippers, or sitting in a favourite coffee shop or pub we find ourselves, like countless citizens before us, observing an ancient hypnotic stream of movement on the street outside.

Cities (and perhaps small cities most of all) may exert a particularly potent influence, for here such associations are layered upon or set against each other, shoulder to shoulder. This may help to explain why Dublin, a city of just over a million inhabitants, has such a formidable literary reputation, as if the proximity of voices, instead of cancelling each other out, only emphasises the importance, even the necessity, of the verbal and literary arts.

Of course it is not only the residents of a city that can be said to know it and to whom we should turn for an accurate description. Visitors too can often make a profound connection with a place, even those who pay only a short or passing visit. Where the long-term resident may fail to see the city as it actually is, as it has developed before him, the first impressions of the visitor may be startling for their unencumbered clarity and precision. The local and the new arrival may walk together side-by-side, but often they do so down very different streets.

For Patrick Kavanagh, the Co. Monaghan-born poet whose move to Dublin resulted in some of his (and the city's) most celebrated poems, poets worthy of the name had to inhabit an actual rather than a merely imagined place. Where Yeats had exhorted Irish poets to "learn your trade, / sing whatever is well made," for Kavanagh it was true connection that was paramount:

> *Irish poets open your eyes.*
> *Even Cabra can surprise;*
> *Try the dog-tracks now and then —*
> *Shelbourne Park and crooked men.*
> ('Irish Poets Open Your Eyes')

This commitment to the reality of place arguably has more to do with the influence of writing in Irish, to the tradition of *dinnseanchas* or 'place lore', and to popular song, than to anything inherent in the English language poetry tradition. Indeed, until the mid 20th century when specific details of place begin to appear more than occasionally in the poems gathered here, the majority of compelling geographical references are to be found in the song and ballad traditions. Indeed that is one of the explanations of the apparent bias towards contemporary over 'historical' writing.

Thus we must accept the absence of a number of quintessentially Dublin poets, James Clarence Mangan among them, in whose work there is little evidence of his native place. At the same time many of the poets most strongly associated with the city (Kavanagh and Brendan Kennelly among them) are among the many whose arrival here has brought something new and revitalising to the city's poetic conversation.

Of the many writers represented in *If Ever You Go,* the majority are Dublin-born; others, like myself, gravitated towards 'the big smoke' and stayed; others contribute from considerably farther afield. As someone who has now spent more than half of his life in the city, the father of two Sicilian-born sons (Dublin-Sicilians? Sicilian Dubliners?), I still feel myself to be in a kind of liminal zone. Indeed it has taken me no less than sixteen different addresses around the city to reach the point of feeling truly at home here. Then again, sometimes being neither one thing nor the other has its advantages, and the tug-of-war between strange and familiar is the animating energy of a great deal of creative endeavour.

&

For even a casual reader, there can be something thrilling about encountering a known place in verse, a sense that it is somehow preserved and, at the same time, held under a revealing spotlight. Austin Clarke (1896–1974) in his semi-autobiographical long poem 'Mnemosyne Lay in Dust' begins with a pen-portrait of the house he grew up in (83 Manor Street, Dublin 7);

> *Past the house where he was got*
> *In darkness, terrace, provision shop,*
> *Wing-hidden convent opposite ...*

Katharine Tynan (1859–1931), meanwhile, describes her home in Clondalkin as "My cottage at the country's edge", a reminder that the city wasn't always as expansive as it is today. While Anthony Cronin (b. 1928), among others, provides a warts-and-all sketch (from a longer sonnet sequence) of his own one-time place of residence, in Stella Gardens, Irishtown:

> *The master bedroom measured twelve by six,*
> *The other, square but smaller had no window*

Since someone built the kitchen up against it.
The loo was out of doors. I don't complain.

Beyond these intimate depictions of the writers' place of birth or residence come the maps that reach ever farther out across the city, including those places where the significant events of their — and our — lives take place, the seismic encounters of the heart and indeed the moves and counter-moves on the national and international stage. And all of them happening not in some idealised city but in a recognisable city of streets and parks, buildings and historic landmarks, made memorable by the intensity of the writing itself.

Those sixteen addresses I mentioned earlier (Rathmines, Ranelagh, South Circular Road, York Street and now Baldoyle among them) are among the reasons I first thought of assembling a volume such as this. Certainly as I moved from place to place I was mindful of the poets and writers who had been, and sometimes still were, there before me. On moving into a bedsit on Longwood Avenue, South Circular Road, in the mid 1980s, for instance, I was only half surprised to find the Wexford-raised poet Philip Casey (at least one of whose poems I knew by heart) living in the basement flat below. And when I bumped into poet and novelist Leland Bardwell in Grogan's pub in South William Street one afternoon some years later (stood up by someone who was supposed to sub-let her place up the way) it seemed that fate had decided my next move should be into her book-strewn Bohemian flat on York Street. And out of that chance encounter came countless further encounters with poets, living and dead, whose work now broadens the scope of this volume.

It always surprises me to remember that many native Dubliners may have a narrower, if more stable, perspective on their city than do us newer arrivals. That said, the prospect of an outsider on his own producing a book like this would seem not only foolish but dangerously imbalanced. For that reason I invited poet Gerard Smyth, a native Dubliner and until recently Managing Editor of *The Irish Times* (now also the Chair of Poetry Ireland) to join me in gathering a range of work that might reflect the breadth of city life and experience.

The results have surprised us both. Readers will note that contributors to this book include many of the best known names in Irish writing, among them Swift, Joyce, Yeats, Beckett, Ó Direáin and Patrick Kavanagh, from whom we borrow our title. They include contemporary figures such as Seamus Heaney, Eavan Boland and Thomas Kinsella, Nuala Ní Dhomhnaill, Paula Meehan and Dermot Bolger, as well as a significant number of mid-career and up-and-coming writers who have joined the poetic dialogue of our capital city. Alongside them we have included a sampling of work by a number of illustrious visitors.

Something that will be immediately noticed by many is the remarkable intersection of poetry and politics, with work from Pearse and McDonagh, Robert Emmet and Arthur Griffith, among the patriots, while contributions by Rudyard Kipling and Samuel Ferguson, to name but two, offer a somewhat alternative view of the city's colonial past.

Though aiming at an English language readership, we have tried too to include at least some flavour of the wealth of Irish language writing that flourishes in the city. Indeed the oldest piece here, 'Moladh Bhinn Eádair' / 'In Praise of Howth Head', dating back to the 12th century, exhibits such a deft command of poetic technique that we had to commission a translation (from the ever-obliging Paddy Bushe) so that those with even a little Irish might brave its exuberant word maze.

On that point, believing himself to be invisible to English language readers, the poet Máirtín Ó Direáin in living memory could write: "Ní foláir nó is taibhse mé / I meabhair an tsóirt sin cheana" ("I'm surely already a ghost / To those of that mind"). Yet it is true that initiatives such as the annual Imram Irish Language Literature Festival do a great deal to develop the audience for Irish language writing in the city. Perhaps we will yet see a companion volume exploring this rich, complementary tradition.

☙

Before Dublin was the Liffey. Taking the river as the historic centre, therefore, and moving outwards from it, the poems and songs that follow are presented in three general sections,

Liffeyside, The Northside and The Southside. Though often earthed in a single location, many of the texts make reference to multiple sites around the city; for this reason it is not possible, or perhaps desirable, to adhere to a rigidly geographical sequencing. (Readers wishing to locate specific locations will find the Index of Place Names of some help in this respect.)

In the main, reference to place in the texts is explicit. In a small few instances where we were aware of the location of a piece (though the text did not state it as such) we allowed ourselves to locate it within a general area, confident that the reader would discern the connection. In these instances we felt it would be intrusive to add a specific reference to the index which therefore should be seen as a starting point rather than as the last word on the relevance of place in the texts.

The majority of poetry and verse anthologies perhaps for good reason present their contents in chronological order, allowing the reader to follow the development of the art form over a historical period. From the outset we wanted to do something different, juxtaposing, for example, an 18th century poem with a contemporary piece in order to allow the texts to speak or sing to each other across the years — as indeed they might do at any real gathering of poets or singers across the city.

The resulting street-by-street 'map' has a number of what might be termed busy intersections. As well as the expected 'popular' locations such as O'Connell Bridge and Street, St Stephen's Green, the Phoenix Park, etc, there are numerous references, for instance, to the south inner city. One explanation, of course, is that this is among the oldest and longest continually inhabited parts of the city, with layer upon layer of historical resonance associated with it. The original Viking settlement was here; and for most of the city's history this was the centre of trade and public administration.

In short it must be admitted that, wherever one lives or visits (the historical quarter, or the wider suburban zone that is now home to the majority of citizens) the city centre retains a particular significance. Whether for socialising or shopping, or for the milestone events of births, deaths and marriage, though increasingly challenged by suburban development the attraction of the centre city should not be underestimated. 'Town', as most Dubliners refer to it, is still a place of deep psychic significance and attraction. That many citizens had their first dates, drinks, concerts or any of a dozen other firsts within the 'eye' of the canals gives the area a weight of significance far beyond its size. And for tourists, there is no doubt that the cluster of Temple Bar, the Spire and the buxom statue of Molly Malone is the Dublin they've travelled to see — even if the smart ones eventually find their way out to the marvels of Howth or Bull Island, Killiney Hill or Marlay Park.

However we tend to view it, it is certainly true that Dublin is a living and evolving city. In attempting to 'map' it like this, we are aware that even our best efforts will soon be in need of updating and revision. Indeed, one of our hopes for *If Ever You Go* is that it will, in time, gather ever more poems and songs around itself, expanding that sense of the open, welcoming conversation. Some of new voices will be celebratory, singing the continuing appeal of Dublin's fair city; others will be critical. Others again, in line with an already strong tradition, will be both at once, expressing affection and perhaps even love for these streets broad and narrow, but far from blind to their disappointments or deaf to their reproach.

A small number of 'enabling' translations aside, no new work was commissioned for this book, and with few exceptions the majority of the pieces gathered here have been previously published elsewhere over the years. In a few instances, copyright restrictions meant we were unable to include the lyrics of, for example, some well-known Dublin songs; fortunately these can readily be found online, and legions of fine Dublin singers continue to air them on a regular basis for all to enjoy.

If, as we do, the reader regrets such absences (or indeed the absence of a beloved location for which, on this occasion, we failed to find a suitable song or verse), we can only hope that this gathering may yet inspire new songs and poems to add further detail to the ever-evolving map of Dublin as a place where — spread the word — poetry matters.

The Heart of the City

GERARD SMYTH

MENTION "PLACE IN IRISH POETRY" and what immediately comes to mind is the bucolic, the pastoral, the rural — Yeats's Sligo, Kavanagh's Monaghan, Heaney's County Derry. The cityscape took some time to be admitted as a subject; the idealised Ireland was elsewhere, beyond the Pale – in the green pastures, on the hills and bogs, by the lakes and on the shores, especially our Western shores.

But the city, and in particular Dublin, has well and truly entered the imaginative space of the poet, finding particular expression in the work of contemporary writers, as this anthology demonstrates. Of course the city was present, if perhaps randomly, since before the time of Swift, but perhaps the mid-20th century publication of Austin Clarke's *Ancient Lights* marks the moment when urban consciousness began to assert its place in the tradition. And it wasn't only the Dublin-born poets like Clarke, Thomas Kinsella and Eavan Boland who took to this new territory.

In an early poem of his, Kavanagh tells us that he knew "nothing about cities". Yet after years living in Dublin the Monaghan poet was capable of creating a powerful sense of the city in his Canal Bank sonnets and in the evocatively haunting 'On Raglan Road', a magnificent love poem but also an homage to the place of its title which has the effect of making even those who have never been there feel as if they know it intimately.

Like Kavanagh, each one of the many poets we have gathered here renders his or her own distinctive sense of place. The anthology is one of multiple perspectives: there are many Dublins in these poems, a city of different strokes for different poets. The mood music of the city that each poet hears and conveys is strikingly different from poet to poet, poem to poem.

After the American poet John Berryman arrived in the city in the 1960s, he wrote to his mother that he was "determined that Dublin shall be fascinating and I shall set out about time to prove it". From its inner city streets out to its outermost suburban edges, Dublin's fascinations have permeated the work of many poets — among the more obvious examples are poets whose work intimately engages with the city: Clarke, Kavanagh, Kinsella, Paula Meehan, Peter Sirr, Harry Clifton, Dermot Bolger and Eavan Boland. These and other poets have between them charted the map that is 'Dublin in verse' and, in doing so, have universalised the local. All of them are a part of Dublin's story "and its outcome / And ready to record its contradictions", as Boland says in one poem.

In these poems and songs we are presented with a sense of some of those contradictions, but above all we have the city as muse, as the consecrated ground and sustenance of the imagination. This is not a collection devoted only to loving portraits or of poets in rapture to the places they behold. Louis MacNeice notes its "seedy elegance", the "Grey stone, grey water,/ And brick upon grey brick", but also "A dance of light in the Liffey". The river's "stinking tide" didn't go unnoticed by Jonathan Swift. Thomas Kinsella has called it "the umpteenth city of confusion" ('Phoenix Park'); but also acknowledged when receiving his "Freedom of the City" that "Dublin gave many important things their first shape and content for me. I learned to look at the world through the rich reality of the inner city."

That "rich reality" is brought to life by poets born in the city, those who came to live in it from other parts of our island and outsiders who have merely passed through it. Here we have the city in which the "aspidistra grows dusty behind the window pane", and in which one poet sees "St Valentine's stubborn heart come floating from Whitefriar Street" and another is aware that

> A million citizens worked, ate meals
> Or dreamt a moment of Joyce.

My Dublin — the city's historic heartland in The Liberties — was gifted to me, not just as a consequence of it being my place of birth and upbringing but as a result of Joycean moments that had much to do with my father's adherence to routine: his

Sunday morning ramble on which I had to accompany him for most of my formative years.

An archetypal and proud Dubliner, he was also a taciturn man of his generation: these were walks of silence; there was little else for the young flâneur at his side to do but become an observer, learn to see his Dublin streets in shifting perspectives. I encountered my city and mapped my first defining landmarks on those saunters and for that I am grateful.

My Sabbath stroll passed through "the malt and barley district"; and my Sabbath soundtrack came from the bells of St Patrick's, Christ Church and Pugin's magnificent steeple in Thomas Street — a street about which a contributor to *The Christian Examiner* in the 1820s wrote: "Here flock the ballad-singers, the news-vendors, and the story-tellers." When I first opened Kinsella's *Downstream* and discovered 'Dick King' I instantly recognised and felt at home in the scene with its

....rain on the cobbles
Ripples in the iron trough, and the horses' dipped
Faces under the Fountain in James's Street

The city that became a fascination was one shifting between the two halves of a century, from the era of Joyce into a modern age — a place that seemed malleable and which the imagination could seize and recreate. In retrospect I could say that the city took possession of me, and in poems written later in adult life, I sought to take possession of it.

The city stroller that I became on those childhood peregrinations has retraced his own footsteps many times since. Kerryman Brendan Kennelly, for whom Dublin is settled ground and who knows its streets intimately, has said that to "stroll through Dublin is to stroll through history ... more a stage than a city".

What is evident among the poets who have located poems in the capital is how the city acts as a storehouse of personal and social memory. The evocative and associative power of place names — Fumbally Lane, Pigeon House, Blackpitts, Bully's Acre — can exert a compelling spell. For many of us they are weighted with memory, like the "known landscape" that was to Tennyson "an old friend that continually talks to me of my own youth and half-forgotten things".

Kavangh perhaps exemplifies the kind of clear-eyed perspective the poet as non-local can bring to a place, and in his case his city surroundings gave him what Seamus Heaney called his "rebirth".

It has been suggested elsewhere that there is no paean to Dublin to match, say, Wordsworth's 'Lines Composed Upon Westminster Bridge' — readers of this anthology might now make their own judgement on that assertion. While the majority of poems here come from contemporary voices, Dublin has long been the nurturing ground for songs of the city — a tradition that dates from the time of Zozimus (Michael J Moran) when ballad sheets were popular up to the more recent era of Bagatelle's 'Summer in Dublin', which we have included as an example of the continuity of that tradition. No poem comes anywhere close to the old favourite, 'Dublin Jack of All Trades', for inclusiveness in its embrace of almost the entire topography of Old Dublin.

In setting out to find poems of the city, we came upon many surprises. We could have produced individual anthologies based on several particular locations that have attracted the attention of many poets and inspired more than a few poems: the Liffey, Grafton Street and the GPO are just a few examples of Dublin landmarks that seem to have some magnetic quality for poets.

There are poets closely associated with the city who wrote nothing about it, or for whom it was never a primary consideration. Though a true Dubliner, Mangan, for example seems to have been impervious to the streets he wandered and did not include any local references in his poems despite intimate connection to Fishamble Street where he was born in 1803 as well as having addresses that were never far from his birthplace — Chancery Street, York Street and Bride Street. While Tom Moore of Aungier Street and like Mangan a frequenter of Marsh's Library, celebrated the "Sweet Vale of Avoca" and places further afield, there is no mention of his Dublin parish in any of his melodies.

Our poet Nobel laureates Yeats and Heaney did not produce many poems of engagement with the city they inhabited or use it as a setting but what little they did write is deeply profound. Professor Terence Brown has noted, for example, that in Yeats's 'Easter 1916' (included here) Dublin stands at "the tragic centrality in the drama of a nation's generation". While Yeats's concerns are with the city's role in history and its monuments to the actors in history, the city's fabric gets the merest glance. In his address to the ghost of Parnell, 'To A Shade', Dublin is the town where "grey gulls flit instead of men/ And the gaunt houses put on majesty".

In Heaney's instance, he strikes a Joycean note in 'The Strand', and in his only extended Dublin-centred poem, 'Viking Dublin: Trial Pieces', the treatment is an excavation of the city's ancient roots. We are delighted also to include his 'Beacons at Bealtaine' and 'Dublin 4', a poem that encapsulates a familiar scene for anyone living adjacent to the DART line.

Setting out to create this anthology we had to establish at least one defining criterion — and that was that a poem should have a topographical focus or reference point. That rule has, with few exceptions, been adhered to. In some instances — or locations — there were several candidate poems to choose from, in others we had to persevere in the search for a suitable poem. There are, too, a small number of poems with no naming of place but about which we can be sure specific locations were very much in the poet's mind: Dennis O'Driscoll's 'Flatlands', for example, among the poet's contributions to the audio CD *Dublin 15: Poems of the City* (1997).

The American novelist Wallace Stegner once said that "no place is a place until it has had a poet". As this anthology shows Dublin and its places have never been in short supply of poets, and it has been enhanced by them.

1. Liffeyside

from The Mourning Muse of Thestylis

Come forth, ye Nymphes, come forth, forsake your watry
bowres,
Forsake your mossy caves, and help me to lament:
Help me to tune my dolefull notes to gurgling sound
Of Liffies tumbling streames: come, let salt teares of ours
Mix with his waters fresh. O come, let one consent
Joyne us to mourne with wailfull plaints the deadly wound
Which fatall clap hath made; decreed by higher powres;
The dreery day in which they have from us yrent
The noblest plant that might from East to West be found.

LODOWICK BRYSKETT (1547–1612 ca)

Liffeytown

Liffey, tawny and asleep in the browsing dusk,
Clings to the dark, enchanted ovals
Of the bridge.
O swan by swan my heart goes down
Through Dublin town, through Dublin town.

Single and bestowing they wander in the olive water,
Dragging a shaft of light behind them in the drowse
Of the evening.
O swan by swan my heart goes down
Through Dublin town, through Dublin town.

Ghosting shadows in the gloom of Liffeytown,
They weave their quiet spell upon the darkening
Of the river.
O swan by swan my heart goes down
Through Dublin town, through Dublin town.

EAVAN BOLAND (*b.* 1944)

from Stella at Wood Park, A House of Charles Ford, Esq., Near Dublin

The winter sky began to frown:
Poor Stella must pack off to town;
From purling streams and fountains bubbling,
To Liffey's stinking tide in Dublin:
From wholesome exercise and air
To sossing in an easy-chair:
From stomach sharp, and hearty feeding,
To piddle like a lady breeding:
From ruling there the household singly.
To be directed here by Dingley:
From every day a lordly banquet,
To half a joint, and God be thank it:
From every meal Pontac in plenty,
To half a pint one day in twenty:
From Ford attending at her call,
To visits of Archdeacon Wall:
From Ford, who thinks of nothing mean,
To the poor doings of the Dean:
From growing richer with good cheer,
To running out by starving here.
But now arrives the dismal day;
She must return to Ormond Quay.
The coachman stopt; she look'd, and swore
The rascal had mistook the door:
At coming in, you saw her stoop;
The entry brush'd against her hoop:
Each moment rising in her airs,
She curst the narrow winding stairs:
Began a thousand faults to spy;
The ceiling hardly six feet high;
The smutty wainscot full of cracks:
And half the chairs with broken backs:
Her quarter's out at Lady-day;
She vows she will no longer stay
In lodgings like a poor Grisette,

While there are houses to be let.
Howe'er, to keep her spirits up,
She sent for company to sup:
When all the while you might remark,
She strove in vain to ape Wood Park.
Two bottles call'd for, (half her store;
The cupboard could contain but four),
A supper worthy of herself,
Five nothings in five plates of delf.
Thus for a week the farce went on;
When, all her country savings gone,
She fell into her former scene,
Small beer, a herring, and the Dean.

JONATHAN SWIFT (1667–1745)

Belts

There was a row in Silver Street* that's near to Dublin Quay,
Between an Irish regiment an' English cavalree;
It started at Revelly an' it lasted on till dark:
The first man dropped at Harrison's, the last forninst the Park.

> For it was: — "Belts, belts, belts, an' that's one for you!"
> An' it was, "Belts, belts, belts, an' that's done for you!"
> O buckle an' tongue
> Was the song that we sung
> From Harrison's down to the Park!

There was a row in Silver Street — the regiments was out,
They called us "Delhi Rebels", an' we answered, "Threes about!"
That drew them like a hornets' nest — we met them good an' large,
The English at the double an' the Irish at the charge.
> Then it was: — "Belts … "

There was a row in Silver Street — an' I was in it too;
We passed the time o' day, an' then the belts went whirraru!
I misremember what occurred, but subsequint the storm
A *Freeman's Journal Supplemint* was all *my* uniform.
        O it was: — "Belts … "

There was a row in Silver Street — they sent the Polis there,
The English were too drunk to know, the Irish didn't care;
But when they grew impertinint we simultaneous rose,
Till half o' them was Liffey mud an' half was tatthered clo'es.
        For it was: — "Belts … "

There was a row in Silver Street — it might ha' raged till now,
But some one drew his side-arm clear, an' nobody knew how;
'Twas Hogan took the point an' dropped; we saw the blood run:
An' so we all was murderers that started out in fun.
        While it was: — "Belts … "

There was a row in Silver Street — but that put down the shine,
Wid each man whisperin' to his next: "'Twas never work o' mine!"
We went away like beaten dogs, an' down the street we bore him,
The poor dumb corpse that couldn't tell the boys were sorry for him.
        When it was: — "Belts … "

There was a row in Silver Street — it isn't over yet,
For half of us are under guard wid punishments to get;
'Tis all a merricle to me as in the Clink I lie:
There was a row in Silver Street — begod, I wonder why!

        But it was: — "Belts, belts, belts, an' that's one for you!"
        An' it was "Belts, belts, belts, an' that's done for you!"
        O buckle an' tongue
        Was the song that we sung
        From Harrison's down to the Park!

* *Silver Street, now Ellis Street, D7.*

RUDYARD KIPLING (1865–1936)

Liffey Bridge

I gazed along the waters at the West,
Watching the low sky colour into flame,
Until each narrowing steeple I could name
Grew dark as the far vapours, and my breast
With silence like a sorrow was possessed,
And men as moving shadows went and came;
The smoke that stained the sunset seemed like shame,
Or lust, or some great evil unexpressed.

Then with a longing for the taintless air,
I called that desolation back again,
Which reigned when Liffey's widening banks were bare:
Before Ben Edair gazed upon the Dane,
Before the Hurdle Ford, and long before
Fionn drowned the young men by its meadowy shore.

OLIVER ST JOHN GOGARTY (1878–1957)

Dublin

Grey brick upon brick,
Declamatory bronze
On sombre pedestals —
O'Connell, Grattan, Moore —
And the brewery tugs and the swans
On the balustraded stream
And the bare bones of a fanlight
Over a hungry door
And the air soft on the cheek
And porter running from the taps
With a head of yellow cream
And Nelson on his pillar
Watching his world collapse.

This never was my town,
I was not born or bred
Nor schooled here and she will not
Have me alive or dead
But yet she holds my mind
With her seedy elegance,
With her gentle veils of rain
And all her ghosts that walk
And all that hide behind
Her Georgian facades —
The catcalls and the pain,
The glamour of her squalor,
The bravado of her talk.

The lights jig in the river
With a concertina movement
And the sun comes up in the morning
Like barley-sugar on the water
And the mist on the Wicklow hills
Is close, as close
As the peasantry were to the landlord,
As the Irish to the Anglo-Irish,
As the killer is close one moment
To the man he kills,
Or as the moment itself
Is close to the next moment.

She is not an Irish town
And she is not English,
Historic with guns and vermin
And the cold renown
Of a fragment of Church latin,
Of an oratorical phrase.
But oh the days are soft,
Soft enough to forget
The lesson better learnt,
The bullet on the wet
Streets, the crooked deal,

The steel behind the laugh,
The Four Courts burnt.

Fort of the Dane,
Garrison of the Saxon,
Augustan capital
Of a Gaelic nation,
Appropriating all
The alien brought,
You give me time for thought
And by a juggler's trick
You poise the toppling hour —
O greyness run to flower,
Grey stone, grey water,
And brick upon grey brick.

LOUIS MACNEICE (1907–1963)

In the City

Gently in the night flows my river, the Liffey.
It is mine by right of love, this river always
Running, since childhood, under my feet, always
Branching along my veins — this river of birds,
Avenue of serene, Ascendancy swans,
Trail of the single gunman cormorant,
Stage of the seagulls' ballet — those faery visitors
Who cry and perch and fly, blown in the air
Like paper toys.
     Tonight there are no birds;
The thickening mist blinds me to all but light.
By day small painted boats, wings
Of coloured parrots, tighten their holding ropes
And lie beside the wall. Pale women
Hurry across the bridges, dawdle at windows,
Treasure their handbags, intend on finding bargains.

Crowds at the rush-hour of a Spring afternoon
Move in the clean patterns of thrown confetti.
                                              But now
In fog the city covers all its candour.
From windowed vehicles the light
Imprints a moving tartan on the water;
And where a street-lamp hangs a luminous triangle,
There, mirrored, a three-sided corresponding
Euclidean figure breaks the river's blackness,
Base to base applied, with lamp-post perpendicular
And tree subtending.
                    Now
Where are the seabirds? Do they fly
At day's end to the sea, to spend the night
One-legged on rock, in thought?
When, rarely, moves a patch
Of faint illumination on the darkest water,
Then are discovered small waiting forms,
Patiently floating, homeless, through the dark
They do not understand. Silence
Holds them, until daylight.

RHODA COGHILL (1903–2000)

Faoileán Drochmhúinte

Is a liacht fear is ban
In Áth Cliath cois Life,
Tuige duit a chladhaire
Féirín a scaoileadh ar fhile?

Coinnigh do phráib agat féin,
A éin an chraois bhradaigh,
Is le do mharthain arís
An file seo ná salaigh.

Leor mar léan liom
Go bhfeicim go seasta
Gur líonmhar d'ál
Ná pór ard na heala.

MÁIRTÍN Ó DIREÁIN (1910–1988)

Ill-mannered Seagull

Of all the men and women
In Dublin by the Liffey
Why, you scoundrel,
Did you bestow your gift on a poet?

Keep your filth to yourself
You voracious devious bird
And never besmear
This poet again while you live.

It's surely sad enough for me
That I steadily see
Your breed outstripping
The noble seed of the swan.

MÁIRTÍN Ó DIREÁIN (1910–1988)
Translated from the Irish by Declan Collinge

Dickey and the Yeomen

At the dirty end of Dirty Lane*,
Liv'd a dirty cobbler, Dick McClane;
His wife was, in the old king's reign,
    A stout brave orange-woman.

On Essex Bridge she strained her throat,
And six-a-penny was her note;
But Dickey wore a bran-new coat,
   He got among the yeomen.

He was a bigot, like his clan,
And in the streets he wildly sang,
O Roly, toly, roly raid,
   With his old jade.

* Now Bridgefoot Street, D8

MICHAEL J MORAN / ZOZIMUS (c. 1794–1846)

Isolde's Tower, Essex Quay
It is our fictions which make us real. — Robert Kroetsch

Is there no end
to what can be dug up
out of the mud of a riverbank,

no end
to what can be dug up
out of the floodplains of a language?

This is no more
than the sunken stump
of a watchtower on a city wall,
built long after any Isolde might have lived,
built over since a dozen times,
uncovered now in some new work —
a tower's old root in black water
behind a Dublin bus stop;

and the story is no more than a story.
Tristan drifted in here on the tide to be healed,
taken in because of his music,

and a long yarn spun on
of which they'd say —

> *Had not the lovers of whom this story tells*
> *Endured sorrow for the sake of love*
> *They would never have comforted so many.*

MOYA CANNON (*b.* 1956)

Down by the Liffeyside

'Twas down by Anna Liffey, my love and I did stray
Where in the good old slushy mud the sea gulls sport and play.
We got the whiff of ray and chips and Mary softly sighed,
"Oh John, come on for a wan and wan
Down by the Liffeyside."

Then down along by George's Street the loving pairs to view,
While Mary swanked it like a queen in a skirt of royal blue;
Her hat was lately turned and her blouse was newly dyed,
Oh you could not match her round the block,
Down by the Liffeyside

And on her old melodeon how sweetly could she play
'Good-by-ee' and 'Don't sigh-ee' and 'Rule Brittanni-ay'.
But when she turned Sinn Féiner me heart near burst with pride,
To hear her sing 'The Soldier's Song',
Down by the Liffeyside

On Sunday morning to Meath Street together we will go,
And it's up to Father Murphy we both will make our vow.
We'll join our hands in wedlock bands and we'll be soon outside
For a whole afternoon, for our honeymoon,
Down by the Liffeyside

PEADAR KEARNEY (1883–1942)

Wood Quay

We had hoped for gardens
Sloping from the cathedral
To the river
With shrubs
And flowering trees,

Pathways along the hill
Following the line
Of ancient Viking streets,
Clusters of wattle houses
Rebuilt on old foundations,

Culverts become
Streams of rushing water,
Old slipways reconstructed
On a lake,
A piece of city wall;

A house in the shrubs
Displaying delicate combs,
Toy ships, water cruses
Our fingers found,
Ornaments carved from bone.

When the concrete is poured
And all the glass
Is in place,
Dream for us sometimes
Of walking through flowers.

PÁDRAIG J. DALY (*b*. 1943)

Liffeyside Bookbarrow

Here I bought my first books
with scarce pennies.

Joe, the barrowman,
could not read:
he judged books by your looks:

the penny section for down-and-outs,
the threepenny section a halfway house,
the sixpenny and shilling sections
for the affluent literate.

One regular buyer
I came to know
bought his books by weight
to sell as pulp
when they'd accumulate.

Between Joe's Charybdis of illiteracy
and the pulper's Scylla
I had to navigate.

MICHAEL SMITH (*b.* 1942)

A Chalk Venus on Eden Quay

Amazing it's been cribbed to the least detail,
   as though the pavement's sullen *tabula*
     woke to the dream of its own Uffizi

This busker Botticelli — his velvet hat
   propped for contributions — has brought to life
     in a rainbow tour de force of softest stone.

Here, too, crowds of nymphs and tritons announce
    the arrival of the goddess on her shell
      demure as ever, a swirl of golden hair

Cascading where waves, fluid promenade,
    deliver her as from some 'forties flick
      into the splendour of a fantasy.

A million ghosts step over her like air
    who lined this river once, and did for years,
      and who long gone are buried elsewhere now.

Though beauty is also an emigré,
    a face floating dumbfounded from the source,
      until the downpour descends like a hand

That wipes the palette clean — a sand painting
    some visionary washes from his sight,
      or the earth erased in a bloom of light.

DANIEL TOBIN (*b.* 1958)

Liffey Bridge

Parade parade
The evening puts on
Her breath-stained jewels
Her shadowy past.

Trailing behind
Tired poses
How they all
Fulfil their station!
The young with masks and
The old with faces
Such an assassin
Such a world!

From the bridge they admire
Their foolish reflection
Drowning in birth,
Man's face and centuries
In rivers with stars
Fugitive wheatfields
Giving no harvest ...
Here's poulticed peace.
If dreaming of death
Unheavened could but rend them
With anger or envy!

The pigeons creak
On rusty hinges
Turn to the window
Bright with oranges
And girls the girls
The gashed fruit
Of their mouths and smiles
Cute as the rims
Of their cock-eyed hats:

In limp doorways
They try out their heaven
They grind at love
With gritted kisses
Then eyes re-opened
Behold slack flesh
Such an assassin
Such a world!

Same with all the
Young and hopeful
Any relief will
Do for a spell
Then timid masks
Live into faces
Then there is quiet
Desperation.

The houses lean
Against the wind
Won't you give over?
Say, what about
That second coming?

Deaf quay walls.
Water wears
The stone away
And out on the river
The arc-lamp rays and the
Wind weave
Try to weave
Something or other
From flight and water.

DENIS DEVLIN (1908–1959)

Ormond Quay

for Seamus Heaney

The ocean mist, amassing in April above Dublin,
moistens bricks, granite, the pitch-black of a car's
sheen. The tide-abandoned riverbed is silty, lays
bare an expanse beneath bridges, empty like an

open palm. This muddy island has known famine,
mutiny. Twenty years ago was shallow as the Liffey,
but now, waking at dawn to the groan of the lorries,
the river's high mark has once again been regained —

or surpassed. A wailing seagull flies into a breach
between warehouses. Pavements are cracked, damp.
By the tower, the bay whispers through raindrops,
branches, time. But it's not us who taught it speech.

Bronze by gold. The staircases are steep, bread bitter,
but the pay sustains. On the quay's corner you sight
the famous siren's den, fully packed, where a migrant
poet drinks to his double's reflection across the bar.

It's all the same. The brown of northern marshes; the
Ionian shore's blue towards which one wearies of rowing.
Like Circe's bed the old rumpled map is expanding:
homeless Europe buries itself in a coarse-grained sheet.

TOMAS VENCLOVA (*b.* 1937)
Translated from the Lithuanian by Ellen Hinsey

from The Return

Once more the red familiar streets
Are round me; and the Irish sky,
Filled with its myriad cloudy feats,
Bends deep above. The sea is nigh:
I fancy that its music comes
Between the triply-breasted ships,
Where Dublin quay clasps close the tide,
Palace and hovel reared beside,
And the salt wind upon my lips.

Dear City of the days long dead,
Whose hopeless Hope o'erlooks the seas,
Thy very life with Death is wed —
Where are thy dazzling pageantries?
Where is the pride that nerved thee once —
The glory of secure renown?
Thou seated here, provincialised,
Beggared and utterly despised —
Queen with rent robe and shattered crown.

JOHN FRANCIS O'DONNELL (1837–1874)

Children

Children in ill-fitting uniforms
drive adults to school, and children
argue the cost of tobacco
in the Newsagent's nearby.

You must have noticed them.

And in the mornings they rise to slaughter pigs,
cook breakfast, solve crosswords at the office ...
Or they send tiny adults into minefields,
barefoot, with pictures
of Khomeini around their necks,
their old toes searching the sand
for death.

And children queue for Bingo
on Ormond Quay, on Mary Street,
and douse their leaking take-aways with vinegar.

And children talk and smoke incessantly
in Eastern Health Board waiting rooms,
always moving one seat to the right,
someone's parents squabbling over trinkets
on the worn linoleum.

And it is always children
who will swear for their tobacco — children
with beards and varicose veins —
and children, dressed as policemen,
who pull their first corpses from the river.

And who is it who makes love in the dark
or in the light, who haunts
and who does all our dying for us,
if not children?

We leave their fingerprints
on everything we touch.

PAT BORAN (*B.* 1963)

The Twang Man

Come listen to my story
'Tis about a nice young man
When the Militia wasn't wantin'
He dealt in hawkin' twang.
He loved a lovely maiden
As fair as any midge
An' she kept a traycle depot
One side of the Carlisle Bridge.

Now another man came courtin' her
And his name was Mickey Baggs.
He was a commercial traveller
An' he dealt in bones and rags.
Well he took her out to Sandymount
For to see the waters roll
An' he stole the heart of the twang man's girl
Playin' 'Billy-in-the-bowl'.

Oh, when the twang man heard of this
He flew into a terrible rage,
And he swore be the contents of his twang cart
On him he'd have revenge.
So he stood in wait near James's Gate
Till the poor oul' Baggs came up,
With his twang knife sure he took the life
Of the poor oul' gather-'em-up.

And it's now yis have heard my story
And I hope yis'll be good men

And not go chasing the twang man's mot
Or any other oul' hen.
For she'll leave you without a brass farthing
Not even your oul' sack of rags,
And that's the end of the story
Of poor old Mickey Baggs.

ANONYMOUS (early 19th century)

Dublin Jack of All Trades

Chorus
I'm a roving Jack of many a trade
Of every trade, of all trades,
And if you wish to know my name
They call me Jack of all trades.

I am a roving sporting blade, they call me Jack of all trades
I always found my chief delight in courting pretty fair maids
For when in Dublin I arrived to try for a situation
I always heard them say it was the pride of all the nation

In Baggot Street I drove a cab and there was well required
In Francis Street had lodging beds to entertain all strangers
For Dublin is of high renown, or I am much mistaken
In Kevin Street I do declare sold butter eggs and bacon

On George's Quay I first began, I there became a porter
Me and my master soon fell out which cut my 'quaintance shorter
In Sackville Street a pastry cook, in James's Street a baker
In Cook Street I did coffins make, in Eustace Street a preacher

In Golden Lane I sold old shoes, in Meath Street was a grinder
In Barrack Street I lost my wife, and I'm glad I ne'er could find her
In Mary's Lane I've dyed old clothes of which I've often boasted
In that noted place Exchequer Street sold mutton ready roasted

In Temple Bar I dressed old hats, in Thomas Street a sawyer
In Pill Lane I sold the plate, in Green Street an honest lawyer
In Plunkett Street I sold cast clothes, in Bride's Alley a broker
In Charles Street I had a shop, sold shovel, thongs and poker

In Liffey Street had furniture, with fleas and bugs I sold it
And at the bank, a big placard, I often stood to hold it
In New Street I sold hay and straw and in Spitalfields made bacon
In Fishamble Street was at the grand old trade of basketmaking

In Summerhill a coachmaker, in Denzille Street a gilder
In Cork Street was a tanner and in Brunswick Street a builder
In High Street I sold hosiery, in Patrick Street sold all blades
So if you wish to know my name, they call me Jack of all trades

ANONYMOUS

A Closing Scene

After the Buñuel film
they walked in the half-glow of sodium light.
It wasn't Sunday but a Sunday hush followed them
through backstreets, black lanes where old trades

were at the end of their time
and a music hall entrance long ago had a sign
that read: *"No skirt-hoops and no swords.*
Standing room only for the Hallelujah Chorus."

Above the inner city steeple
the multiplying gulls were peeking
to see who was slouching down Lord Edward Street
or taking shelter behind the cathedral.

On Ormond Quay they quickened their steps,
finding their way among the shifty spectres
of Vikings and Insurrectionists —

ghosts who appeared on ground
where a treasure hunt would yield antiquities, the past
or traces of it in broken bits.

GERARD SMYTH (*b.* 1951)

House on Usher's Island
after Huston's Version of 'The Dead'

for Seamus and Marie

This is no mythical house but bricks and mortar
built to last, steps to a door that opened once
to let the river gods hear laughter, a waltz,
the fuss of hospitality, the shuffle from stair to stair.

Those who were here before are here again —
not as dinner guests, not to drink the wine
but as revenants — in from the snowy weather,
wearing the kind of clothes the last Edwardians wore.

Now and forever they are up there, gathered where
they can see as far as the housetops of Stoneybatter.
Sequestered in a place of memory,

of song and dance and doleful aria
they walk the floors, keep the table-talk going
with their badinage of argument and revelry.

GERARD SMYTH (*b.* 1951)

Aston Quay: January 2008

Look closely at this streetscape
now
to underline it

see it as it is
As it is? for now and not
for *As it is*
as when you see it in your head
Commercial icons

Burn Our Ear Off
where once
the multi-coloured rays
fanned out from *Bovril*
into the sky
above the Ballast Office

Drays and barges
and the smell and taste
of big red copper pennies
for the slot machines
in the Fun Palace

And tiny on Eden Quay
the missing Astor Cinema:

Where I saw *(He saw)*
I saw
The Wages of Fear
Ballad of a Soldier
The Cranes are Flying
Fanfan La Tulipe
Les Enfants du Paradis
Casque D'Or Golden Marie
flicker of shadows
of shadows

My breath tightens
along the river
Wind and gulls
May it not be lost
May it not be lost forever

MACDARA WOODS (*b*. 1942)

Haiku

Millennium Bridge —
behind me and before me,
cold fog

ANATOLY KUDRYAVITSKY (*b.* 1954)

Ha'penny Bridge

Collecting coppers on an Irish flag —
a spectre in a *Simpsons* sleeping bag.

PAT BORAN (*b.* 1963)

Perversion at the Winding Stair Bookshop & Café

Three floors above the Ha'penny Bridge
The wind off the Liffey howling like new religion
        through the streets
A prophet in a raincoat holds court in Russian
A jazz guitar tunes every napkin to poetry
The Dutch tourist keeps time with his pen on the ashtray
A French girl might be sketching me
I do my best to look across the room capable of something

I realise I have no favourite woman and no mother tongue

Speaking the language of short affairs and civic buildings
Proposed afternoons Che Guevara credit cards

I miss the alcoholics
The five in the morning bullshit

Thinking now of a woman's dry oligarchy
The order of her heart
The meritocracy of her sex

ALAN JUDE MOORE (*b.* 1973)

Lannaigh Faoi Dhroichead Uí Chonaill

Bhailigh dornán daoine ar Ché Éidin
Chun breathnú ar na héisc faoin droichead.
Ghabh duine beag tharstu faoina chaipín liath:
'Lannaigh!' ar sé,
'Dea-shíon ar feadh sé seachtaine.'

Agus is mar sin a bhí.
Tháinig an ghrian amach.
Shoilsigh an solas céanna
Ar Ard-Eaglais Chríost
Ar na Ceithre Cúirteanna
Ar Choláiste na Tríonóide
Ar Bhanc na hÉireann
Ar shiopa beag a bhí dúnta le cláir
Ina ngearrtaí eochracha tráth
Is ina gcuirtí faobhar ar sceana.

Chuardaigh iarsmaí Lochlannach
Is Gael
Shoilsigh ar scoileanna
Ar ospidéil, ar thábhairní is ar phríosúin,
Ar pháirceanna, ar thithe is ar an Zú:
Bhí moncaithe ann is leathadar a ngéaga roimis.

Shoilsigh an ghrian ar shráideanna
Is ar chaolsráideanna duirleogacha
Ar ghúnaí samhraidh na mban óg
Ar an Life

Is ar na héisc
Nár chorraigh ach ar éigean:
Lannaigh ar léir dóibh an todhchaí.

GABRIEL ROSENSTOCK (*b.* 1949)

Mullet Under O'Connell Bridge

A group had gathered on Eden Quay
To watch the fish under the bridge.
A little fellow with a grey cap went by.
'Mullet!' says he,
'Fine weather for six weeks.'

And so it was.
The sun came out.
The same light shone
On Christ Church Cathedral
On Trinity College
On the Bank of Ireland
On a little shop boarded up
Where once keys were cut
And knives sharpened.

It searched for the remains
Of Viking and Gael
Shone on schools
On hospitals, on taverns and prisons,
On parks and houses and on the Zoo:
Monkeys there to welcome it with open arms.

The sun beamed down on cobbled streets
And alleyways
On the summer dresses of young women
On the Liffey
And on the fish

That scarcely moved.
Mullet, vision of the future.

GABRIEL ROSENSTOCK (*b.* 1949)
Translated from the Irish by the author

After Reading JT Gilbert's 'History of Dublin'

Long have I loved the beauty of thy streets,
    Fair Dublin: long, with unavailing vows,
    Sigh'd to all guardian deities who rouse
The spirits of dead nations to new heats
Of life and triumph: — vain the fond conceits,
    Nestling like eaves-warmed doves 'neath patriot brows!
    Vain as the 'Hope', that from thy Custom-House
Looks o'er the vacant bay in vain for fleets.
    Genius alone brings back the days of yore:
Look! look, what life is in these quaint old shops —
The loneliest lanes are rattling with the roar
    Of coach and chair; fans, feathers, flambeaus, fops,
Flutter and flicker through yon open door,
    Where Handel's hand moves the great organ stops.

DENIS FLORENCE MACCARTHY (1817–1882)

New Liberty Hall

Higher than country lark
Can fly, a speck that sings,
Sixteen-floored Liberty Hall
Goes up through scaffoldings
In memory of Larkin,
Shot Connolly. With cap
On simple head, hallmark

Of sweat, new capitalists
Rent out expensive suites
Of glassier offices,
Babel'd above our streets,
The unemployed may scoff, but
Workers must skimp and scrape
To own so fine a skyscraper,
Beyond the dream of Gandon,
Shaming the Custom House
The giant crane, the gantries.
Labour is now accustomed
To higher living. Railing
Is gone that I leaned against
To watch that figure, tall and lean,
Jim Larkin shouting, railing.
Why should he give a damn
That day for English grammar,
Arm-waving, eloquent?
On top, a green pagoda
Has glorified cement,
Umbrella'd the sun. Go, da,
And shiver in your tenement.

AUSTIN CLARKE (1896–1974)

On First Looking Onto the Samuel Beckett Bridge

Some people have roses named after them,
but down where the ferry used to cross,
from Misery Hill to Guild Street,
they have built a new bridge
and are naming it after Samuel Beckett.
It might have been better
if they had brought back
the little ferry with its log
chronometer, and compass:

The *SS Samuel Beckett*
cleaving the river,
back and forth, back and forth,
over and over,
from dawn till dusk.

I would have named
a country road after him,
something steep, windblown,
a wintry track,
a wood of black crows on one side,
high stone wall on the other,
a rutted path
under a threatening sky,
leading from or towards nowhere,
nothing getting clearer,
closer, or ebbing away.
Just the leaves turning
and falling
on 'Samuel Beckett Way'.

This morning I saw the bridge
for the first time.
I wasn't discouraged.
Out of the mist
a white arc reaches into the air,
a whalebone washed in on the tide.
Beneath it,
twenty-five suspension wires hang
taut as musical strings.
From a distance it looks like
a great Irish harp lying on its side,
something Carolan might pick up
to compose a *planxty*, a tune
to the glory of the ceaseless river.

In time people moving over the bridge
will become the books, the plays.

Footfalls will be everywhere,
from a tired woman's shuffling feet
to a child's small steps;
from the two men waiting all day,
to those who *Come and Go, Ill Seen Ill Said,*
the midnight voices at *Play* recalling old love,
some remembering *Happy Days, Rockaby,*
and some *The Lost Ones,* their faces woebegone,
their eyes fixed on *Endgame, Catastrophe.*
They will live *Worstward Ho, Eh Joe*
ferrying their worries, their woes, their glad
tidings back and forth, back and forth.

TONY CURTIS (*b.* 1955)

Liffey Swim

In the dream, the Blessington Street Basin
fills with the Liffey's stout-bottle waters,
but still the swimmers come, in droves,
on the stray sovereign of an Irish summer's day.

The river courses through the city,
turning concrete roadways to canal banks
that shrug their shoulders into dark water;
a man rises, seal-like in his caul of silt, to wave.

At the sluice gate, where the river bends
out of sight between toppling buildings,
a black dog jumps, again and again, into water.

And there, at the edge of vision, my parents,
ready to join the swimmers,
gesture their cheerful farewells.

JESSICA TRAYNOR (*b.* 1984)

2. Northside

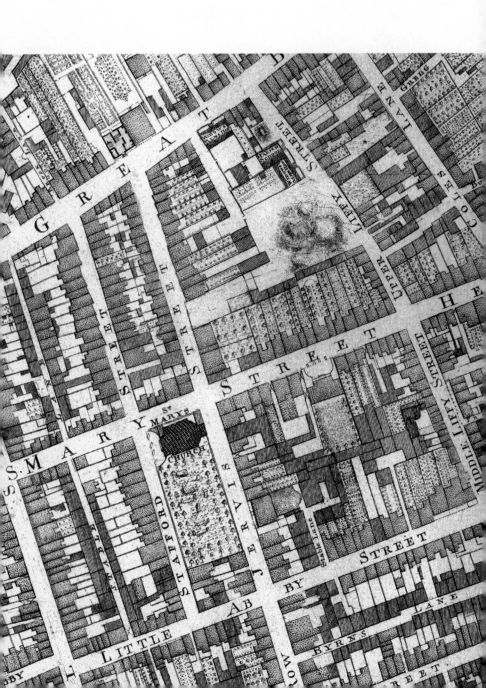

Easter 1916

I have met them at close of day
Coming with vivid faces
From counter or desk among grey
Eighteenth-century houses.
I have passed with a nod of the head
Or polite meaningless words,
Or have lingered awhile and said
Polite meaningless words,
And thought before I had done
Of a mocking tale or a gibe
To please a companion
Around the fire at the club,
Being certain that they and I
But lived where motley is worn:
All changed, changed utterly:
A terrible beauty is born.

That woman's days were spent
In ignorant good-will,
Her nights in argument
Until her voice grew shrill.
What voice more sweet than hers
When, young and beautiful,
She rode to harriers?
This man had kept a school
And rode our wingèd horse;
This other his helper and friend
Was coming into his force;
He might have won fame in the end,
So sensitive his nature seemed,
So daring and sweet his thought.
This other man I had dreamed
A drunken, vainglorious lout.
He had done most bitter wrong
To some who are near my heart,
Yet I number him in the song;

He, too, has resigned his part
In the casual comedy;
He, too, has been changed in his turn,
Transformed utterly:
A terrible beauty is born.

Hearts with one purpose alone
Through summer and winter seem
Enchanted to a stone
To trouble the living stream.
The horse that comes from the road,
The rider, the birds that range
From cloud to tumbling cloud,
Minute by minute they change;
A shadow of cloud on the stream
Changes minute by minute;
A horse-hoof slides on the brim,
And a horse plashes within it;
The long-legged moor-hens dive,
And hens to moor-cocks call;
Minute by minute they live:
The stone's in the midst of all.

Too long a sacrifice
Can make a stone of the heart.
O when may it suffice?
That is Heaven's part, our part
To murmur name upon name,
As a mother names her child
When sleep at last has come
On limbs that had run wild.
What is it but nightfall?
No, no, not night but death;
Was it needless death after all?
For England may keep faith
For all that is done and said.
We know their dream; enough
To know they dreamed and are dead;
And what if excess of love

Bewildered them till they died?
I write it out in a verse —
MacDonagh and MacBride
And Connolly and Pearse
Now and in time to be,
Wherever green is worn,
Are changed, changed utterly:
A terrible beauty is born.

September 25, 1916

WILLIAM BUTLER YEATS (1865–1939)

Imperial Measure

"We have plenty of the best food, all the meals being as good as if served in a hotel. The dining-room here is very comfortable."
— PH Pearse, the GPO, Easter 1916, in a letter to his mother

The kitchens of the Metropole and Imperial hotels yielded up to
    the Irish Republic
their armory of fillet, brisket, flank. Though destined for more
    palatable tongues,
it was pressed to service in an Irish stew and served on fine bone
    china
with bread that turned to powder in their mouths. Brioche,
    artichokes, tomatoes
tasted for the first time: staunch and sweet on Monday, but by
    Thursday,
they had overstretched to spill their livid plenitude on the fires
    of Sackville Street.

A cow and her two calves were commandeered. One calf was
    killed,
its harnessed blood clotting the morning like news that wasn't
    welcome

when, eventually, it came. The women managed the blood into
    black puddings
washed down with milk from the cow in the yard who smelt
    smoke on the wind
and fire on the skin of her calf. Whose fear they took for loss and
    fretted with her
until daylight crept between crossfire and the sights of
    Marrowbone Lane.

Brownies, Simnel cake, biscuits slumped under royal icing.
    Éclairs with their cream
already turned. Crackers, tonnes of them: the floor of Jacobs'
    studded with crumbs,
so every footfall was a recoil from a gunshot across town, and
    the flakes
a constant needling in mouths already seared by the one drink
    — a gross
or two of cooking chocolate, stewed and taken without
    sweetener or milk.
Its skin was riven every time the ladle dipped but, just as quickly,
    it seized up again.

Nellie Gifford magicked oatmeal and a half-crowned loaf to
    make porridge
in a grate in the College of Surgeons where drawings of field
    surgery
had spilled from Ypres to drench in wounds the whitewashed walls
of the lecture hall. When the porridge gave out, there was rice:
a biscuit-tin of it for fourteen men, a ladleful each that scarcely
    knocked
the corners off their undiminished appetites; their vast,
    undaunted thirst.

The sacks of flour ballasting the garrison gave up their downy
    protest under fire.
It might have been a fall of Easter snow sent to muffle the rifles
    or to deaden the aim.

Every blow was a flurry that thickened the air of Boland's Mill,
    so breath
was ghosted by its own white consequence. The men's clothes
    were talced with it,
as though they were newborns, palmed and swathed, their
    foreheads kissed,
their grip unclenched, their fists and arms first blessed and,
    then, made much of.

The cellars of the Four Courts were intact at the surrender, but
    the hock
had been agitated, the Riesling set astir. For years, the wines
    were sullied
with a leaden aftertaste, although the champagne had as full a
    throat as ever,
and the spirits kept their heady confidence, for all the stock-
    piled bottles
had chimed with every hit, and the calculating scales above it all
had had the measure of nothing, or nothing if not smoke, and
    then wildfire.

VONA GROARKE (*b.* 1964)

O'Connell Street*

A noble failure is not vain,
But hath a victory its own.
A bright delectance from the slain
Is down the generations thrown.

And, more than Beauty understands,
Has made her lovelier here, it seems.
I see white ships that crowd her strands,
For mine are all the dead men's dreams.

FRANCIS LEDWIDGE (1887–1917)
Title added by scholars to poem unpublished in author's lifetime.

Statue (from 'Counsellor')
for Maurice O'Connell

You're pedestalled in stone above the traffic,
A bronze statue with attendant figures
Marked by the bullets of civil war.
The city's central street, the bridge

Spanning the coming and going of tides,
Carry your name. O'Connell, Liberator
Counsellor, Dan. It's a long way
From Derrynane to this windy eminence.

Windy's the word they used
There behind you in the GPO.
Where poets died strapped to pillars,
Leaving ravens to perch on our shoulders.

But history won't be repealed by you
Or me. Let the hare sit for now.
Emancipated from responsibility,
You can harangue the passing crowds.

PADDY BUSHE (*b.* 1948)

Dream Song 321

O land of Connolly & Pearse, what have
ever you done to deserve these tragic masters?
You come & go,
free: nothing happens. Nelson's Pillar blows
but the buses still go there: nothing is changed,
for all these disasters O.

We fought our freedom out a long while ago
I can't see that it matters, we can't help you
land of ruined abbeys,

discredited Saints & brainless senators,
roofless castles, enemies of Swift & Joyce,
enemies of Synge,

enemies of Yeats & O'Casey, hold your foul ground
your filthy cousins will come around to you,
barely able to read,
friends of Patrick Kavanagh's & Austin Clarke's
those masters who can both read and write,
in the high Irish style.

JOHN BERRYMAN (1914–1972)

Fód an Imris: Ard Oifig an Phoist 1986

Anso, an ea, 'athair, a thosnaigh sé?
Gur dhein strainséirí dínn dá chéile?
Anso, an ea?

Fastaím a shílis riamh dár mórchuid cainte —
Fiú nuair aontaíomar leat:

Oidhrí ar eachtra nár aithin bolaith an phúdair
Ná na heagla,
Nár chaith riamh ruchar feirge
Is is lú ná san
A sheas …

D'éalaíomar uait thar Pháil na Gaelainne isteach;
B'shin *terre guerre* ba linn fhéin,
Is chuaigh sé de mhianach an Olltaigh
Ionatsa
Ár lorg a rianadh,
Ár dtabhairt chun tíríochais —
Civilitie Spenser
D'oibrigh irtsa a chluain.

Leanamarna treabhchas na máthar:
Kranz barrghaoitheach na Mumhan;
Ba tusa san seanabhroc stróinsithe,
Scheamhaíl ort ag paca spáinnéar.

Le haois ghnáthaoímar a chéile thar n-ais;
D'fhoghlaimís carthain,
Ach b'éigean fós siúl go haireach;
Do mheabhair agues th'acfainn chirt
Níor thaithigh cúl scéithe;
Comhaos mé féin is an stat,
Is níor chun do thola do cheachtar.

Óigfhear in easnamh, anaithnid, thú, 'athair,
San àit seo —
Ceileann neamart is tuathal an eochair ar m'intinn —
Ach an seanóir a charas le grà duaisiúl,
Cloisim a thuin aduaidh:
An cuimhin leat an t-aitheasc a thugais
Nuair nà raibh faiseanta fós?
Mar seo do ràidhis é:

I see no cause for rejoicing
That Irishmen once again
Are killing other Irishmen
On the streets of Belfast!

MÁIRE MHAC AN TSAOI (*b.* 1922)

Trouble Spot: General Post Office 1986

Here, father, is this where it started?
Here we became strangers to each other?
Was it here?

You thought most of what we said was nonsense —
Even when we agreed with you:
Inheritors of the event who never knew the smell
Of gunpowder, or of terror,
Who never fired a shot in anger,
Worse yet,
Never stood up to one ...

We retreated from you into the Pale of Irish;
That was our familiar *terre guerre*,
And the Ulsterman
In you
Could not follow our tracks
Or tame our barbarism —
Spenser's *civilitie*
Had beguiled you.

We took after our mother's tribe:
The high-blown ways of Munster;
You were the recalcitrant old badger
Run to ground by howling spaniels.

In later years, we tried again;
You learned to be charitable,
But we still had to tread carefully;
Your intelligence and sense of justice
Never practised deception;
I am the same age as the state
And neither turned out as you wished ...

In this place, father, you are the unknown
Youth who went missing —
Neglect and awkwardness hide the key from my mind —
But I hear now the Northern accent
Of the elder man I loved with hard devotion:
Do you remember the rebuke you delivered
Before it became fashionable?
You spoke thus:

I see no cause for rejoicing
That Irishmen once again
Are killing other Irishmen
On the streets of Belfast!

MÁIRE MHAC AN tSAOI (*b.* 1922)
Translated from the Irish by Louis de Paor

Nelson's Pillar

My duty done, I rose as a Doric column
Far from at home, planted to reach the sky;
A huge stake in the crossed heart of a glum
Garrison city overlooked by my blind eye.

One-armed on a cold square abacus to rule
The waves, I never controlled the verminous
Poor beggars round my plinth, schooled to rebel.
I was loved well as a tramway's terminus.

Who cares, now, what good masons carved my four
Sea victories in granite from Golden Hill?
When masked men cracked my head off, the blast wore
Red, white and blue in a flash of puerile skill.

Dismasted and dismissed, without much choice,
Having lost my touch, I'll raise my chiselled voice.

RICHARD MURPHY (*b.* 1927)

Post Colonial

At the GPO in Dublin
The options for letters are as follows —
DUBLIN   REST OF WORLD.

What provincial clarity in this pair
of polished brass openings that
double the world by halving it,
closing the gap between
Ballyvaughan and Beijing
Lisburn and Lisbon
Spiddal and Salt Lake City —
these and all the rest, surplus to Dublin,
remaindered, leftover.

The jiffy bag of birthday treats
slouching towards Mrs Rafferty
of Sligo town shuffles up next the letter
carefully addressed to
President O'Bama, The White House,
falls alongside the aerogram
headed Down Under —
all part and parcel of what is not Dublin.

Vestige of the packet steamer,
remnant of a capital confidence,
fragment of a Zen koan —
DUBLIN   REST OF WORLD.

Stark choice,
for Joyce and for all the departed
who post themselves
with no return address,
Workboys of the Rest of World,
restless until they rest in the
Land of the Fee or the
Home of the Saved.
Meanwhile Dublin rests, lies,
peels and sticks, awaits collection,
a long envelope of time til
next working day.

WILLA MURPHY (*b.* 1967)

Dublin Honeymoon

For a whole week we walked the same beat,
Through Stephen's Green, whatever the weather,
Collecting travel stains on Grafton St.,
Past Trinity, O'Connell Bridge, the Quays.
Back at the hotel we bathed together,
Dispensing with the last formalities.

Our first time in Dublin. Not quite at home
But feigning ease, our moves were tentative.
As yet lacking the confidence to roam
Freely, we kept to our accustomed lap,
Were grateful for it.
Later we branched out and didn't need the map,

And laughed to remember. Without a wince
We've been exploring alleys ever since.

FRANK ORMSBY (*b.* 1947)

Plane

December, and the stand of planes in O'Connell Street
might just as well be lit with crossfire as with these fairy lights.
Xerxes has finished shopping and has left the battlefield
of Clery's with his list ticked off, when he sees it, straddling
the no-man's land between Abbey Street and Lydia.
Crowds mill round him, but he can't take cover or advance.
Which leaves him gazing for another age on the bedecked face
of his beloved and its glow. While to his left, just out
of sight, goes the last bus to Thermopylae, heading south.

VONA GROARKE (*b.* 1964)

Sráid an Amhrais

Le dhá lá níl sámhnas ach síorbháisteach.
Phréamhaigh sceachaill an amhrais go doimhin
is theilg arraingeacha ar fuaid an bhaill.

Im shuí i mbialann Bhritish Home Stores
ag machnamh dom trí ghalfhuinneog
chím an phearsa stairiúil sin Clery & Co.

ag análú is ag easanálú saoránach
faoi scátha fearthainne, beag beann
ar an bhfathach Larkin ar a stáitse eibhir —

d'fhéadfadh na lapaí cré-umha san
bheith ag tabhairt dúshlán na scamall á rá:
'Ídigh sinn má tá sé ionaibh, a ghrúdairí na díomá.'

MICHAEL DAVITT (1950–2005)

Disillusion Street

It's been raining for the past two days, with no let-up.
A tumour of disenchantment has taken root
and spread to all arts and parts.

From the restaurant in British Home Stores
I watch through a steamed-up window
the historical persona of Clery & Co.

inhale and exhale the citizenry,
umbrellas and all, all totally ignorant
of Big Jim Larkin on his plinth of granite —

those great bronze hands
might well be calling the clouds' bluff;
'Try wearing us out, O masters of let-down,
     let's see you strut your stuff.'

Michael Davitt (1950–2005)
Translated from the Irish by Paul Muldoon

Dublin

I open our sash window to the inner city sky:
Sunday morning clouds, electronic clang of a great bell
Between the rain-drenched quays and the Gresham Hotel;
Aroma of coffee with water just off the boil

And that distant fluttering, specks of conflict
In the air above us, like Lavery's German bi-planes
In that great painting from the First War, dim frames
Caught in lighted haze, painting their frail aspect

As they bank and turn. And then, that great Dublin call,
Uniquely Dublin, the squeal of Norah MacGuinness sea-
Gulls as they lift off the canvas of her closed gallery:
The sheer beauty of it, this cacophony as her gulls fall.

THOMAS McCARTHY (*b.* 1954)

Dublin Spire

Cold steel colossus
Squat between the heavens
and the street
the street and the heavens

Part dragon
    Part dreadnought
        Part STARWARS
            Part Panopticon
                Part Messerschmitt

you pierce the clouds
occupy the atmosphere
possess the rooftops
dominate the capital
diminish everyone in range

and so are suited to the worship of neo-liberal Pharaohs
Bullies Templars Christian Brothers Mafias Ku Klux Klans
Conspiracies and modern governments in general

that are more heartless than any admiral
that have no pulse,
and are unmovable
that, numb to the touch,
watch over all,
feeling for none.

With a face as blank and comfortless
as an executioner's hood
you brag of your unscalable heights
your impenetrable flanks

of how at dusk you lance the sunset from the sky
set alight your tapering lure
reel in the falling stars
hack off their flaming tails,
                impale their flying wishes.

DAVE LORDAN (*b.* 1975)

The Spire
(10 years on)

The spire in the quagmire,
The dagger in the corpse,
The skewer in the sewer,
The middle finger up.

The stiffey by the Liffey,
The ace in the hole,
The chopstick stuck in traffic,
The North(side) Pole.

The pin that burst the bubble,
The last tooth in the comb,
The first sign of trouble,
The barbed welcome home.

The spike in the crime rate,
The spine without a back,
The hypo from the Corpo,
The stake though the heart.

The needle in the noodle,
The point of no return,
The stick in the muddle,
The javelin, the harpoon.

The rod, the birch, the *bata*,
The Christian Brother's cane,
The crozier of St Patrick
Weaponised again.

The flagpole flying nothing,
The blade-like glint of steel,
The arrow pointing nowhere,
The raver's broken heel.

Stiletto in the ghetto,
Monument of blight,
The nail in the coffin,
The 'we' reduced to 'I'.

PAT BORAN (*b.* 1963)

William Butler Yeats, in Old Age, Meets
Maud Gonne MacBride in O'Connell Street

The poet, head among the stars no longer,
but turned to see where best to cross the street,
and the lady of his delight, no longer treading
his web of coloured dreams beneath her feet,
with the teasing wind from the River Liffey blowing
its rags and scraps of paper round them, meet.

How can he talk of soft lake water lapping,
or speak the rage of his defeated heart,
above the shouting newsboy, and the rattle
over the cobbles of a loaded cart?

What can he say, the artificer of legend?
The blood runs quiet now, the wind strikes cold.
They turn and go their slow and separate journeys,
who now are grey, and full of sleep, and old.

EVANGELINE PATERSON (1928–2000)

The Volta

A gleam, this new idea in his head:
a chance of turning coin, his city still
in blackness, awaiting sound and light

so he comes back, acquires a hall
off Sackville and fills it; wooden
benches, Windsor chairs for the quality

a carpet sticking its red tongue out
along the centre aisle, potted palms
beside the orchestra, and a screen

and opens in December, frost and ice
and snow that soon would be
general all over Ireland

counting heads, the queue outside
curious under gaslight
then curses the bad weather as the stream

dries to a trickle, the money
running out, and closes six months later
the doors locked and the posters

gone, but not the taste for it.
How well he knew us
as we crowd in once again

loving the womb-warm inky dark,
the press of flesh, and stories stories
stories created out of all of us, pictures

alive in flame-flicker, a huddle around
cave paintings made from the crushed
bones and blood of the animals we painted.

JOHN O'DONNELL (*b.* 1960)

The Uniform

"My Willie was so proud
Of his Head Usher's uniform,"
Bridie Sandford said,
"I had my work cut out
Keeping it pressed and immaculate.
When he was killed that time
We had a photo of him in it
Blown up and framed.
I used to get a laugh
Out of visitors
When they saw the photo
And asked,
'Was Willie in the army?'

'No,' I used to say,
'He was in the Adelphi.'"

GERRY McDONNELL (*b.* 1950)

Searmanas na Feola

"*In Moore Street where I did dwell
a butcher boy, I loved right well ....*"

'*Mo-oo,*' a chanaimis seachas, '*Mew-ew*'.
Bhíodh blas ag an dornán a mhair go hArdteist
na *ew-ers* ba dhúchasaí greadta leo.

"*In Moore Street where I did dwell
a butcher boy, I loved right well.*"

"Tinceir, táilliúir, búistéir, báicéir,
múinteoir, saighdiúir nó sean-siúinéir ...."
"Búistéir!"

Cé thabharfadh suas í féin don bhúistéir?

Triallaim air anois
leis na mna tí eile, na máithreacha clainne.
A chrága ag minghearradh feola le scian fhada dhubh
ar an mbloc adhmaid i gcónaí.

Lámha a scorann ball toll ó bhun feimide.
Lámha a bhaineann cnámh na leise as ceathrú an uain chásca.
Lámha cnáimhseora a sheolann stéig an lae
slán amach chugainn idir cheithre chosa na beatha.

Éisteann sé
faoistiní feola,
an rósta nó a easpa,
cé mhéid ispín is gá a theascadh anuas
dá shúgán síoraí? ...

"Give me a nice tender little bit, please, Billy."

Is bímid teanntásach i siopa an bhúistéara
ábhairín gáirsiúil fiú
mar go n-aithníonn fear na feola a dhíol bean na feola
          a cheannach
is a mhalairt thart.

Cuirtear an dearg in uachtar anseo.
Bímid ag fuilscaipeadh,
ag crú,
"Lean lap, Billy love,
belly bacon."
Lá i ndiaidh lae,
gach lá dar saol,
Áiméan.

BIDDY JENKINSON (*b.* 1949)

Rites of the Flesh

"In Moore Street where I did dwell, a butcher boy I loved right well..." Those of us who had stayed till Leaving Cert sang 'Mo-oor', not 'Mew-wer'. We had been to elocution. The confirmed 'ew-ers' had dropped out. *"In Moore Street where I did dwell, a butcher boy I loved right well..."* *"Tinker, tailor, butcher, baker, teacher, soldier or cabinet maker ..."* Butcher! Who would offer herself up to the butcher? I go to him now along with the other housewives, mothers of families. On the wooden block he minces meat, a long black knife in his great big fist. His hands pull ball from socket, remove the thigh bone of the Pascal lamb. The hands of an obstetrician, they deliver our daily meat from under the four legs of life. He listens to confessions: the roast or the lack of one, how many sausages are to be cut from the endless rope. "Give me a nice tender little bit, please, Billy." We become skittish in the butcher's shop, lewd at times, for the man selling meat understands the woman who is buying meat, and vice versa. Red is dominant. We spill blood. Milk it. "Lean lap, Billy love, belly bacon." Day after day. All the days of our lives. Amen.

BIDDY JENKINSON (*b.* 1949)
Translation by the author

City Dweller

I have never seen wild Donegal
nor the Atlantic cliffs of Kerry,
though in a haze of alcohol
I might have admired Enniskerry.

I've never dreamt beneath Ben Bulben's head,
or in a pool of poppies hid my face,
and the sweetest poems I have ever read
were down in Christchurch Place.

I've never looked down from the hills of Mourne
to the laughing sea at my feet

for the grandest of scents to my nostrils borne
came from the stalls in Moore Street.

Galway's glories rugged and raw
were in one single afternoon seen,
and the only lakes that I ever saw
were those in St Stephen's Green.

No call of soft-vowelled curlew
came to me across evening leas,
and all the lilting strains I knew
were in *The Shaky Man's* on the Quays.

Yet my Liffey dreams were just as sweet
as those in a Wicklow valley,
and my heart was first forged in Merrion Street
and blinded with love in Bull Alley.

CHRISTY BROWN (1932–1981)

Love Letter to My Henry St. Dealer

Keep your eyes peeled for the coppers love
they're all over the shop today
her hand disappears into wintry layers
roots round reinforced brassieres
fumbles under corsets and slips out
magically holding my pouch,
a Dutch love letter from my Henry Street dealer
still warm from the heat of her oxter.

Fifty fat grams of *halfzware shag* in my back pocket —
I'm flush for the week,
padded against the cold days to come,
a flourish of rolling and smoking
down the basement flat
till the soft tendril strands whisper away

56

and I make my way back to the street
for more of what's beneath her liberty bodice.

KEITH PAYNE (*b.* 1975)

On Hearing of the Death of Gerald Davis
Saturday, June 18th, 2005

Any other Bloomsday you'd up and bloom,
Leopolding, immaculate Poldy: not this time.

Two days ago your Dublin lost its bowler hat,
Went bare-headed to your not-being-there.

Two small paintings creep up my wall,
A Mask, a Window, twin elements, camouflage,

A world framed: you said I knew your art,
Which was more compliment than I deserved.

I went away from every meeting with a Jazz
CD like a bright, surreal coin in my pocket —

We drank herbal tea sung over, you said, by
A rabbi, hot-spiced from the Holy Land.

How right you were, Bloom of Capel Street,
To hold out for the passing of Poldy's Day,

Let the sun slip into the sea like a hand
Into a pocket, slip off yourself: dwindlebloom

That last gush, blast, Yes Yes Yes of work
Seared the eye, went beyond itself, must have

Left a gash in you, the best you'd done; a
CD spinning now, like a model of the universe,

Fogs in my cold sitting-room with Kaddish,
A held top note on the last word, a flourish,

A defining brush-stroke, wing-life of an ending:
You'd layered so much colour on all that silence,

Voicing each painting, participles of style,
A Capel Street of contrast, a Grafton Street

Of shade, tone, a kidney-breakfast of composition,
A riddling Sandymount of the imagination; still

From wall to wall this labyrinth of self-shaping
Ran indecipherable yet obvious, a willing

Into the face of a sheet blank as death of
Mythographic, musical, bullish, last images,

A plump cave-painter busy in the half-light
Of a skittishly pagan Plurabella moon —

No escape this time on self-impaling wings,
Feather-tips curled inwards in a tabernacular heat —

You heard the wax melt, saw bright drops
Fuse in Howthy sand, felt the laughing descent into light.

FRED JOHNSTON (*b.* 1951)

Flute-fixing in McNeill's of Capel Street

I would have passed it by —
secreted between pound shops,
purveyors of pine
or fifty types of trainer.
But you knew the way,

easing the heavy door,
leading me in.

Time was suspended
with the motes
as light slipped in
through timbered slats
and varnish teased our noses
till our breath
was pure mahogany.

The job was not yet done.
He twined the hemp, unwound
and twined again around
the bevelled shaft, retouched
with beeswax so the cord
stayed moist and pliant
as he talked of sessions,
of bodhráns played in the Sligo style.

As he worked you browsed
from shelf to shelf, ear cocked
to some internal tune
among the lutes and mandolins
till a bouzouki's soundboard
curved to swell a song
you promised I might one day sing.

NESSA O'MAHONY (*b*. 1964)

Parnell Street

'Death will come and will have your eyes.' — *Cesare Pavese*

This is my first address: this is where
My mouth first opened. After half a century
I'm here again, as if the Rotunda midwife
Had never cut the cord.

Fair shades, my first loves
Stand at the Finglas bus stops
Or shelter in the doorways of extinct pubs.
Here is the basement where young poets
Cuffed each other with sheathed claws,
The attics where we rehearsed our lives
As *Songs* by Leonard Cohen.

In the surprisingly beautiful fifties flats
Behind the Georgian facades,
I returned to film children
Who saw religious statues move —
The old gods' last performance.
Now the gods have gone
But those children's children
Still play on the streets,
Fearless and insolent as ever.

The world has followed me back here
Like multicoloured gum on my shoe:
Now I hear again every language I ever heard
Drink beer I crossed a continent to taste.

The old Shakespeare Pub is a Korean restaurant
But nothing has changed. Men and women
Still face each other at tables, trying
To rewrite the night to a different ending.

In dreams I often returned here, looking
For my life, which was hiding
In an alley like a wounded animal.

Now I am afraid that
This is where death will find me,
Wearing your eyes.

MICHAEL O'LOUGHLIN (*b.* 1958)

In North Great George's Street
(a thought from Moschus)

Ah me, the aspidistra grows dusty behind the window pane,
And the delicate tracery of the fan-light is obscured from light;
Yet these shall, perchance, be dusted, and shine brightly again;
But they, the gallant, the witty and the brave,
Whaley and Egan, and all who fought the oncoming of death
    and night,
These death has taken. They lie forever, each in a forgotten grave.

SEUMAS O'SULLIVAN (*b.* 1879–1958)

At the Gate Theatre
for Dearbhla Molloy

' ... Ah, what new pain must I now undergo?
What monstrous torture have I yet to know?
All I've endured, the madness and the fear,
self-pity, rage, humiliation, self-hate,
the insult of rejection, even, were mere
ripples of the approaching storm ...' Not many
in the trade now can decently impersonate
the great ones of the tragic repertoire
— Medea, Cleopatra, Lady Macbeth —
much less achieve the famous 'diamond edge'
of the doomed Phaedra's lightning-inviting rage,
her great apostrophes to love and death;
so here am I, like any stage door Johnny,
to call your playing out of Phaedra's agony,
your bright contralto, stringed and starlit vertigo
of outrage and despair from head to toe
not only wonderful but actually sublime
in the old sense of resistance overcome,
articulate terror, storm answered with storm,
a heaven-splitting performance. When she cries

defiance to the gods, the wings, the quivering flies,
we know we are in the presence; but we know too
a whole theatrical tradition is in crisis —
this play peaked and exhausted all at once
an entire genre; for its fierce eloquence
yielded in no time to the *comic* Muse,
the death of tragedy and the Birth of the Blues.
Backstage tonight, I glimpse the ghostly faces
of Micheál and Hilton, Geraldine and Siobhán
amid the festive racket of make-up and paint-sprays,
Hedda Gabler, The School for Scandal, Happy Days,
moonlit revels and laughter in the dark,
the thrill of envenom'd chalice and poisonous book;
for tragedy too, of course, is enormous fun
though now we've no use for the tragic posture.
The Greeks mixed tragedies with satyr plays;
and look at the old age of Euripides
who, after a lifetime struggling with new ideas,
sends out his Bacchae to the woods and glens
to dance devotion to the god of vines
under the rocks, under the moonlit pines,
for Dionysus, son of Semele, is come.
Bring on ivy and goatskin, pipe and drum!

DEREK MAHON (*b.* 1941)

Municipal Gallery Revisited

I

Around me the images of thirty years:
An ambush; pilgrims at the water-side;
Casement upon trial, half hidden by the bars,
Guarded; Griffith staring in hysterical pride;
Kevin O'Higgins' countenance that wears
A gentle questioning look that cannot hide
A soul incapable of remorse or rest;
A revolutionary soldier kneeling to be blessed;

II

An Abbot or Archbishop with an upraised hand
Blessing the Tricolour. 'This is not,' I say,
'The dead Ireland of my youth, but an Ireland
The poets have imagined, terrible and gay.'
Before a woman's portrait suddenly I stand,
Beautiful and gentle in her Venetian way.
I met her all but fifty years ago
For twenty minutes in some studio.

III

Heart-smitten with emotion I sink down,
My heart recovering with covered eyes;
Wherever I had looked I had looked upon
My permanent or impermanent images:
Augusta Gregory's son; her sister's son,
Hugh Lane, 'onlie begetter' of all these;
Hazel Lavery living and dying, that tale
As though some ballad-singer had sung it all;

IV

Mancini's portrait of Augusta Gregory,
'Greatest since Rembrandt,' according to John Synge;
A great ebullient portrait certainly;
But where is the brush that could show anything
Of all that pride and that humility?
And I am in despair that time may bring
Approved patterns of women or of men
But not that selfsame excellence again.

V

My mediaeval knees lack health until they bend,
But in that woman, in that household where
Honour had lived so long, all lacking found.
Childless I thought, 'My children may find here
Deep-rooted things,' but never foresaw its end,
And now that end has come I have not wept;
No fox can foul the lair the badger swept —

VI

(An image out of Spenser and the common tongue).
John Synge, I and Augusta Gregory, thought
All that we did, all that we said or sang
Must come from contact with the soil, from that
Contact everything Antaeus-like grew strong.
We three alone in modern times had brought
Everything down to that sole test again,
Dream of the noble and the beggar-man.

VII

And here's John Synge himself, that rooted man,
'Forgetting human words,' a grave deep face.
You that would judge me, do not judge alone
This book or that, come to this hallowed place
Where my friends' portraits hang and look thereon;
Ireland's history in their lineaments trace;
Think where man's glory most begins and ends,
And say my glory was I had such friends.

WILLIAM BUTLER YEATS (1865–1939)

Francis Bacon at the Hugh Lane Gallery

I

The August light anonymous
and warm. Buses droning up past the Rotunda,
or idling next to the Ierne, taking the sun.
Inside the Garden of Remembrance
the cross of water, ripple-free,
and Lir's children rising still.

II

as nightmare
maremouth open air —

less scream
dissslocate soundless

            Fface of
       man ?) in cyanide aSPHixiate blue
                drowNEd, livid, blurrrr
            surfaceglass shadow

        ccccrawling cross redness
         rawred, bare: arid torso
straightjacket limblessness
and the Umbrella!
    as though as though as though

        Studio searchlight; an eye
        on oval operating table
        bare flesh contorted
        and around it zinc white
        curves antiseptic rail

heheheads in   series
     mMegacccccephaLlous
     three   tryptich333
deformedistortediseased
     Bbrow jawbone a

               III
Outside, again.
The light momentarily disorients,
the air warm and noisy. A smile,
ambivalent, in what might be termed
apologetic admiration:
And he was from Dublin, too,
though you'd never believe it.

DAVID BUTLER (*b.* 1964)

Matt Talbot, 1856-1925

I need to rinse out the rancid tin can you drank from
In a ramshackled shed beside the timber yard gates,

To place a mattress over the plank you slept on
And release rusted dog chains cutting into your flesh.

We have each sobered awake in the abyss of dawn,
Longing for a revelation to overwhelm our futility,

But you substituted torture with an addict's fixation
That ensnared us in the servitude of poverty.

Lift your head, Matt, and read on the newsboys' placards
How Dublin burns as you trudge each evening from work

To shuffle to your meal on bare knees across floorboards,
With blunt labourer's eyes out-staring those who would mock,

Until you fall in Gramby Lane, missing your final Mass,
Like you carried the whole city's pain upon your back.

DERMOT BOLGER (*b.* 1959)

In Memory of Those Murdered in the Dublin Massacre, May 1974

In the grime-ridden sunlight in the downtown Wimpy bar
I think of all the crucial aeons — and of the labels
That freedom fighters stick onto the lost destinies of unborn
    children;
The early morning sunlight carries in the whole street from
    outside;
The whole wide street from outside through the plate-glass
    windows;
Wholly, sparklingly, surgingly, carried in from outside;

And the waitresses cannot help but be happy and gay
As they swipe at the tabletops with their dishcloths —
Such a moment as would provide the heroic freedom fighter
With his perfect meat.
And I think of those heroes — heroes? — heroes.

And as I stand up to walk out —
The aproned old woman who's been sweeping the floor
Has mop stuck in bucket, leaning on it;
And she's trembling all over, like a flower in the breeze.
She'd make a mighty fine explosion now, if you were to blow
    her up;
An explosion of petals, of aeons, and the waitresses too, flying
    breasts and limbs,
For a free Ireland.

PAUL DURCAN (*b.* 1944)

from **The Week-end of Dermot and Grace**
Part One: Friday

Amiens Street. I tipped the porter a shilling
And walked the length of the platform twinned
In the reflective windows of the carriages,
The I and the I shall be.
I was the sunrise and its shadow the evening,
I was the spring field and the stooked corn,
The alphabet and the *Iliad*,
First kiss on a bench at startime,
The last gag when candles are lit to sweeten the air.
The engine wagged its grey beard and said,
Vah! Himself he cannot save.
But the righteous were confident,
Each with his thirdclass ticket duly clipped
By the collector in the company's uniform
Might let his footfalls ring disdainfully

On stone flags under a blackglass vault
And carry his trim attaché-case
Stamped with his initials quaintly
As a smug virtue in an old woodcut.
The glass roof blotched like a print on crude paper
Shaded us all walking,
The righteous and I:
I the imagemaker,
I the masks that look out of the imagemaker's line.

EUGENE R. WATTERS (1919–1982)

Remembrance Day, Sean McDermott St.

Could be a heartbeat, she ventures, and I explain
about the station and trains crossing that five-and-a-half-
second gap between tall buildings all day long.

And that? she gasps, putting a hand to her throat.
No, not gas, I laugh, mimicking Angela as she signs off
with a prolonged hiss from the aerosol can.

And my heart — half-said, so as not to interrupt —
can't you hear it? as I listen closer to a woman's voice
from the third floor shouting , *Ed–die, Ed–die.*

HUGH O'DONNELL (*b.* 1951)

Dicey Reilly

Ah poor aul' Dicey Reilly she has taken to the sup,
And poor aul' Dicey Reilly, she will never give it up
It's off each morning to the pop and she goes in for another
    little drop,
But the heart of the rowl is Dicey Reilly.

She walks along Fitzgibbon Street with an independent air,
And then it's down by Summerhill and the people stop and stare.
She'll say, "It's nearly half past one, time I had another little one."
Ah the heart of the rowl is Dicey Reilly.

Now at two, pubs close and out she goes as happy as a lark.
She'll find a bench to sleep it off down in St Patrick's Park.
She'll wake at five feeling in the pink and say, "'Tis time for
    another little drink,"
But the heart of the rowl is Dicey Reilly.

Now she'll travel far to a dockside bar to have another round
And after one or two or three she doesn't feel quite sound
And after four she's a bit unstable; after five underneath the
    table,
But the heart of the rowl is Dicey Reilly.

Oh they carry her home at twelve o'clock as they do every night,
Bring her inside, put her on the bed and then turn out the light.
Next morning she'll get out of bed and look for a curer for her
    head,
But the heart of the rowl is Dicey Reilly.

Ah poor aul' Dicey Reilly she has taken to the sup,
And poor aul' Dicey Reilly, she will never give it up
It's off each morning to the pop and she goes in for another
    little drop,
But the heart of the rowl is Dicey Reilly.

ANONYMOUS

Buying Winkles

My mother would spare me sixpence and say,
'Hurry up now and don't be talking to strange
men on the way.' I'd dash from the ghosts
on the stairs where the bulb had blown
out into Gardiner Street, all relief.
A bonus if the moon was in the strip of sky
between the tall houses, or stars out,
but even in rain I was happy — the winkles
would be wet and glisten blue like little
night skies themselves. I'd hold the tanner tight
and jump every crack in the pavement,
I'd wave up to women at sills or those
lingering in doorways and weave a glad path through
men heading out for the night.

She'd be sitting outside the Rosebowl Bar
on an orange-crate, a pram loaded
with pails of winkles before her.
When the bar doors swung open they'd leak
the smell of men together with drink
and I'd see light in golden mirrors.
I envied each soul in the hot interior.

I'd ask her again to show me the right way
to do *it*. She'd take a pin from her shawl —
'Open the eyelid. So. Stick it in
till you feel a grip, then slither him out.
Gently, mind.' The sweetest extra winkle
that brought the sea to me.
'Tell yer Ma I picked them fresh this morning.'

I'd bear the newspaper twists
bulging fat with winkles
proudly home, like torches.

PAULA MEEHAN (*b.* 1955)

Dublin Town

Rollin' down to Dublin Town
Comin' from the Northside, headin' Southbound
The glare of the city, you can see it in the sky
See it in the faces when I'm passing them by
Dublin Town
Bright lights all around
All the different sounds
Concrete surrounds
You need a few pounds or there's nothing to do
No muns, no fun in the foggy dew
I be signing on, off Gardiner Street
See all the people struggling just to make ends meet
The more unfortunate ones be begging at your feet
We'll have to send a warning to the socially elite
And I repeat, if you keep a people down
In any old town
Or country
They'll rise don't you see
It's the will to survive
That keeps them alive
And they're starting to see through all the lies
That they've contrived, so I say to you all
To educate yourself, become well read
And start to use the head
Contemplate your own situation
Find the true enemy and stop banging heads
With the victims of its greed
Am I getting too serious?
Well this was meant to be a love song
Well it is a love song because I love my people
Not so long ago, back in the good old days
I dreamed of Irish laws and Irish ways
And saw that the present days weren't so good
And the only thing I could think about them that was good
Was most of the people that surrounded me
But still I call them good old days because of the craic
That we had

We refused to stay sad
If you have your own around you and also possess your health
At the end of the day you'll discover that that is the most
Essential wealth
I throw my mind back
And recall the days I used to have the craic
Back in Dublin town
Getting down to the Irish and Jamaican sounds
Listenin' and learning about life
Helping me make it through the strife
Suckin' on a big fat spliff full of rocky
Flagon in my hand
Be makin me feel grand
Discussing this and that
And thinking about the now
Thinking about the future, making myself a vow
I wasn't going to waste my life
But I was going to live and love
Do the best that I could
I was going to bring some music to the people
and tell them that they were equal
But some of them wouldn't listen
And this is what is pissin'
The rest of us off
You would wanna start listening to us, you would
Coz to you we aren't going to be good forever
Yeh maybe even here, in the Dublin Town
Things could get turned upside down

DAMIEN DEMPSEY (*b.* 1975)

Oíche

Cha raibh ann ach seomra beag suarach
i gceann de lóistíní oíche Shráid Ghardiner;
cincleach ar ńa ballaí, na braillíní buí agus brochach;
gan le cluinstin ach ochlán fada olagónach

na cathrach agus rúscam raindí na gcat
ag déanamh raicit i mboscaí bruscair an chlóis;
ach ba chuma agus tusa, a rún na gile, sínte ar shlat
do dhroma, ar cholbha na leapa agus gan tuinte ort …

Agus tú ag dlúthú liom go docht, d'aoibhnigh do gháire
salachar an tseomra agus smúid oíche na sráide,
agus ansiúd ar sheanleabaidh lom na hainnise, bhí tú liom,
go huile agus go hiomlán, a ógánaigh chiúin an cheana.
Ansiúd ar an tseanleabaidh chruaidh, chnapánach úd
agus domboladh an allais ag éirí ón éadach tais,
bhlais mé do bhéilín ródheas, do bheola te teolaí,
a chuir an fhuil ar fiuchadh ionam le barr teasbhaigh …

Bhí gach cead agam, an oíche úd, ar do chaoinchorp caomh;
ar ghile cúr séidte do bhoilg; ar do bhaill bheatha
a ba chumhra ná úllaí fómhair 'bheadh i dtaisce le ráithe;
ar mhaolchnocáin mhíne do mhásaí, ar bhoige liom go mór iad
faoi mo láimh, ná leithead d'éadaigh sróil, a mbeadh tomhas
den tsíoda ina thiús … Anois agus mé 'mo luí
anseo liom féin i leabaidh léin an díomhaointis
tá mé ar tí pléascadh aríst le pléisiúr … le tocht

ag cuimhneamh ortsa, a ógánaigh álainn, deargnocht
a d'aoibhnigh an oíche domh … ocht mbliana déag ó shin, anocht.

CATHAL Ó SEARCAIGH (*b.* 1956)

Night

it wasn't much of a room
one of those B&Bs off Gardiner Street
damp on the walls the sheets yellow with grime
nothing to listen to but the slow moan
of the drunkening city and the racket
from bin-hoking cats in the yard but so what?

weren't you lying flat on your back on the edge
of the bed undressed to the nines?

and you clung to me so tight your laugh transforming the dirty room and murky night outside
to bliss there on the wreck of a bed you
in all your power and glory my quiet young lover
there on that hard hurting bed with stale
sweat rising from the damp sheet your warm
comforting lips kissed my blood alight

that night I could do anything with your slender
smooth body your belly bright as a foaming wave
and below more tempting than autumn apples
in store mine were the rolling drumlins of your cheeks
soft under my hand and light as the scantiest silk
now alone on a no-such-lucky bed in pain
in joy I remember you beautiful naked

transforming my night eighteen years ago tonight

CATHAL Ó SEARCAIGH (*b.* 1956)
Translated from the Irish by Frank Sewell

Nelson Street

There is hardly a mouthful of air
In the room where the breakfast is set,
For the blind is still down though it's late,
And the curtains are redolent yet
Of tobacco smoke, stale from last night.
There's the little bronze teapot, and there
The eggs on the blue willow-plate,
And the sleepy canary, a hen,
Starts faintly her chirruping tweet
And I know, could she speak, she would say,

'Hullo there — what's wrong with the light?
Draw the blind up, let's look at the day.'
I see that it's Monday again,
For the man with the organ is there;
Every Monday he comes to the street
(Lest I, or the bird there, should miss
Our count of monotonous days)
With his reed-organ, wheezy and sweet,
And stands by the window and plays
'There's a Land that is Fairer than This'.

SEUMAS O'SULLIVAN (1879–1958)

Charleville Mall Sestina

Woman at sad canal
clothed in a swan-cape,
lost to this water world
in green, reptile tunnels:
the white as lightning swan
swooped, and the bulrush burned.

The copper beeches burned,
the tropical canal
spun as a molten cape
of steel; locked in their world
of green violent tunnels,
woman and waning swan.

White potency of swans
that no thing female burned,
the white and pure canal,
to this undid her cape,
a new conquesting world
to her, stirred new tunnels.

Water-rats in tunnels,
an old decrepit swan,
an old hair mattress burned,
along the scummed canal;
to this her opened cape,
this legendary world.

'Look, I am naked, world,
my breasts from cloth tunnels
naked: mated by swan
whiteness, my body burned;
along this hid canal
I undid my cloth cape.'

Wet swan-web on her cape,
curtsey of swan to world
of swan, to wet tunnels:
for her attempting swan
satisfaction's scar burned
her face, her hid canal.

A swan on its canal
tunnels through its wet world:
burnt, a woman's cast cape.

MICHAEL HARTNETT (1941–1999)

The Pipers' Club

The leaping finger tightens on the string.
Bow slips sideways in a sudden swoop;
The fiddler's found his air; with head on swing,
His glazed eyes ignore the captive group.

But oh! my knuckles whiten at my plight.
What silken word can match the fiddler's fling

Who saw a blackbird in a gap of light
And trapped its sweetness on a tightened string?

ULICK O'CONNOR (*b.* 1928)

Summerhill Moon

October evening:
I ride the bus
over summer's high hill

eye-to-eye
with the moon
in the pinching black sky.

When I get home
it's balanced on the roof
of the Spring Street flats —

I call you out;
press my hand in yours,
watch the moon as it languishes

like a lemon slice
fallen from some deity's cocktail.
It's far from cocktails we are

and the moon is a bitter gift to give,
but a gift nonetheless;
held in the heat between our palms.

JESSICA TRAYNOR (*b.* 1984)

Dublin Girl, Mountjoy Jail, 1984

I dreamt it all: from end to end, the carriageway,
The rivulet behind the dairy streaked with crystal,
A steel moon glinting in a guttered stream of rain,
And the steep hill that I would crest to find her:
My child asleep in my old bedroom beside my sister.

I dreamt it all: and when I woke, furtive girls
Were clambering onto the bars of the windows,
White shapes waving against the dark skyline,
Praying for hands to reply from the men's cells
Before screws broke up the vigil of handkerchiefs.

I dreamt it all: the times I swore never again
To walk that carriageway, a rivulet of heroin glowing
In my veins until I shivered in its aftertaste,
And hid with my child in the closed-down factory
Where my brain snapped like a brittle fingernail.

I dreamt it all: the longing to touch her, the séance
In the cell when we screamed at the picture falling,
The warmth of circled hands after the frozen glass
Between my child and me, a warder following her words
To be rationed out and lived off for days afterwards.

I dreamt of you, who means all to me, my daughter,
How we might run to that carriageway by the rivulet,
And when I woke, a blue pupil was patrolling my sleep,
Jailing my dreams in the vacant orbit of its world,
Narrowed down to a spyhole, a globed eyelid closing.

1984

DERMOT BOLGER (*b*. 1959)

Condemned (*from* 'God's Pattern')

Hung there above
The nuns, you,
Red drops like darts
On your white outsides.

That frightened boy I was
Knelt in sin, clumsy
Street kid laced into
Boxing gloves to show off
The silly arts of self-
Defence to beaming mothers
At the convent drill display.
(Whose mother was too sick
To come? Whose d'you think,
Jackass?) Red drops, real blood,
On a white shirt when the round
Ended with the Angelus Bell
And rosary novenas on scraped knees
Benched before the thorn-crowned martyr-god.

Blood, blood, blood. The son
Tugged swathed in red
From the mother's womb
Soon learns cut-and-thrust
Wounds in a scrape with gang-boys
All along Church Street — gouts of it,
Streams, streaks, gouts of bloody offal
Over the slaughterhouse floor
Where we peeped in, straggling home
From bloody McGinty's bloody
Sixth Class National School.

JAMES J. MCAULEY (*b.* 1936)

Temple Street Children's Hospital

I

This is your territory, I brought you here:
Shoddy tenement windows where washing flaps,
Crumbling lanes where cars get broken for parts.

There is an archway beneath which we passed —
Like the one above which you shared a flat
With your sisters up from Monaghan for work

In a war-becalmed Dublin. Surely you must once
Have gazed up, puzzled by how the years since
Had landed you here with a son, a stuttering misfit,

Unable to pronounce the most simple of words,
A bright penny whose cloud you'd never see lift
As you fretted, unaware of how close death hovered.

The speech therapist's office had fancy toys and books
And a special mirror which allowed me to be watched.
The waiting room contained a white merciless clock

Which ticked off the final hours we spent alone,
Gazing down at a garden where I yearned to walk,
Trapped indoors by the shame of my garbled tongue.

II

I stand outside that hospital in Nerney's Court,
At Kelly's Row where a blacksmith once worked,

And no logic can explain why you feel this close,
Why I see us in the mother and child who pass,

Or how, as I age, I slowly become your son,
Gazing through your eyes with incomprehension.

I was too young to have known you, so it makes no sense
That every passing year only deepens your absence.

1996

DERMOT BOLGER (*b.* 1959)

Eccles Street, Bloomsday 1982

Onesided, stripped of its ghosts,
The half that was left of Eccles Street
Stood empty, on that day of days
My own unconscious feet
Would carry me through
To a blind date, or a rendezvous.

Invisible pressure, invisible heat
Laid down the blue coordinates
Of an Hellenic city
From Phoenix Park to the Merrion Gates,
Where disconnected, at one remove
From wisdom, or eternal love,

A million citizens worked, ate meals,
Or dreamt a moment of Joyce,
And felt themselves wholly real,
The equals of fate, the masters of choice,
As I did too, on Eccles Street,
Before ever you and I could meet

In the larger scheme .... Coincidence
Ruled invisibly, the casual date
Upstaged by Greek infinities
Moving among us like common sense,
Imprisoning, setting me free
To dream and circumambulate

In a myth too young to be formed.
I would build it myself, from the ruined door
Of Bella Cohen's bawdyhouse,
From other basements, other whores
Unbuttoning their blouses
Forever, while traffic swarmed

And the lights outside turned green and red
On shifting planes of reality —
And you, eternal student, read
Of Joyce in the National Library,
Or stood in the crowd, my love unseen,
At the unveiling in Stephen's Green.

An hour went by, on Eccles Street —
Two drunks, at ease in the Mater portals,
Swigged, and sang Republican songs.
I watched a line of taxis wait
And saw where real grass had sprung
Through mythic pavements, already immortal,

Green as life, and unresearched.
I had come, only that morning,
From Ringsend docks, and Sandymount Church,
Along the arc of odyssey,
With my invisible yearning
To break the circle, set myself free,

As you had yours, until one day
In the prefigured city,
Where every step is a step of fate
And recognition comes only later,
We would meet, you and I,
Weigh anchor at last, and go away.

HARRY CLIFTON (*b.* 1952)

Daily Bread

This morning, the sky cleared to reveal spring.
I went to the bakery hard by the market
and the streets were vital in the clear light.
A woman pushed a pram, her son holding on,
and she was happy to be with her children.
We dodged Japanese forklifts shifting oranges
from Jaffa, apples from Spain, potatoes from Rush.
Adjusting her shades, a driver reclined,
enjoying the breeze in the hold of her van.
The district was thronged, and juggernauts
edged their way through a street made for horses.
Amid merciless banter, a man was absorbed
in his racing page, reckoning his luck
as a dray-horse relished abandoned cabbage.

PHILIP CASEY (*b.* 1950)

North Brunswick Street Lullaby

When the sirens don't blast the air,
When they've put out the fire
And broken up the break-in and the mêlée,
Then the passing traffic sounds like the sea
Saying hush uselessly to the crowds
On the streets, who're out of their heads,
Who're seeing different things in the same light,
Who won't stop telling everyone about
The taxis having it sewn up altogether,
The next big thing who's a Cavan boxer,
The latest cheapest one-way ticket west,
The boyfriend's new girlfriend's bad conscience,
That song, the song you've never heard,
That goes something like this.

JOHN MCAULIFFE (*b.* 1973)

The Early Houses
for Belinda McKeon

They're all strung out, our alcoholic brethren,
On an infinite chain of early-morning drinks
In joints like this one. Little grey people
Unlike you, though — people without a future,

Dapper folk, with nothing to say for themselves,
The daily chemical hit, not ecstasy,
What they are after. Not exactly one of them
Myself, but the degree of separation

Less by the year, I can barely stay awake
As Smithfield market dawns, on a last blind date
Between night and morning, early and late —
The forklift whiz and rumble on the ramps,

The Chinese hauliers, their tailboards down
For the weight of the world. Little Britain Street,
North King Street — haunts of the underdog
Who lives off scraps, returns to his age-old vomit ...

One last glance, before we break away
Into past and future .... Drizzle, dark before dawn,
The lights kept low, in deference to the wishes
Of the damned, in this strobe-lit gin-palace

Afternoon whites out, when the children come
To fling themselves at ecstasy, as I did myself,
And the binges start. For your company, much thanks,
In the underworld. *Slán,* and don't look back.

HARRY CLIFTON (*b.* 1952)

The Dead and the Undead of St Michan's

They attended us, like martyrs, for centuries
as if their bones were stone and their skin
cured leather. They stood like sand-shapes
abandoned by tides, their language courtesy

and silence. We were witnesses to patience,
withheld decay, to timekeepers tremulous
to be loosed onto the air; we shook hands
with Strongbow, Patrick, Jesus, Thor

and left again, awed, and less afraid.
But the cider-drinkers, the language-killers,
came at night from our impatient streets,
they heaped the bones into a pyre, and the skulls

void with a centuries' old screaming, till —
with a communal sigh — the ancients yielded
to the flames. Farewell, our old familiars,
our seafarers, our progenitors, our clowns.

JOHN F. DEANE (*b.* 1943)

Smithfield Saturday

He only took this route in early mornings,
haring through green lights and the occasional red
as if we owned the paper-strewn streets.
But when we crossed the bridge
our car gave way to rumbling juggernauts.
Forklifts turned laden pallets on a penny
through plastic-ribboned doors.

Following at a distance, we clutched hands,
obeyed his curt commands over roaring engines
and the baritone of traders.
Nearer, burning rubber and diesel fumes
were laced with citrus
mixed with the sweet breath of ripe bananas,
the damp-earth odour of potato sacks.

Inside, we ranged from stall to stall,
Aladdins counting out the loot,
hovering once the choice was made,
the crate jemmied to reveal
its crinkle-papered hoard.
Our father, transformed to haggler,
picked up the fruit and sniffed each expertly,
his voice in muted undertone for the transaction.

He always knew his man, exchanging racing tips
before the spit and handshake polished off the deal.
Back past rows of exotica we never tasted,
past straw-filled crates showing labels garish
with palm-trees and pyramids,
arguing the toss on whether Jaffa
was the place or just a trader's name.

NESSA O'MAHONY (*b.* 1964)

Lines Written on the Burying-Ground of Arbour Hill in Dublin, where the bodies of Insurgents shot in 1798 were interred

No rising column marks this spot,
    Where many a victim lies;
But oh! the blood which here has streamed,
    To Heaven for justice cries.

It claims it on the oppressor's head,
    Who joys in human woe,
Who drinks the tears by misery shed,
    And mocks them as they flow.

It claims it on the callous judge,
    Whose hands in blood are dyed,
Who arms injustice with the sword,
    The balance throws aside.

It claims it for his ruined isle,
    Her wretched children's grave;
Where withered Freedom droops her head,
    And man exists — a slave.

O sacred Justice! free this land
    From tyranny abhorred;
Resume thy balance and thy seat —
    Resume — but sheathe thy sword.

No retribution should we seek —
    Too long has horror reigned;
By mercy marked may freedom rise,
    By cruelty unstained.

Nor shall a tyrant's ashes mix
    With those our martyred dead;
This is the place where Erin's sons
    In Erin's cause have bled.

And those who here are laid at rest,
    Oh! hallowed be each name;
Their memories are for ever blest —
    Consigned to endless fame.

Unconsecrated is this ground,
    Unblest by holy hands;
No bell here tolls its solemn sound,
    No monument here stands.

But here the patriot's tears are shed,
 The poor man's blessing given;
These consecrate the virtuous dead,
 These waft their fame to heaven.

ROBERT EMMETT (1778–1803)

The Parkgate Book of the Dead

Away from the scourge of daylight we sit,
transfixed by man-made darkness and uncomplex calm,
in hieroglyphic poses. I am the Jackal, confounded,
you are the Ibis scarred by your greed for beauty,
and we watch, with other beasts, our lives departing
into the tunnel of the original mystery tour.
We drink to their final journeys,
to the tattered passports of our souls,
and pray that mercy has a sense of humour.

Immured in space, voids of banter
orbit between our elbows,
feeding on photons of strain and silence,
and all that was said before is said again,
the reason and the rubbish, the smashing of promises,
in the cultivated language of destruction,
while we suck each other's bruises
and find each other always on a fallow footing.

Once was the heady green of possibility
sprouting earthly peace.
Once was an open book
loaded with restful heat.
But the seeds of deceit had been planted,
the white pages waiting to burn.

Now, as we relate
our singular falls,

browbeaten Jackal to ageing Ibis,
our eyes become a single eye,
a telescope of pain and longing
scouring earth sea and sky for our cunning.

Now, the screen hollers death in vivid Kodachrome,
and the corpulent general informs the room
that he, also, doesn't give a rat's butt.
This is how it is, how it must be;
the kerb beyond the door is cracking, oozing gas.
We drink again and breathe it in,
and breathe it in,
and breathe it in …

AIDAN MURPHY (*b.* 1952)

Ode to the Phoenix Park

Green sanctuary, where my artist's eye first opened.
I come again to flirt amid the fauna,
to pass your stone phallic monument of war.
Mighty oak and beech tower over me,
as memories flower from the wet soil,
worms crawl beneath my feet,
the sky bends to my bellow,
the sun plays its angelic score.
Park where I scraped my knee as a child,
park where I had a butane gas brain vision,
park where I sit in an empty bandstand in a valley of white
        benches,
park where I cover my face with muck, birds nest in my hair,
my toes twist to roots, my beard a pond filled with ducks,
my mouth agape to receive the communion of broken twigs
        and sap.

KARL PARKINSON (*b.* 1978)

Epigram on the New Magazine Fort in Phoenix Park

Behold! a proof of *Irish* sense!
   Here *Irish* wit is seen!
When nothing's left, that's worth defence,
   We build a magazine.

JONATHAN SWIFT (1667–1745)

Magazine Hill

Commanding, in a single vision,
Dublin hills to the south, where remote executions
Simplified our future, and the position
Of our Third Estate, west of Heuston Station,

I am to believe
It's on our side, the magazine fortress
On a height, where the guards have been deceived,
The country left defenceless,

On the brink of Europe's war
We never entered ... neutral energies
Pace themselves, moving like longdistance runners
In a race, as far as I can see

Through the Phoenix Park
Below the garrison. Islandbridge traffic roars
And a meaningless crowd, as it gets dark
Along Chapelizod Road, splits itself more and more ....

Somewhere behind barbed wire
And concrete slits, a single child is crying
In the guardroom, I could swear,
Or the dormitories. Everyone else is lying.

HARRY CLIFTON (*b.* 1952)

from **At the Polo-Ground**

(Samuel Ferguson's long poem 'At the Polo-Ground' treats of the assassination by The Invincibles of Lord Frederick Cavendish, the Chief Secretary of Ireland, and Thomas Henry Burke, the Permanent Undersecretary, in the Phoenix Park in 1882. The first of the two extracts below helps to set the scene while the second enters the mind of James Carey, the Fenian leader who masterminded the operation.)

6th May 1882

Here I am

Beside the hurdles fencing off the ground
They've taken from us who have the right to it,
For these select young gentry and their sport.
Curse them! I would they all might break their necks!
Young fops and lordlings of the garrison
Kept up by England here to keep us down:
All rich young fellows not content to own
Their chargers, hacks, and hunters for the field,
But also special ponies for their game;
And doubtless, as they dash along, regard
Us who stand outside as a beggarly crew.
'Tis half-past six. Not yet. No, that's not he.
Well, but 'tis pretty, sure, to see them stoop
And take the ball, full gallop; and when I
In gown and cocked hat once drove up Cork Hill,
Perhaps myself have eyed the common crowd,
Lining the footway, with a similar sense
Of higher station, just as these do me,
And as the man next door no doubt does them …

Oh, he comes at last!

No time for thinking now. My own life pays
Unless I play my part. I see he brings
Another with him, and, I think, the same
I heard them call Lord — something — Cavendish.
If one; two, likely. That can't now be helped.
Up. Drive on straight, — if I blow my nose

91

And show my handkerchief in front of them,
And then turn back, what's that to anyone?
No further, driver. Back to Island Bridge.
No haste. If some acquaintance chanced to pass,
He must not think that we are running away.
I don't like, but I can't help looking back.
They meet: my villains pass them. Gracious Powers,
Another failure! No, they turn again
And overtake; and Brady lifts his arm —
I'll see no more. On — by the Monument.
On — brisker, brisker — but yet leisurely.
By this time all is over with them both.
Ten minutes more, the Castle has the news,
And haughty Downing Street in half an hour
Is struck with palsy. For a moment there,
Among the trees, I wavered. Brady's knife
Has cut the knot of my perplexities;
Despite myself, my fortune mounts again.
The English rule will soon be overthrown,
And ours established in the place of it.
I'm free again to look, as long as I please,
In Fortune's show-box. Yes; I see the chain,
I see the guilder coach. God send the boy
May take the polish! There's but one thing now
That troubles me. These cursed knives at home
That woman brought me, what had best be done
To put them out o' the way? I have it. Yes,
That old Fitzsimons' roof's in need of repairs.
I'll leave them in his cock-loft. Still in time
To catch the tram, I'll take a seat a-top —
For no one must suppose I've anything
To hide — and show myself in Grafton Street.

SAMUEL FERGUSON (1810–1886)

The Zoological Gardens

Thunder and lightning is no lark
When Dublin city is in the dark
So if you've any money go up to the park
And view the Zoological Gardens.

We went out there to see the zoo,
We saw the lion and the kangaroo
There was he-males and she-males of every hue
Up in the Zoological Gardens.

We went out there by Castleknock,
Says she to me, "Sure we'll court on the lock,"
Then I knew she was one of the rare old stock
From outside the Zoological Gardens.

We went out there on our honeymoon.
Says she to me, "If you don't come soon
I'll have to get in with the hairy baboons
Up in the Zoological Gardens."

Says she to me, "It's seven o'clock
And it's time for me to be changin' me frock,
For I long to see the old cockatoo
Up in the Zoological Gardens."

Says she to me, "Me lovely Jack,
Sure I'd love a ride on the elephant's back,
If you don't get up there I'll give you a smack
Up in the Zoological Gardens."

Well, thunder and lightning is no lark
When Dublin city is in the dark,
So if you've any money go up to the park
And view the Zoological Gardens.

ANONYMOUS

Beacons at Bealtaine

Uisce: water. And *fionn:* the water's clear.
But dip and find this Gaelic water Greek:
A phoenix flames upon *fionn uisce* here.

Strangers were *barbaroi* to the Greek ear.
Now let the heirs of all who could not speak
The language, whose ba-babbling was unclear,

Come with their gift of tongues past each frontier
And find the answering voices that they seek
As *fionn* and *uisce* answer phoenix here.

The May Day hills were burning, far and near,
When our land's first footers beached boats in the creek
In *uisce, fionn,* strange words that soon grew clear;

So on a day when newcomers appear
Let it be a homecoming and let us speak
The unstrange word, as it behoves us here,

Move lips, move minds and make new meanings flare
Like ancient beacons signalling, peak to peak,
From middle sea to north sea, shining clear
As phoenix flame upon *fionn uisce* here.

SEAMUS HEANEY (1939–2013)
*This poem was delivered by Seamus Heaney at a ceremony in the
Phoenix Park to mark EU Enlargement, on May 1ˢᵗ, 2004.*

Wellington Testimonial

Needling my native sky over Phoenix Park
I obelize the victory of wit
That let my polished Anglo-Irish mark
Be made by Smirke, as a colossal spit.

Properly dressed for an obsolete parade,
Devoid of mystery, no winding stair
Threading my unvermiculated head,
I've kept my feet, but lost my nosey flair.

My life was work: my work was taking life
To be a monument. The dead have won
Capital headlines. Look at Ireland rife
With maxims: need you ask what good I've done?

My sole point in this evergreen oak aisle
Is to maintain a clean laconic style.

RICHARD MURPHY (*b.* 1927)

Making Love Outside Áras an Uachtaráin

When I was a boy, myself and my girl
Used bicycle up to the Phoenix Park;
Outside the gates we used lie in the grass
Making love outside Áras an Uachtaráin.

Often I wondered what de Valera would have thought
Inside in his ivory tower
If he knew that we were in his green, green grass
Making love outside Áras an Uachtaráin.

Because the odd thing was — oh how odd it was —
We both revered Irish patriots
And we dreamed our dreams of a green, green flag
Making love outside Áras an Uachtaráin.

But even had our names been Diarmaid and Gráinne
We doubted de Valera's approval
For a poet's son and a judge's daughter
Making love outside Áras an Uachtaráin.

I see him now in the heat-haze of the day
Blindly stalking us down;
And, levelling an ancient rifle, he says "Stop
Making love outside Aras an Uachtaráin."

PAUL DURCAN (*b.* 1944)

Daisy Chain

Sometimes on Sundays we'd take
the old canal bank walk
from Broom Bridge to the Ashtown Cross,
my father picking daisies as we went,

between questions of *How is school?*
and *Did you score any goals this week?*
my embarrassment at his interest,
a quiet *Fine* or *Only one this time.*

Often he would talk of the past,
of how his grandfather passed this spot
every day for nearly twenty years
as he drove the train from Castlebar

to Connolly Station, the canal water
his sign that he was nearly home,
until his early death in a red-brick
terraced house near Great Western Square,

my father saying, *I only knew him*
by a photograph the way you know my father
through me, as an image and likeness,
as a man about whom stories gather;

and all the while his fingers working
the stems, binding them together one
by one, a chain of flowers slowly forming
in his hands until joining first to last

the circle was complete and he'd
give it to me to throw into the canal waters.
And forgetting school and football,
we'd watch it floating on the surface,

bobbing slightly in our world of lost
connections, the frail wreath pulled
slowly downstream by the current,
towards the distant, steady thunder of the lock.

NOEL DUFFY (*b.* 1971)

Tilly

He travels after a winter sun,
Urging the cattle along a cold red road,
Calling to them, a voice they know,
He drives his beasts above Cabra.

The voice tells them home is warm.
They moo and make brute music with their hoofs.
He drives them with a flowering branch before him,
Smoke pluming their foreheads.

Boor, bond of the herd,
Tonight stretch full by the fire!
I bleed by the black stream
For my torn bough!

JAMES JOYCE (1882–1941)

1941 (North Strand)

Bulls running wild down the Wall
children juggling hot metal and bricks

"Shades of Guernica," said Mr. Nolan
"Bet that Blueshirt Duffy's changed his mind about them now"

Burning black and red again, flowers of smoke
in rows of jagged houses

"Didn't I tell ya," someone said
"they'd get yer man in the pawn sooner or later"

ALAN JUDE MOORE (*b.* 1973)

Elegy for Donal McCann

1
One night on Jones's Road,
on the terrace of houses below the road,
he opened a window and slipped in.

"No one heard me at the door,"
he said later,
"so I had to try a window."

Undeterred by the dimness and silence on that doorstep,
determined not to disappoint his hostess, her guests,
he hopped up on the windowsill,
grasped the lower sash and pushed.

2
One night on Usher's Island he went to a party.
It was the right night.
It was snowing.

It was Twelfth Night, the night for visits.
It was snowing.

His aunts fretted at his lateness,
feared he would not come.
They came out onto the landing,
closing out the notes of a polonaise,
to listen for the footfall of horses, their harness.

Snow
settled on the shoulders of his overcoat,
stiffened the spaces in its buttonholes.

BETTY THOMPSON (*b.* 1951)

Croke Park

We stand for the anthem, buoyant and tribal, heart beating
    with heart,
our colours brave, our faces turned from the uncertain sun.
The man beside me takes my hand; good luck to yours, he says;
I squeeze his calloused palm and then — he's gone.
A shadow socket where he was, the one beside him vanishes
and another before me, behind me; all around Croke Park
one by one we wink out of existence: tens, hundreds, then
thousands, the great arena emptying out, the wind curling in
from the open world to gather us all away. Each single one of us.
I could feel myself fail at the end, but then maybe everyone
    thought that,
each one of us the last to go. The whistle blew and we all
came back with a roar, everything brighter and louder,
    desperate and vivid.
I held his hand a moment longer, I wished his team all the luck
    in the world.

THEO DORGAN (*b.* 1953)

Herself and Himself

They're driving in
from the cricketing fields of Dublin
past the Five Lamps, Empress Lane
and the Corner of the Talkers
where you'll still get wind
of the bombing of the North Strand
in a war we were no part of
or so we thought. It isn't always
we know what wars we're in.
There's shopping to be done,
young mouths waiting for baker's bread.
She knows the shops, the men and women
behind the counters. She knows himself too.
On a tough journey, a few words will do
to ensure the future will be fed.
She does the shops, gets what she wants,
they have two creamy pints together
then hit for home
between the worked fields and the sea,
herself and himself
words and silence
peace and war
you and me.

BRENDAN KENNELLY (*b*. 1936)

East Road, East Wall

There was sunlight in the yard
when I broke my toe
five years of age
fifty years ago
in the hall the Japanese umbrellas
in the parlour

the mandolin and concertina
always sunlight in the yard
and heaps of coal
lights from the locomotives after dark —
I know
the heat from the fire-box glow
in Westerns

In the roof there were pointed windows
behind the house
the verandah
trainlines leading to the docks
down there where my green balloon
sailed off
all those missing years ago

And a journey with my mother
across Dublin
past the Custom House —
oh don't put me
in there — I said
don't ever put me in there —
three of us up
on a donkey and cart
moving my grandfather's piano
me and my mother
and the one-armed driver
my mother engaged —
piano-mover with a heart condition

Anchored in time
and light — a child
in Gandon's open space
where my
one-legged great-grand-uncle
navigated yet another
nautical academy
the first left sailing empty
abandoned in Belfast

Behind us all the afternoon
the East Wall in the sun
the parish register
of Lawrence O'Toole's —
recording the marriage of Wooloughan and Dias
and where was she from I wonder
the Iberian name at last
the further I go
the nearer I get
get back
to that peninsula
travelling south to Pembroke Street

Travelling now to
Clonskeagh
half a century later
across the river and city
across the Grand Canal
(that's my house there
        in Ranelagh
that's where my son lives
        and I
hold onto this
I think
and that is where I was born
down there
in Upper Leeson Street)

On the anniversary of my father's death
I am looking toward
Clonskeagh
where my mother is slowly dying
and saying her fragments of prayers
from childhood — oh
in this January month
as always
the trees are bare
I see too clear

In the pumping-station
I paused today
there was sunlight
in the yard
the engineer says
there is always sunlight here
he says —
not true I know
but I know what he means
for this was the place for photographs
on kitchen chairs
hauled into daylight
my people sat here
afternoons

This week
they begin to knock the house
that was Billy Woods's home:
and Norah Wooloughan's

the Japanese umbrellas
the mandolin and concertina
the columned clock on the mantel
their three sons

the heaps of coal
the puff and steam of locomotives
and the shaking great pump-engines
gone

outside the bricked-up
parlour window
a palm tree in the earth lives on

January 1999

MACDARA WOODS (*b.* 1942)

Fairview Park: 6 a.m.
for Dan McMahon

1

Night into a trumpet-mouth
had funnelled,
loudly in silver to the east and south:
in viscous drops light had tunnelled
into a sudden scar of blue.
An audacious blackbird started,
and the cock crew.
A young lady,
vague in nineteenth-century dress,
massive and locked with lace,
her oaken-old, her lily face
stretched with nineteenth-century stress,
had clasped my wrist.
She was obviously out of place,
obviously distressed.
'It is not as if we parted —
indeed we never met,
but who shares my dawn with me
must not forget
the trees are brokenhearted.'
I fumbled with some careful words,
having no muse at hand.
She flew, a flock of migrant birds,
across the wailing land.

2

I spoke to a lone plover
in no uncertain fashion:
'What feather of a lover
do you seek with such passion?'

Its piebald, reptile glance
marbly regarded me.
Its plumed, nunlike stance
disconcerted me.

'Can you not see the female curve
beneath this down,
nor in this birdlike frown
detect a moving nerve?'

It clawed me, shrieking, human,
and fled across the park.
Perhaps the internecine dark
made it a running woman.

MICHAEL HARTNETT (1941–1999)

Cycling to Marino

Leaves and leaves and leaves —
huge chestnut fans, bright sycamore, and oak
plastered against pavement, kerb, cushioning slick road
beneath my tyres, stifling the slight squirt of rain
which should mark my passing.

My sisters I've cast off, shed them at the turn
up Glandore Road, and I continue free-
wheeling on the stretch of Griffith Avenue that's mine
until I hit the school. I'm seven and exultant in the drowse
of leaves, thick colours, dormancy, fine rain,

In the classroom, the heat from hot water pipes
dries sodden clothes on skin. We know someone's
not clean, and someone's poor, and always late,
someone's too fat or tall or pale
and someone's palms get reddened much too often
but what does poor mean? Where are those places
other people live? Places to the north or east
with names like Artane, Donnycarney, Whitehall —
houses much like our own but not, strange
mothers making stew in sculleries while we
swim through the classroom,
absorbing drench and drift —

Metallic taste of ink on lips so much more urgent even
than the waxy paper bread and jam
comes wrapped in. Or glimpse of stacks
of brand-new copies, unpared pencils bound
with bands, lodged deep within the unlocked cupboard.
Delirium of new books, bold colours barely dry
the smell of pages, fresh from the printing works,
while we sit chewing wood or graphite, wool,
the whorls on finger-tips soak up
the business of the day, eyes clinging to the nun's
soft winter habit, the way the pleat turns
at her breast, the independent curve of strand, of thread,
the heavy cross along the length of robe
that's petrol blue. We're learning how to sew, to knit,
each stitch has singularity, then holds its shape
in partnership with the next, and next —

My mother walks along the avenue to meet me.
She carries apples. And I dismount,
escorting her through bowers that I know best,
stern arch of branch, cascade of leaf,
the stench of fermentation, rain.
We planted bulbs today — I could try this —
how I wished to drive my sharp white teeth
against brown jackets into compact flesh!
Today I broke my flask. I hear its subdued rattle
in my bag and I am scared, seeing ahead
her glass-roofed kitchen, home,
keeping to myself my own disasters or
the sight of silver shards abandoned
in a pool of milky tea, the way tea leaks
into the awkward gloss of concrete,
the way steam rises in snarls,
mysterious, remote like heat, then disappears.

MAIRÉAD BYRNE (*b.* 1957)

from Stardust Sequence

(i.m. those young people killed by fire after emergency exits were chained in the Stardust Night Club, a converted jam factory, Artane, North Dublin, 1981)

I

Shadows whisper a new language of possibilities
From hidden couples reminding us we are not alone
In searching for romance and the kinship encountered
While dancing to the secret rhythms of our peers.
Through steel shutters clamped across windows
Rock music invents a vocabulary that unites us.

Strobelights on the ceiling break up the air until
The brain keeps pace with the body's theatricality
In this slow, fragmented black-and-white movie.
Every Friday you would dance away the hours
In gathering tempo until the harsh glare of bulbs
Evicted you from a space that felt briefly yours.

Thrust out into the night you'd doss or go home
Among couples & groups of girls singing of love.
But tomorrow you will wander incubator estates
And stare disbelieving, in the brutality of dawn,
At silent families maintaining vigils in doorways
With only numb anger left burning inside them.

II

Last night in swirling colour we danced again,
And, as strobelights stunned in black & white,
I reached in this agony of slow motion for you.
But you danced on as if cold light still shone,
Merging into the crowd as my path was blocked
By snarling bouncers & dead-eyed club owners.

When I screamed above the music nobody heard,
I flailed under spotlights like a disco dancer
And people formed a circle clapping to the beat
As I shuddered round the club in a violent fit.
Hurtling through a dream without trembling awake,
I revolved through space until I hit the ground.

Lying among their feet tramping out the tunes,
I grasped you inside my mind for this moment,
Your white dress bobbing in a cool candle-flame,
Illuminating the darkness spinning towards me:
A teenage dancing queen, proud of her footwork,
Sparks rising like stardust all over the floor.

III

We are here along the edge of people's memories,
A reference point in the calendar of their lives.
Our absence linked with acceptances or refusals
On summer evenings when love seemed attainable
And moist lips opened after dances in the parks.
We are the unavoidable stillbirth of your past.

The young golden girl you loved, pregnant at seventeen;
Young friends growing sour, paralysed by the dole;
Your senile boss, already rotting inside his skin,
Returns the look of hatred that's burning you up,
Drawing new breath from every young life wrecked.
All those smooth men who would quietly forget us,

Who turn you on a spit over cold flames of dissent,
Are guilty of murder as if they chained the exits
When we stampeded through their illusion of order.
We have buried in your skull these ashes of doubt
And you believe nothing but one slow fuse of anger
Since the night your thin candle of youth ran out.

DERMOT BOLGER (*b.* 1959)

from **The Battle of Clontarf**

"Stand ye now for Erin's glory! Stand ye now for Erin's cause!
Long ye've groaned beneath the rigour of the Northmen's
    savage laws.
What though brothers league against us? What, though
    myriads be the foe?
Victory will be more honoured in the myriads' overthrow.
Proud Connacians! oft we've wrangled in our petty feuds of yore;
Now we fight against the robber Dane upon our native shore;
May our hearts unite in friendship, as our blood in one red tide,
While we crush their mail-clad legions, and annihilate their pride!
Brave Eugenians! Erin triumphs in the sight she sees today —
Desmond's homesteads all deserted for the muster and the fray!
Cluan's vale and Galtees' summit send their bravest and their
    best —
May such hearts be theirs forever, for the Freedom of the West!"

WILLIAM KENEALY (1828-1876)

Dublin Bay

A good time to come is January;
there is a geranium sky behind Longford Terrace,
a black pine gone mad between chimneys,
from where you stand by the abandoned soap factory.

Turn right: the town is walled in mist;
no twentieth century, but hard, sure,
the winter rip of Vikings, tearing dire
by Howth, fogged also, yet solid, fast.

You are back where Brian seemed holy
praying in Clontarf. There are no bulls either
nor the strewn excesses of a modern summer
at Seapoint. Only the cormorants, happy,

and the ceaseless pagan sea; you climb
as do two or three others, each alone
trudging towards that queer geranium zone ...
January, there, is a good time.

EITHNE STRONG (1923–1999)

Kiss

I

On O'Connell Bridge against the wind and the sleet
With a terrified newspaper wrapped round your feet
You stood past all embarrassment to kiss and kiss again
The boyfriend whose arms you found yourself in.
And watching his black hair toss round your flying fair hair
(The ponies gallop on the beach
The crab bursting out laughing)
I fly through exams
But miserably fail
Even to begin to comprehend the very tip of your toenail.

II

There's a clam on the seabed
Kissing itself under tide-kisses
And claw-marks on Dollymount Strand
Where the bull crab straddled his missus
While I'm forced to watch the closed door
Open to persuasion in the dark
Where somebody's tinkering with somebody's heart
On whose body's inscribed the motto:
Let us lie and be happy till dawn us two part.

1973

MAURICE SCULLY (*b.* 1952)

from **Lament for the Bull Island**

They have burned and razed
the mansion of St Anne's
and dumped its rubble
in the Blue Lagoon

so cars may cross to you
and make a parking lot
of Dollymount Strand.

The long white laces
of the sea are stained
and the dunes are sown
with broken glass.

Away to the west and the city
the great oil drums
are massed like tanks
waiting to roll forward
and encircle the proud
Head of Howth.

Across the wooden bridge
above the flotillas
of seagull and duck
under the swooping squadrons
I go to you
to say goodbye.
For how many years
have you given me sanctuary?
How often have I stumbled
across to you
holding my mind
like an aching limb?

And lain among your grasses
and walked your strands

until the thunder of the surf
vanquished despair
and my heart was hopeful
with the song of birds.

KEVIN FALLER (1920–1983)

Touchdown
The Brent Geese return to Bull Island

Bay, open bay, spread out below
the cloud banks, cloud-dappled, drenched
in greens and greys, scarred
by the sudden and the gradual
in equal parts, but firm;

one foot-sized expanse
and then another, shimmering,
waiting for the fall of shadow,
the relaxing of muscles, the folding
of wing and reach, the dip
and careful drift down into touch
and sodden

solidity of place — the screech
of other selves, the echoing of hunger,
and the ache, the sheer
collective ache, after
so much longing, after so much
of nothing else to depend upon
but open air.

PAT BORAN (*b.* 1963)

Drumcondra Bridge

Three lanes become two here, motorists joust
In a daily game to see who will blink first.

Every afternoon when I approach this bridge
I relive the second when the cyclist strayed
To avoid a pothole that blocked her passage;
Her glimpse of water through the balustrade

As a car brushed the college books on her carrier
With the faintest touch as she swerved and fell.
Traffic crept past while passers-by encircled her
Motionless and hushed as if locked into a spell.

Her back wheel still spun when it had fallen,
With her face hidden, no hint of hair or clothes,
But peeping out from an oil-streaked tarpaulin
Two breathtakingly white slender bare soles.

DERMOT BOLGER (*b.* 1959)

1968

He sixteen — sixteen she — on a green bench
by a wall under the chestnut's canopy opposite
The Cat & Cage in winter, half-past six
and dark, the sudden, intimate taste of lipstick —
pippin, unpredatory — those lovely, licit,
Irish, uncontinental soft touches first pervade.

Margaret Dunne.
I name you for the magic of it,
your marvellous school uniform
still on.

MAURICE SCULLY (*b.* 1952)

Cross Guns Bridge

Once too often for my taste I shall cross
That bridge two miles north of Dublin where
On one side an orphanage, other, a gas-station,
Stand like twin guardian demons on this undoubting road.

Had they been chosen, what could be more appropriate
On the approach to a graveyard than these two buildings?
Some surrealist impulse welled up like spring-water
And tossed out this gas-station, this bridge and this orphanage.

There, opposite but more than similar, they stand, fit symbols:
One to remind the mourners how they all are homeless
Like the homeless one in the brass-bound coffin whom they
    follow
From the hub of life to the rim of clay-stopped quietness,

And one to tell them how the days rush by,
The acceleration of seconds, the whining meanness of years,
How our minds run dry, how our lives start pinking,
How we need the hands of love to set them right again.

Not London Bridge of London Town but a decrepit structure
Spans the artificial river dividing city and cemetery,
Dividing dead and not-so-dead. It will collapse
Any day and a good many be caught unwittingly.

Yet who would anticipate evil in days like these
When it alights around us like birds unexpectedly
And steals through our chimneys and windows with the day
Of the light and the night of the dark as its cloaks.

Well to the south of Dublin, to-day I watch
The evening cloud over, the inclination of rain.
Outside my window, the green spume of the earth
Drenches the irises of my eyes and my girl is laughing.

VALENTIN IREMONGER (1918–1991)

114

Leinster Street
for Bernie

Let us wake again in Leinster Street,
    Both of us still twenty-six,
On a spring Monday in 1985.
    We lie on, relaxed, illicit,
Listening to the melody below
    Of friends cooking breakfast.
Flaking paint on the lattice,
    Old wire, crumbling stone,
The silos of the abandoned mill
    Framed by windows which open
Onto flowers that are lodged
    Between bricks in the lane.

And no need for us to rise
    For one more drowsy hour:
Lie on with me in that moment
    When you were still too shy
To dress yourself while I watched
    Your limbs garbed in light.

          *

In those rooms five years passed
    In a single drawn-out breath,
Before we plunged into new lives.
    Remember how the ceiling wept
Beneath each rafter in the winter,
    The rustle of cards that crept

Up unlit stairways after midnight.
    May some tenant of the future
Turn when switching out his light
    And, framed by the doorway, glimpse
The phosphorescence of our lives
    Still glowing with this happiness.

DERMOT BOLGER (*b.* 1959)

The Botanic Gardens

It was too early in the year
to see much. The herbaceous walk
was scattered with a few daffodils
and tulips, everything else lay
in sodden mounds waiting their turn.
The gardens had a bare scrubbed look,
I got tired of endless rows of polyanthus.

You, pushing our daughter in her buggy,
stopped and examined every tree,
Though all I saw was skeleton and bark,
except for the evergreens. The 'giant' sequoias
were a mite small for my taste.

All the while our son ran on ahead,
impatient to be gone, our daughter
wore her petulant look. Out of the corner
of my eye I could see the tall tower
of the crematorium nearby and curling smoke
from a bonfire burning last year's leaves.

JEAN O'BRIEN (*b.* 1952)

Holotropic Botanicus

I close my eyes to find before me
    A wooden door with a silver handle,
        Which I feel unable to open,
            Which opens by itself inwardly.

Beyond it, a nightscape of stars
    Weakens down to the glimmer
        Of a sweating pane of glass,
            Curved within corroding girders.

The Waterlily House of the Botanic Gardens;
  My son's face moisted in the sultry light,
    We are seated by the plopping waterwheel
      And we are smiling across at each other.

I only realise as the scene is dissipating
  That I am him and the tall figure my mother,
    Goldfish flit through the green water
      And we are smiling across at each other.

1993

DERMOT BOLGER (*b.* 1959)

First Poem

I went out with nowhere to go,
Past the houses
And well past the snow.
The river in the reeds
Beneath the Tolka bridge
Slowed down and froze,
And I too waited
On silence an age.

The Wooden Church was closed
And yet its bell began to chime
The Seven Dolours of Glasnevin.
I thought of God, waylaid by time.
He could not be something, so
He must be nothing.
There was no heaven,
There was only the snow.

Beyond the city, still as death,
The sea at Ireland's Eye
Let out its breath.
A child was being born
That would not cry.
The baby crowed
And I began to shiver
Outside of the houses
Alone in the snow.

The windows glowed
As if they knew.
The sky, grown clear, allowed
The stars resume their dance
In the river,
And the moon came out too,
For the child was stubborn still
That laughed with chance
On Mobhi Hill.

I went home with nowhere to go,
Past the houses
And well, well past the snow.

BRIAN LYNCH (*b.* 1945)

Glasnevin Cemetery

With deportment learnt from samurai films
I surface in the ancestral suburbs.
My grandmother is older than China
Wiser than Confucius.
I pace my stride to hers
Soaking in the grey-green air.

Under my name cut in stone
My grandfather lies
Within hearing of the lorries' roar
Out on the main road.
I forget my unseemly haste
To see the Emperor's tomb.

We search for family graves
In the suburbs of the dead.
From the jumble of worn stones
Unmarked by celtic crosses
Like an egyptologist she elucidates
Obscure back-street dynasties.

We see where Parnell lies buried
Under Sisyphean stone
Put there my father says
To keep him from climbing out.
I am surprised by ancient bitterness
Surfacing among the TV programmes.

The plotters of the nation
Are niched in their kitsch necropolis.
Matt Talbot, Larkin, Michael Collins
A holy graven trio
Shoulder to shoulder enshrined
In the tidy bogomil parlour of her heart.

The day flowers sluggishly
From the stone of contradictions.
The trees sway like green Hasidim
I shuffle in a kind of lethargic dance
A sprung sign among the signified
A tenant in the suburbs of silence.

MICHAEL O'LOUGHLIN (*b.* 1958)

Elvis in Glasnevin

No kisses are harder to remember.
Any night will bear witness to that
With a rolling dustbin and a black cat.
Elvis is singing *Return To Sender;*
Most of the stalls are closed; the fortune teller,
Down on her luck, has taken leave from fate
And closed up shop; the candy-floss seller
Twirls a final cloud, like himself, soft and fat;
The dodgems clump together, sparkless, duller
Than the neon stars, turned off, grown cold.
The last ghost train bursts out, it has no freight.
But the barely formed kids are so carnal
And bewildered in the half-dead carnival
That it seems natural to have and to hold,
And though the fact is our paths have not crossed
And no kisses are hard to remember
Everyone like that tonight seems tender
And so what if, like Glasnevin, we're lost.

BRIAN LYNCH (*b.* 1945)

Glasnevin North

Jack Lynch looks down from every pole.
Mammy likes him because he comes from Cork.
Daddy says he should be taken out and shot.
I'm walking to the shops with Timothy.
He always looks sleepy.
"My father will give me the belt tonight," he says.
"What did you do? Poison his tea?"
"Nothing."
"Do his trousers not fall when he takes off his belt?"
"He has a special belt for hitting me.
He hangs it on the kitchen door."
"Oh."

Doug and Tony are both shot through the heart.
Merlin sends the bolts back to their crossbows.
"Are you not having any tea?" Mammy says.
"I'm not hungry," I say.
Although I am.

Cherry blossom petals shower my path.
Is it eight years since I lived here?
The daffodils all nod.
My Captain Scarlet wallpaper is gone.
The witch cottage is smothered by ivy.
Nettles nestle where I once feared to tread.

ALAN MOORE (*b.* 1960)

Other People's Grief

1950s Dublin: two girls sit silently on an open-backed bus,
Winter coats draped over their laps so that the conductor,

Sauntering downstairs to collect their fares, will not notice
The tiny infant's coffin cautiously concealed on their knees:

The wooden box their hands cradle with covert tenderness,
En route to Glasnevin Cemetery's unmarked angels' plot.

The journey never revealed to future husbands or children:
The journey they never dare refer to, even with each other:

This ache that might have allowed daughters to decipher them:
The unutterable weight of that small box carried to their deaths.

DERMOT BOLGER (*b.* 1959)

The Song of Dermot and the Earl

The Old French poem Chanson de Dermot et du Comte describes the coming of Strongbow and the Normans to Ireland and the native resistance to same. In it we learn of an army, some 60,000 strong, made up of contingents from all parts of the country, camped out in a number of locations around Dublin, preparing to close on the city.

A chastelknoc, acele feiz,
De connoth iout li riche reis;
E macdunleue de huluestere
A clontarf ficha sa banere;
E obrien de monestere
A kylmainan od sa gent fere;
E murierdath, cum lentent,
Vers dalkei fu od sa gent.

At this time to Castleknock
Came the wealthy king of Connaught;
MacDunlevy down from Ulster
At Clontarf unfurled his banner;
To Kilmainham, with his soldiers,
O'Brien travelled up from Munster;
Murtough, too, as I hear tell,
Was out near Dalkey with his men.

Anonymous (early 13th century)
Translated by Pat Boran

Motorway Daffodils

The daffodils are glittering by the motorway —
those long-thighed ladies of the autostrada.
They outdo even the derelict washing machines
with their in-your-face-ness. I'm winter breathless,
unready. The autumn leaves I meant to clear,
the pounds I meant to lose, are rotting quietly

in heaps, when next thing, here's your one, Spring,
showing her legs to the jaded drivers. The fields
have lost their mud-covers and even Dunsink
sports a sward for travellers' foals. On the estates
it's all cherry blossom, Corporation tractors
and a new crop of kids roller-blading the walkways.

Yet again I remember
that I've never learnt to dance, or play the trombone,
never kissed him on the top of the No. 10 bus
coming back home from the zoo. And now
that I'm more than halfway to little old ladyhood
(10 mass, umbrellas, and prodigal ailments)
it's too late, too late ...
Bring back winter and its blackout on truth!
A plague on all you jangling daffodils!

MÁIRÍDE WOODS (*b*. 1948)

Finglas, 1979

Steel winds at dawn sting like a wasp,
    In this factory where men curse
And rust grows like hair on a corpse.

She's off to work as he finishes night shift.
    Today is their child's first birthday,
They'll put his name on the housing list.

Taking a chair he sits in the garden,
    Smoking Moroccan dope and tripping,
The housing estate keeps disappearing.

He feels himself at the bottom of a pond,
    Floating below rows of water lilies
With new names like Finglas and Ballymun.

DERMOT BOLGER (*b*. 1959)

Stony, Grey, Soiled
after Kavanagh

Ballymun you rock-hard bitch
My childhood love you thieved.
Your harsh nature quarried my passion.
You carved me from barren streets.

You concreted the feet of my boyhood
And twisted my stride to a stumble.
Your sprawl corrupted my naïve tongue,
Indian-inking my guttural mumble.

You preached from the trough of the scrounger,
The heaving, life-strangling trough.
Your mantra stained, your culture stunted,
You kept diamonds dull, in the rough.

You screamed 'cross piss-stained balconies
The wail of the deserted brood.
You stewed my clothes in smoke and booze
You reared me on stale food.

Your silhouette sours my vision
Of beauty, love and truth.
Ballymun, you barren whore
You spoiled the stock of my youth.

Not for me golden views of mothers
As poverty-free young hens,
So I vow to stab at your crusted back
And embrace the poisoned pen

That scars these loveless verses
And curses the tarmac where
The first clean flight of my fury
Got caught in this poet's prayer.

124

Ceannt, McDermott, Balbutcher, Shangan,
Wherever I run I see
The stony grey rubble of Ballymun
Rebuilt as dark towers in me.

COLM KEEGAN (*b.* 1975)

from The Smock Race at Finglas

Now did the bag-pipe in hoarse notes begin
The expected signal to the neighbouring Green,
While the sun, in the decline of day,
Shoots from the distant West a cooler ray.
Alarmed, the sweating crowds forsake the Town,
Unpeopled Finglas is a desert grown;
Joan quits her cows which with full udders stand
And low unheeded for the milker's hand.
The joyous sound the distant reapers hear,
Their Harvest leave and to the Sport repair;
The Dublin Prentice at the welcome call
In hurry rises from his cakes and ale;
Handling the flaunting seamstress o'er the plain,
He struts a Beau among the homely swain.

JAMES WARD (1691–1736)

My Father Perceived as a Vision of St Francis
for Brendan Kennelly

It was the piebald horse in next door's garden
frightened me out of a dream
with her dawn whinny. I was back
in the boxroom of the house,
my brother's room now,

full of ties and sweaters and secrets.
Bottles chinked on the doorstep,
the first bus pulled up to the stop.
The rest of the house slept

except for my father. I heard
him rake the ash from the grate,
plug in the kettle, hum a snatch of a tune.
Then he unlocked the back door
and stepped out into the garden.

Autumn was nearly done, the first frost
whitened the slates of the estate.
He was older than I had reckoned,
his hair completely silver,
and for the first time I saw the stoop
of his shoulder, saw that
his leg was stiff. What's he at?
So early and still stars in the west?

They came then: birds
of every size, shape, colour; they came
from the hedges and shrubs,
from eaves and garden sheds,
from the industrial estate, outlying fields,
from Dubber Cross they came
and the ditches of the North Road.
The garden was a pandemonium
when my father threw up his hands
and tossed the crumbs to the air. The sun
cleared O'Reilly's chimney
and he was suddenly radiant,
a perfect vision of St Francis,
made whole, made young again,
in a Finglas garden.

PAULA MEEHAN (*b.* 1955)

Fingal Driving Range

From the dark car park where you used to sit
To check all your texts and voice messages,
Fantasias of white balls trace solitary orbits
Across a floodlit arc of sky above the rooftop,
Like silent souls failing to ascend into heaven.

DERMOT BOLGER (*b.* 1959)

'A Man is Only as Good'

A man is only as good
as what he says to a dog
when he has to get up out of bed
in the middle of a wintry night
because some damned dog has been barking;

and he goes and opens the door
in his vest and boxer shorts
and there on the pock-marked wasteground
called a playing field out front
he finds the mutt with one paw

raised in expectation
and an expression that says Thank God
for a minute there I thought
there was no one awake but me
in this goddamned town.

Baldoyle, 2002

PAT BORAN (*b.* 1963)

Grange Abbey, Donaghmede

It's a shell marooned on a suburban shore,
a shell that we scarcely listen to:
Open your ears!

Under the tide of traffic there's a faint rush of sea;
the wind singing in the golden meadows;
the shouts of men hoisting keystones;
the stone-cutter at the grave slabs.

Here lies a way of life:
the church itself a gravestone now,
the graveyard a park, unloved as parks go,
a local traversy, a travesty
of stripped bicycles and shopping trolleys.
Here lies the Grange of Baldoyle:
a medieval supermarket, a busy farm
with daily deliveries on carts or foot
into the spreading town.

Open your ears!
Can you hear the King of Leinster's coach,
hear his great lungs breathe in the country air?
That's the scratch of his quill
gifting his gleaming fields to city monks.

Open your ears!
Hear the din of dinner at the Priory of All Hallows:
Trinity monks sup milk from Baldoyle cows,
feed on Grange cheeses, bread and butter,
quaff St Donagh's mead.

And we should drink deep from this well of history:
These walls guard secrets still,
have barely teased the archeologists
with splinters of bowls and bones,
a riddle of shifted stones.

Open your ears!
A whole world quivers like a slammed door
in this shell washed up on a suburban shore.

CATHERINE ANN CULLEN (*b.* 1961)

Station Road, Sutton

There is that moment when the barrier comes down
on Station Road, when the train to Howth has passed
and nothing happens; when the men in lycra vests
and shorts on their blade-thin wheels look round

and through each other; when the yummy mums
with their dozy, school-bound offspring by their sides
or trussed up in the seats behind like dolls,
glance down one more time to check the time;

when the very birds up on that ever slack
tangle of cables shuffle two steps left
or one step right; when the sea retreats
and only sunlight advances along the track;

when something in the chest unlocks or shifts,
and you find you're no longer waiting; when the barrier lifts.

PAT BORAN (*b.* 1963)

Moladh Bhinn Éadair

Aoibhinn bheith i mBinn Éadair,
fírbhinn bheith ós a bánmhuir,
cnoc lánmhar longmhar líonmhar
beann fhíonmhar fhonnmar ághmhar.

Beann i mbíodh Fionn is Fiana,
beann i mbíodh cuirn is cuacha;
beann i rug ua Duinn dána
lá Gráinne do ruinn ruaga.

Beann tomghlan seach gach tulach,
's a mullach crunnghlas corrach,
cnoc lannach creamhach crannach,
beann bhallach mhíolach mhongach.

Beann is áille ós úir Éireann,
glébheann ós fairrge faoileann,
a tréigean is céim cruaidh liom,
Beann álainn Éadair aoibhinn.

ANONYMOUS (12th century)

In Praise of Howth Head

Delightful to be in Binn Éadair,
Pure pleasure over the bright sea,
Standing proud above many ships,
Intoxicating, spacious, auspicious.

Hill that hosted Fionn and the Fianna,
Their hunting horns, their drinking horns,
Hill where once the daring Diarmuid
Ran his race for love with Gráinne.

Hill whose outcrops are the clearest,
Summit roundest, steepest, greenest
Hill of sharp blades, garlic, trees,
Dappled, thicketed, many-creatured.

Loveliest hill on Irish soil,
Over sea and seabirds shining,

It's with a heavy step I leave
Binn Éadair — dazzling, delightful!

ANONYMOUS (12th century)
Translated from the Middle Irish by Paddy Bushe

Ar Thrá Bhinn Éadair

Ar thrá Bhinn Éadair
Briseann tonn le fuaim;
Screadann faoileán aonrach
Os cionn an chuain.

Ó lár an léana
Le hais Ghlas Naíon
Labhrann an traona
Ar feadh na hoích'.

Tá ceiliúr éanlaithe
I nGleann na Smól,
An lon 's an chéirseach
Ag cantain ceoil.

Tá soilse gréine
Ar thaobh Sléibh' Rua,
Is an ghaoth ag séideadh
Óna bharr anuas.

Ar chuan Dhún Laoghaire
Tá bád is long
Fá sheoltaibh gléasta
Ag treabhadh na dtonn.

Anseo in Éirinn
Dom féin, a bhráthair,
Is tusa i gcéin uaim
I bPáras áigh:

Mise ag féachaint
Ar chnoc is chuan,
Ar thrá Bhinn Éadair,
Is ar thaobh Sléibh' Rua;

Is tusa go réimeach
I bPáras mór
Na ríbhrugh n-aolda
Is na dtreathanslógh.

'S éard atáim a éileamh
Ort féin, a ghrá,
I bhfad i gcéin duit
Go smaoinír tráth

Ar phort an traona
Le hais Ghlas Naíon,
Ó lar an léana
Ag labhairt san oích';

Ar ghlór na héanlaithe
I nGleann na Smól,
Go sásta séiseach
Ag cantain ceoil;

Ar thrá Bhinn Éadair
Mar a mbriseann tonn,
'S ar chuan Dhún Laoghaire
Mar a luascann long;

Ar an ngréin ag scéitheadh
Ar thaobh Sléibh' Rua,
Is ar an ngaoth a shéideas
Óna bharr anuas!

PÁDRAIG PEARSE (1879–1916)

On the Strand of Howth

On the strand of Howth
Breaks a sounding wave;
A lone sea-gull screams
Above the bay.

In the middle of the meadow
Beside Glasnevin
The corncrake speaks
All night long.

There is minstrelsy of birds
In Glenasmole,
The blackbird and thrush
Chanting music.

There is shining of sun
On the side of Slieverua,
And the wind blowing
Down over its brow.

On the harbour of Dunleary
Are boat and ship
With sails set
Ploughing the waves.

Here in Ireland,
Am I, my brother,
And you far from me
In gallant Paris,

I beholding
Hill and harbour,
The strand of Howth
And Slieverua's side,

And you victorious
In mighty Paris
Of the limewhite palaces
And the surging hosts;

And what I ask
Of you, beloved,
Far away
Is to think at times

Of the corncrake's tune
Beside Glasnevin
In the middle of the meadow,
Speaking in the night;

Of the voice of the birds
In Glenasmole
Happily, with melody,
Chanting music;

Of the strand of Howth
Where a wave breaks,
And the harbour of Dunleary,
Where a ship rocks;

On the sun that shines
On the side of Slieverua,
And the wind that blows
Down over its brow.

PÁDRAIG PEARSE (1879–1916)

Beautiful Lofty Things

Beautiful lofty things: O'Leary's noble head;
My father upon the Abbey stage, before him a raging crowd:
'This Land of Saints', and then as the applause died out,
'Of plaster Saints'; his beautiful mischievous head thrown back.
Standish O'Grady supporting himself between the tables
Speaking to a drunken audience high nonsensical words;
Augusta Gregory seated at her great ormolu table,
Her eightieth winter approaching: 'Yesterday he threatened
      my life.
I told him that nightly from six to seven I sat at this table,
The blinds drawn up'; Maud Gonne at Howth station waiting
      a train,
Pallas Athene in that straight back and arrogant head:
All the Olympians; a thing never known again.

WILLIAM BUTLER YEATS (1865-1939)

Seo Anois Linn

Seo anois linn faobhar caol na haille siar
tráthnóna gréine ar Bhinn Éadair
faoi bhrat fraoigh chorcra is Lochlannach trí chéile,
is meirleach na mara i mbéal na haille
ar ruathar foluaineach i bhfad ó bhaile
ag scaipeadh geabhróg is faoileann.
Aoibhinn bheith i mBinn Éadair,
blas meala ar ár mbéala ón táthfhéithleann
is blas eile inár gceann ar ghreann na Féinne —
Ó Duibhne an buachaill báire, Iníon Rí na Gréige
a nocht lena cabhlach ban thíos fúinn ar an dtaoide,
is na scannáin ná déanfar a dhéanfadh Tarantino —
inár spaisteoirí ag baint sásaimh as divéirseacht
iomadúil fraoigh, aitinn, inseacha, cheann tíre,
Éadar, Hoved, Howth, Dún Criofainn, Baily,

a chlóim amach ina gcló ceart as a chéile
ina gcomhsheasamh le sruth coipthe na taoide
is fós i bpáirt sa ghréasán iomlán soilse
idir an Cheis amuigh, na Muiglíní, Dún Laoghaire,
marcanna ár gcaladh baile féin le blianta.
Aoibhinn bheith i mBinn Éadair trathnóna gléineach
gan miam a scaipfeadh cleite, a líonfadh seol;
fágaimis faoi na déithe é is seolfaidh Aeólas
fairsing ar a ghualainn sinn, abhaile slán.

LIAM Ó MUIRTHILE (*b.* 1950)

Here We Go Now

Here we go now west on the narrow cliff edge
walking towards Howth on a sunny evening,
a profusion of purple heather and bell-heather,
the skua in the mouth of the cliff
on a gliding mission far from home,
gulls and terns scatter.
Pleasant to be in Howth,
our mouths taste of the sweetness of honeysuckle,
the humour of Fenian lays colouring our minds —
Ó Duibhne, woman-crazy, the Greek King's Daughter,
who appeared on the waves below with a fleet of Amazons,
all the unmade films of Tarantino —
strollers enjoying the infinite diversity
of heather, furze, islands, headlands,
Éadar, Hoved, Howth, Dún Criofainn, Baily,
which I print out one after the other just as they are,
as they stand against the foaming current of tide
yet all part of an entire web of light
between Kish yonder, the Muglins, Dún Laoghaire,
for years now the landmarks of our own port town.
Pleasant to be in Howth on an evening when all is dear
not a breath of wind to disturb a feather or fill a sail;

let's leave it to the gods, Aeolus will keep us
close to the wind, as we head for home.

LIAM Ó MUIRTHILE (*b.* 1950)
Translated from the Irish by Gabriel Rosenstock

Haute Couture

On Howth Head
the sky is my big blue hat,
still bright around the rim
although the world begins
to dress down for evening.

An early moon's a jewel
in the navel of a muddy puddle.
Birds fly low, mocking a distant jet
with their easy unfuelled aeroplane chic.

Old's the new new, I'm told,
so my hat's the latest thing,
attached to my shoulders by tall,
avant-garde, invisible poles.

The promontory itself gives me height
more striking than any platform shoe.
I wobble slightly with the joy of walking here;
my hat quivers imperceptibly.

KATHERINE DUFFY (*b.* 1962)

The Baily Lighthouse

At times I still dream about the watch room,
Assailed by the spume of waves on every side,
With one and a quarter million candelas
Of power, every fifteen seconds, flashing white,
Forty-one metres above the mean spring tide:
Yielding fourteen and a quarter seconds of darkness
Punctuated by a three-quarter second splurge of light.

During each flash the missing part of me is revealed,
Still hunched there, typing with slow finger strokes
Over the incessant crackle from the short-wave radio.
The part of me that reality could never quite reclaim,
Absorbed in some novel with my back to the window,
Alone with phantoms who keep haunting my brain,
Protected by sea birds and seals on the rocks below.

DERMOT BOLGER (*b.* 1959)

Feltrim Hill

The land around is all so flat
That Feltrim makes a noted hill
And you may look far out to sea
Standing beside the mill.

Here, once, by hedged and dusty lanes
The rustling acres made their way
And none who met but blessed the load
And passed the time of day.

Within the shadow of this arch
The miller watched to see them climb,
The white dust drifted in the sun
As to the end of time.

The ploughman at Kinsaley stood
To watch the lumbering sails go round,
Then turned contented to his toil
Knowing whose corn was ground.

Lovely and strong these wine-dark walls
Preserve intact their circle still,
But time has wrung that wheel of life
Whose hub was Feltrim Mill.

The sails of forty feet are gone,
The dome is fallen, and on high
The great wrack bares its idle fangs
Against a cruel sky.

PATRICK MacDONOGH (1902–1961)

Vigil

Her father's watch goes tick, tock.
Beneath the window, wave on rock.
The summer morning pock, pock
of tennis in Portmarnock.

The sunlight raw above Red Rock.
Swifts flash past, a sudden shock
Of headlong life. Tick, tock,
the tide is ebbing at Portmarnock.

THEO DORGAN (*b.* 1953)

High Tide at Malahide
to Lynn Doyle

The luminous air is wet
As if the moon came through
To hold as in a net
Such as the spiders set
By ditch and rivulet,
The grey unfallen dew.
The sun is not down yet;
As yet the eve is new.

The water is all a-quiver,
There scarce is room to stand
Beside the tidal river
So narrowed is the strand:
And, over there, the wood
Is standing in a flood,
Erect, and upside down;
And at its roots, a swan.

A silvern mist enhances,
By tangling half the light,
The glowing bay's expanses
Which else had been too bright;
For air is subject to
A tidal ebb and flow.

OLIVER ST JOHN GOGARTY (1878–1957)

Hedgehog

On those nights,
not lit by any moon
through Malahide
along the coast,
past Howth,

140

the city stood
against the dark —
so many strands
strung with diamonds
resting on a plain
black dress.

Our house lights
shaped an up-turned boat
out of two Nissen huts
welded together,
it seemed to float
over marram
and scutch;
beyond the fence
the real sea touched
and kept touching
sand.

Wrapped in each other
and in our walk,
we were back
in the garden
when I noticed driftwood
you almost kicked —

but it glittered,
had eyes set into
a coat of spines, a body
we would nourish
with bread, milk, time.

ENDA COYLE-GREENE (*b.* 1954)

Place Names

Where the M50 crosses the M1
to join the N32
their car broke down, the classic
steaming open-bonnet scene,
with two or three, no four
kids in the back, wide-eyed
and frightened, darkness approaching,
the Sunday evening homebound traffic
a river in flood. I pulled up close
in front, walked back
along the verge to find
a couple dressed in full-length robes,
their cellphone dead, a map
on the dashboard folded
to the mess of veins and arteries
they sat there in, one road above,
another below, a third
spun out before them into empty space,
and cars and trucks and caravans
flung wide about them all
like satellites or stars,
in which confusion the names
I might have chanced meant little —
Clonshaugh or Collinstown,
Belmayne or Darndale —
all borders lost within the web of lights,
instead my finger homing in
on the black pool up ahead,
my voice, now foreign even to myself,
repeating: "Don't worry now,
you're almost there."

PAT BORAN (*b.* 1963)

142

You've been this way before

You've been this way before. The road curves. The moon swerves,
staring in your windscreen open-mouthed. You

check your mirror, see the city's lights transposed. In the air
a plane tamps wary circles, kites in

as another turns its nose up, skimming streaks of light,
    piercing clouds.
You focus on the white line,

broken where the road slopes up in shallow turns; the sky falls
nearer as you slip the steering wheel between your fingers,

pass the metal skeleton of half-built barn. Half way up the hill
fields ripple, trees lean over, dark blue

water laps the sleeping Viking hump of Lambay. At the top,
    lights stop.
Nascent stars pull out. Moving back to fourth you roll

the skin of window down; the night falls in, blares past you
at Balcunnin. In another driver's pumped-up wake

notes float like ghosts. You press the radio for voices. A car comes
at you, beaming headlights. Dimmed

in Shady Lane, obscured by branches heavy-armed with leaves,
the sky has gone. You will yourself to stay

awake to pass the twin abandoned cottages that become a river
when the stream that feeds the mill's lake floods, tell yourself

you're almost there before you reach the quarry's gates: dust-
white hedges eerily familiar

as you take the final bend in one drawn breath, an echo
in the tunnel, then the roundabout, the slowing, going home.

ENDA COYLE-GREENE (*b*. 1954)

3. Southside

Bewley's coarse brown bread (unsliced)

There are days when Ace
can't begin to be human
till he feeds the seagulls

worrying the Liffey. He buys
a loaf of Bewley's coarse brown bread
(unsliced), plods through the eyes

of Westmoreland Street, turns left
at O'Connell Bridge, heads for
the wall, breaks the bread,

starts to feed the shrieking
creatures of whatever heaven
hangs over scuttery Dublin

like a letter begun by a fallen
angel with a nice writing style
millions of years ago, still

being written by hordes of
angels and demons, manky chancers,
chatty conmen, parodists of love

and hate, parodists of parody itself. Alone
at the wall, he watches the ravenous
birds come into their own,

breaking the bread from the generous
waters of old mother Liffey
(how she flows for you for me for all of us!)

and slowly, like light stealing
through the overcoat dark of a winter morning
a feeling, a small real feeling

of being human invades old Ace (hard
enough to come by these days). He feeds the birds
till the sign of a smile crosses his face.

Not for the first time he thanks
the insatiable gulls. Soon he'll walk
past restaurants shops churches banks

more human with every step.
(Would the gulls eat him, properly prepared?)
Who knows their ferocious snow? He may let it rip

tonight, find something new in this parodyplace,
this black pool of cynical skins
and quite unoriginal sins,

some new slant on the gathering dark,
gossip lighting up living and dead,
the fabulous power of coarse brown bread

bobbing on the river
slowly creating the sign of a smile
auguring a hurt unkillable style.

BRENDAN KENNELLY (*b.* 1936)

Bewley's Oriental Café, Westmoreland Street

When she asked me to keep an eye on her things
I told her I'd be glad to keep an eye on her things.
While she breakdanced off to the ladies' loo
I concentrated on keeping an eye on her things.
What are you doing? a Security Guard growled,
His moustache gnawing at the beak of his peaked cap.
When I told him that a young woman whom I did not know
Had asked me to keep an eye on her things, he barked:
Instead of keeping an eye on the things

Of a young woman whom you do not know,
Keep an eye on your own things.
I put my two hands on his hips and squeezed him:
Look — for me the equivalent of the Easter Rising
Is to be accosted by a woman whom I do not know
And asked by her to keep an eye on her things;
On her medieval backpack and on her space-age Walkman;
Calm down and cast aside your peaked cap
And take down your trousers and take off your shoes
And I will keep an eye on your things also.
Do we not cherish all the children of the nation equally?
That young woman does not know the joy she has given me
By asking me if I would keep an eye on her things;
I feel as if I am on a Dart to Bray,
Keeping an eye on her things;
More radical than being on the pig's back,
Keeping an eye on nothing.
The Security Guard made a heap on the floor
Of his pants and shoes,
Sailing his peaked cap across the café like a frisbee.
His moustache sipped at a glass of milk.
It is as chivalrous as it is transcendental
To be sitting in Bewley's Oriental Café
With a naked Security Guard,
Keeping an eye on his things
And on old ladies
With, under their palaeolithic oxters, thousands of loaves of
    coarse brown bread.

PAUL DURCAN (*b.* 1944)

Gérard Depardieu in Eustace Street

His fleshy face aslant fills the screen
here in this vaulted room
still light enough to see the patina on oak
though the lights are down

as I sit in a plush row where benches used to seat
the friends who met here
in silence mostly
unless one felt impelled to speak about the light within.

We too sit in silence
looking up at the screen of light
receiving its forms and tints
tracking their force
tasting the full-mouthed vowels and moist consonants
of its habitués this day
    who
inhabiting or sojourning in the drab part of town
relocate for a scene or two
to its volcanic hinterland
to daze themselves with light and air.

BETTY THOMPSON (*b.* 1951)

Dublin, You're a Bitch

Your lipstick is smeared across your face,
Your rouge is untidy,
And the mascara is badly applied.
Dublin, your evening dress does not fit
And your hair looks lousy.
Dublin, you are a bitch.
You are greedy for money
And a house on the hill.
Once you were happy
With the Saturday night tennis hop,
A Sunday hike in the Dublin hills;
Now it's champagne and pills,
Tenerife, the Big Apple.
That's why you married a thief.
Daily you look more pale;

If you get caught
I do not think that you could cope with jail.
It's not justice that you give:
You only want to receive.
Your children all hate you
Because you are so vain,
You're not Joyce or Swift,
More like a dealer
The drug squad want to lift.
Dublin, you are a bitch.

JOHN McNAMEE (*b.* 1946)

Hawkins Street

The cinema where, aeons ago,
The Omen could be glimpsed
between fanned fingers, has gone
dark after the afternoon show;
the coming evening's neon drench
won't reach the straggled line
behind the bus stop.

At that end of the street —
so narrow it's almost a stretch
a tall man might make horizontally —
road works dangle pipe-veins,
wires are stitches pulled. Outside
the office block, glass and concrete
dulled by dust,

there's a gash kept fresh and open
for the workers who will staunch
the weekend's silences
on Monday, at nine.
But for now at least, it's Saturday.

In heels, her toes on show
beneath a filigree of softest leather,

a woman won't be swayed
by the shower about to break again
above grey brick, grey slate, grey river;
with care she picks her footsteps
as she walks towards the corner
in a city where, eventually, she got sense:
she explodes her blue umbrella,

at exactly the right moment
the rain begins.

ENDA COYLE-GREENE (*b.* 1954)

Trinity New Library

Walking in a library door is like
Being raped by an army: it makes
Your intimate visions look silly.

Knowledge was what was needed;
But you can have too much at once
And a guess works nearly as well.

When I read *Arcadia* all other words
Became absurd and the library
Could blow up in the morning.

Over your shoulder I can see
The rocks of the last shore
The last surviving sea.

EILÉAN NÍ CHUILLEANÁIN (*b.* 1942)

Visiting The Book of Kells
in the Trinity College Library

At first you see almost nothing;
then letters, tumbling down the shelves,
a high dark nave, light on the old spines
umbered gold, on either side
the pale bowed heads of philosophers.
A harp set with stones has the burned
tracery of interweaving on the shaft.
In the uneven, ancient glass trees flicker by;
I spell out 'Carolus Secundus', pass
the close-written text of a manuscript,
Synge's photographs, an old map of Paris.

A new chamber holds the treasure of the place.
Copies anaesthetise the eyes: to see
clearly you must cleanse them, start again.
The dimness of it! as if dipped in tea,
or old varnish — even to look at it
requires patience, the eye making out
only a little at a time. You might follow
the twists and whorls like a maze
but there is no ending, the thread
strays, wavers but remains the same;
only we, following the path, are changed.

ROSEMARY CANAVAN (*b.* 1949)

The Long Room Gallery
Trinity College Dublin

There is nothing to breathe
here in the Gallery
except old years.
The air from today

goes in one lung
and 1783 comes out the other.
As for spirits,
stand perfectly still
and you will feel them
carousing near your ear.
Tourists down below
think they've seen a ghost
when they spot you
floating through bookcases
over their heads.
On a creaky wooden balcony
you tunnel through centuries,
mountains of books
rising into the cumulus.
You could scale a ladder
up the rockface of knowledge
or search the little white slips
stuck in books
for a personal message
from Swift.
Ancient oxygen,
antique dust particles,
petrified wood ...
Who are you kidding?
You belong down there:
baseball caps, chewing gum, videos.

JULIE O'CALLAGHAN (*b.* 1954)

Molly Malone (Cockles and Mussels)

In Dublin's fair city,
Where the girls are so pretty,
I first set my eyes on sweet Molly Malone,
As she wheeled her wheel-barrow,

Through streets broad and narrow,
Crying, "Cockles and mussels, alive, alive, O!"

"Alive, alive, O,
Alive, alive, O,"
Crying, "Cockles and mussels, alive, alive, O!"

She was a fishmonger,
But sure 'twas no wonder,
For so were her father and mother before,
And they each wheeled their barrow,
Through streets broad and narrow,
Crying, "Cockles and mussels, alive, alive, O!"

Chorus

She died of a fever,
And no one could save her,
And that was the end of sweet Molly Malone.
Now her ghost wheels her barrow,
Through streets broad and narrow,
Crying, "Cockles and mussels, alive, alive, O!"

Chorus

JAMES YORKSTON (attrib., *1880s, dates unknown*)

Molly Malone (*from* 'The Lost Children of the Inner City')

Out of the debris of history
a song, a name,
a life we piece together

from odds and ends,
the cast off, the abandoned,
the lost, the useless, the relicts.

She died of a fever
the urge to save her
the same urge to gather

up the broken and the maimed
and what remains
after: a song, a name

and tokens of the sea
salty as life blood, as tears
she is moved to

though cast in bronze now
her unafflicted gaze
on the citizens who praised her

and raised her aloft
who are blind as her own bronze eyes
to the world of her children.

PAULA MEEHAN (*b.* 1955)

To the Pen Shop

Toward College Green,
by the pillars of the Bank of Ireland.
I made it out toward the centre, through a gap in the traffic.

And stepped out under the arms of Grattan
against a malevolent gear change
and a broadside of bus windows against my face

— the green backside swaying and settling
with an organic blast
back at the face of the College.

And my curses pursue you, Number 21!
Down Dame Street, by Thomas Davis slack and sad.
By the Castle; and the Fountain; and the Forty Steps;

toward Kilmainham, heading Westward.
Past Inchicore.
               Toward the thought of places

beyond your terminus.
By the pale Western shore where I have seen
the light of cities under the far horizon.

I crossed over, more calm
under the eyes of Burke and Goldsmith;
to the corner of Grafton Street,

the shops at the far end opening toward the South:
toward Wicklow; toward Wexford, and the company of
    women.
Toward Finistère.

                  Into Nassau Street.
The thick back of an enemy
disappearing in the side entrance of Trinity;

the traffic gathering speed along the high railings
to the Canal bridge
and Eastward out of the city

along the South shore of the Bay,
by the last reaches of the river entering the sea
among the black flats around the Pigeonhouse.

Toward the thought of voices
beyond Liverpool,
               rising out of Europe,

the first voices rising, self chosen, beyond Jerusalem.

*

I turned aside
into the Pen Shop
for a few of their best black refills.

The same attendant in his narrow cell,
over alert all my life long
behind the same counter.

THOMAS KINSELLA (*b.* 1928)

Morning on Grafton Street

Grafton Street is yawning, waking
limb by limb; jewellers' steel
shutters clatter upwards, the sweet
doughy smells from hot-bread

shops steam the frosty morning,
warm our passing; disc-stores'
sudden rhythms blare an introit,
launch the busy liturgy of day.

Look! Two breakfast wooers
fallen in love with farewells
smooch, soul-kiss on the kerb.
Gently, my street puts on her face.

Grafton Street, witness of my time,
seer, watcher of every mood,
traps me the grandeur, the melancholy,
ever-new carnival of man.

Walk here alone in broodiness,
inwoven, anonymous, swept along;
stroll here infatuated, self-communing,
lost in the lyric flow of street.

MICHEAL O'SIADHAIL (*b.* 1947)

Summer in Dublin

Take me away from the city and lead me to where I can be on
    my own.
I wanted to see you, and now that I have, I just want to be left
    alone.
I'll always remember your kind words, and I'll still remember
    your name,
But I've seen you changing and turning, and I know that
    things just won't be the same.

I remember that summer in Dublin, and the Liffey as it stank
    like hell,
And the young people walking on Grafton Street, and
    everyone looking so well.
I was singing a song I'd heard somewhere, called 'Rock 'n' Roll
    Never Forgets',
When my hummin' was smothered by a 46A and the scream of
    a low-flying jet.
So I jumped on a bus to Dún Laoghaire, stoppin' off to pick up
    my guitar,
And a drunk on the bus told me how to get rich. I was glad we
    weren't goin' too far.

So I'm leavin' on Wednesday morning and tryin' to find a
    place where I can hear
The wind and the birds and the sea on the rocks, where open
    roads always are near,
And if sometimes I tire of the quiet, and I wanna walk back up
    that hill,
I'll just get on the road and stick out my thumb 'cos I know for
    sure you'll be there still.

LIAM REILLY (*b.* 1955)

Mother and Daughter in Bewley's Café

Farther and further they go into silence,
Eat their grill and then their gateaux
Knowing how to do this together.

There's something alike.
A look about the mouth that will
Fold with time in the same way,
Hair that may only have faded from
How the younger's is. But really,
You could never tell.

The mother, appalled
At the unfair passage of the years,
Gazes sullen as an adolescent.
In carriers around her feet,
New clothes for winter no one
Will notice. Except her sister
Who'll ask first how much.

Nothing to say, they nurse
Their secrets. Dreams
Of deceit, of love, of glory.
An unfilial future. A makeshift past.

Idly, Girl spoons the sugar,
Applauds Mother's empty plate
And, splendid eyes downcast, frankly
Unreins her filly's mane for a boy
In the corner bored with his tea.
Mother sees what her mam saw —
No sooner here than gone.

ANNE HAVERTY (*b.* 1959)

Grafton Street

Grafton Street's a Wonderland
Mé ar adhastar leat a chailín
Ar adhastar
Buairichín do láimhe mo tharraingt chughat
Mo mhealladh
Ar eagla m'éalaithe ní féidir gurb é
Ní baol
Ní lao mé ó choiseagán
Ní fheileann urchall mé
Ná tú mé ag rothlú faoi chornasc
Mo ruball mar théad duit a chailín
An é
Mar théad
Ní hé go bhfuil éad ort
Ní hé
Ní léimfead is eol duit
Ó chonair na péire
Níl gá leis an chuing
Le hiodh, laincis ná loncaird
Is leor dom bheith faoin aon spéir amháin
Spéir bhog théagartha shlán sin an ghrá
Nach gá a thaispeáint
Sráid Grafton nó Sord
An gá
Nó táim ad leanúint
Faoi cheangal do lámh
Ó tá
Faoi cheangal do lámh.

PÁDRAIG Ó SNODAIGH (*b.* 1935)

Grafton Street

Grafton Street's a Wonderland
You have me haltered girl

161

Haltered
Your hand a little spancel pulling me towards you
Enticing me
Couldn't be the fear of me scarpering
No chance
I'm not a calf on the loose
Spancelling doesn't suit me
Nor me you if my head is twisted
Is my tail a rope to you girl
Is it
A rope
It isn't that you're jealous
No way
You know I won't jump
From the double path
There's no call for the yoke
Nor for the collar, the spancel, the fetter
It's enough for me to be under the one sky
That strong safe soft sky of love
That demands no guidance
In Grafton Street or Swords
Does it
Because I'm following you
Am I not
Tied to your hand
Yes I am
Tied to your hand.

PÁDRAIG Ó SNODAIGH (*b.* 1935)
Translated from the Irish by Paddy Bushe

Dublin

After our affair
I swore that I'd leave Dublin
And in that line I'd left behind
The years, the tears, the memories and you

In Dublin

At the quays friends come to say farewell
We'd laugh and joke and smoke
And later on the boat
I'd cry over you

How can I leave the town that brings me down
That has no jobs
Is blessed by God
And makes me cry

Dublin

And at sea with blowing hair
I think of Dublin
Of Grafton Street and Derby Square
And those for whom I really care and you

In Dublin

PHIL LYNOTT (*b.* 1949–1986)

The List (A Letter to Phil Lynott)

It was here, Phil, off Grafton Street
— a few yards from your statue,
under Dublin's menacing sky,
amid the silence and cries of drunks —
after leaving Bruxelles at midnight,
I sat on an empty Guinness barrel
and wrote down plans
on the back of a beer mat.
Things I had to do.
Stay away from bars, I swore.
Write poetry.

Cry when I see a sunset.
Fall in love for real.
Play *Jailbreak*.
Believe in something.
Never give up following my dreams.
Never give up.
Throw stones in a lake.
I promised I would. Like hell I will.
Life always ends up hurting us,
and we always tackle it
by making lists that are of no use at all.

JORDI PUJOL NADAL (*b*. 1975)
Translated from the Catalan by Ruth Murray

A Neary's Afternoon

There's Barry Fitzgerald hunched in the corner
with his silver-top cane, he buys one drink,
sips the rest of the afternoon from what's
under the silver head — that's Siobhán
McKenna, a clutch of theatre owls —
she'll make them rotten with drink,
turn them out later from her Rathgar house.

Salad days in the hostelry of the Golden Fleece.

A nice man comes in, Con Leventhal, tailored,
coiffured, less Bloom light than Trinity air
either way a street cloud in Dublin. I whisper
how honourable to sell *Ulysses* under
the counter in a pissed Guinness puritan
town — he's off to Paris for Sam's beck and call,
we return to the beautiful nests we have made.
Gold sun down on them as they barge café doors.
We say how extravagant it is to choose avatars —

Joyce in his chain-charms of alcohol, Con's
Parisian in colonial chains of less Alcohol.
Clairvoyant modernism costs a Jot, we put
on war-weary paint. Padraic Fallon from Wexford
bow-tied joins the table. He doesn't want me
here, who's been telling thespian tales?

Around a corner McDaid's dome under heaven.

JAMES LIDDY (1934–2008)

Going to the Gaiety

I thought of you as the hard man
ruling a house through the bottle
but when the opera opened
we climbed as one
up a hundred steps
and sat, dreamy from song
and the height of the gods,
to hear sad Traviata
peer down at Mimi in damson
Othello in saffron damask

and were lost in the lustre
of gaud and strut
as the scent of the heated crowd
rose in our faces like opium
and I squeezed close to your old serge
with its years of tobacco,
feeling emotion swell
with the taut of the long sweet note

releasing you
to be the father I loved
who wandered home

through the gold lit dark of Dublin
arm in arm with his daughter,
whistling the tune of your man
the Italian tenor.

SHEILA O'HAGAN (*b.* 1933)

'shiver in your tenement'

You might have thought them mature student, clerk
or priest once, long ago in the demure sixties
before the country first discovered sex —
Cathal O'Shannon, Harry Kernoff, Austin Clarke
arriving by bus at noon in search of roguery
from Howth, Raheny, Monkstown or Templeogue,
some house by bridge or woodland *à l'usage*
of the temporal, of the satiric or lyric Muse.
Gravely they strolled down Dawson or Grafton St.,
thoughtful figures amid the faces, the laughter,
or sat among the race-goers and scroungers
in Sinnott's, Neary's, the Bailey, the Wicklow Lounge —
pale, introspective almost to the point of blindness
or so it seemed, living the life of the mind,
of European *littérateurs,* their black Quartier hats
(all purchased from the same clerical outfitter)
suggestive of first editions and dusty attics.

They sipped watery Jameson — without ice, of course —
knew London and Paris but preferred the unforced
pace of the quiet city under the Dublin mountains
where a broadsheet or a broadcast might still count.
Those were the days before tourism and economic growth,
before deconstruction and the death of the author,
when pubs had as yet no pictures of Yeats and Joyce
since people could still recall their faces, their voices;
of crozier-wielding bishops, vigilant censors,
pre-conciliar Latin, smoke pouring from swung censers;

of sexual guilt, before French letter and Dutch cap,
fear muttered in the dark of dormitory and side chapel.
There was much dark then in the archdiocese
though some, like you, had found a gap of brightness —
now, of course, we live in a blaze of tropical light
under a green pagoda sunshade globally warm
like the slick glass on a renovated farmhouse.

Mnemosyne, mother of nine, dust at St Patrick's,
labour 'accustomed to higher living', poverty old hat,
does art benefit from the new dispensation?
What, in our new world, have we left to say?
Oh, poets can eat now, painters can buy paint
but have we nobler poetry, happier painting
than when the gutters bubbled, the drains stank
and hearts bobbed to the clappers in the sanctuary?
Has art, like life itself, its source in agony?
Nothing to lose but our chains, our chains gone
that bound with form the psycho-sexual turbulence,
together with those black hats and proper pubs,
at home now with the ersatz, the pop, the phoney,
we seldom love or hate, as once, with a full heart.
Those were the days; now patience, courage, artistry,
solitude things of the past, like the love of God,
we nod to you from the pastiche paradise of the post-modern.

DEREK MAHON (*b.* 1941)

St Teresa's — Clarendon Street

The silence of St Teresa
as if she were alabaster
sent me out a side door
into the drench of an alley
four umbrellas wide
where I stood under awnings
by windows full of yellow

rings starry in the lights
and next to me a woman down
on cardboard begging shoppers
cutting in from Grafton Street
'Change, please, would you,'
and it's only now I hear her.

TED McNULTY (1934–1998)

Gulliver in Dublin

1
Waking on the strand, with sand in my ears
　　　and sewage washing my head,
I found my limbs and body bound
　　　by a thousand lengths of thread:

woven with all of a spider's skill,
　　　in monkish knots and coils —
too fine to hold me down for long,
　　　too intricate to spoil.

How many years had I overslept,
　　　when I stirred, and made them cower?
The last I knew, I'd nodded off
　　　over *The Will to Power,*

and the next I knew was the whispering
　　　of the Union of Catholic Mothers,
as a thousand tiny needles
　　　stitched my flies together.

Leopold Bloom went through my pockets,
　　　and rolled away a copper.
The Archbishop marched across my chest,
　　　to shrink me with holy water.

As he blessed my stubble in Gaelic
    and flicked his aspergillum,
I stood up for *The Soldier's Song.*
    And the rest is all on film.

2
I learned to be more circumspect
    here, where nobody grows
taller than the tinkling steeples,
    or the flags at Lansdowne Road.

Where the rows of rooftop aerials
    spread out like beds of nails,
and God, in the lap of his mother,
    conforms to the local scale.

Where voices are never raised above
    the foghorns on the quay,
and the ships tied up at the Custom House
    turn their backs on the sea.
Where even the hills are tied down fast,
    like tarpaulins over hay,
with a mesh of dykes and boreens
    to stop them blowing away.

I had to stoop very low, to hear
    the gossip in Grogan's Bar:
It's all in the poor lad's head. He's read
    too many books, by far.

It was then that I took that mouthful
    out of the Galtee Hills,
and spitting it into the ocean,
    retired to Hy-Brasil.

GERALD MANGAN (*b.* 1951)

169

from **Dublin in July**

II
Take a walk down South Great George's Street,
Where seedy bars and not-so-great hotels
Consort with trendy restaurants and shops
And India commingles with Japan.
Here is a laundry, there an Oxfam outlet.
And everywhere the crowds, the jostling shoulders,
The cell phone bleating from a stylish belt.
Tonight we'll dine at Yamamori Noodles,
Tomorrow eat panini at the Bailey
Or Chicken Tikka at the Shalimar.
What has become of that revered, imagined
Dublin of O'Brien and Ó Faoláin,
Its taste as Irish as a ball of malt?
Look for it in Liverpool or Boston
Or conjure it yourself from pints of Guinness.
But here beware of Vespas when you cross
This street that's no more Irish than its name,
Where traffic comes in rolling, tidal swells
But now and then grows still, as if recalling
The ochre ethos of a slower time.

BEN HOWARD (*b.* 1944)

A Photograph of Fade Street, Dublin, 1878

The exposure, half a minute? Enough for light's breath
to cloud the glass with this narrow
Georgian canyon: dark fanlights

above dark doors, sash windows raised
while the far end assumes its name, greys
to a smoky membrane.

Steady as a gramophone needle behind his tripod,
the afternoon swirling about him,
time's pupil concentrates on

the cogs and gears. Three girls perched on a kerb
will be restless smears; two boys
sitting on a doorstep may take

if they keep staring, contracted in the same hard gaze
as their grown ups', two men in bowlers
huddled on the next step.

Opposite, nearer, the pair of women who stand
talking with a third (held sharp
in her street-level window)

sway themselves into ghosts with a pale-faced lad
flickering from a doorway.
Others, too fast, walk

through the boxed walls, empty themselves round corners,
withdraw — an old man tapping the pane
gone, a cat in the railings —

children who whirr, sparrow across the street —

MARK GRANIER (*b.* 1957)

The Beau Walk of St Stephen's Green

'Mid Trees of stunted Growth, unequal Roes,
On the coarse Gravel, trip the Belles and Beaus.
Here, on one Side, extends a length of Street,
Where Dirt-bespattering Cars and Coaches meet.
On t'other, in the Ditches lazy Flood,
Dead Cats and Dogs lie bloated; drench'd in Mud.

But lo! a Statue from afar salutes your Eyes,
To which th'Inclosure all Access denies.
So distant, whose, or whom, no Eye can ken,
Plac'd in the Centre of a marshy Fen.
But know, 'tis Royal George on whom you stare,
Tho' oft mistaken for some good Lord Mayor:
And tho' his Charger foams in ductile Brass,
The Charger for an ambling Pad may pass;
The whole equestrian Statue for a Toy,
A Horse of Hobby, mounted by a Boy.
For shame ye Cits, where meet th'assembl'd Fair,
Fill up your Dikes and purge th'unwholsome Air.
Let George's royal Form be fairly shewn.
And like his Virtues, be reveal'd and known.

THOMAS NEWBURGH (c.1695–1779)

The Death in Dublin by Fire of Six Loreto Nuns

They are released from their vows.
Children in their care
Grew to maturity of years.
So many kindnesses they performed,
Hearts that gave an abundance of love.
They were taken on a summer's night
While the city slept.

The dawn chorus was just
Beginning in St Stephen's Green
When the flames rose higher.
Stars had begun to die
As the smoke grew more intense
In the choking inferno.
The last glasses of wine
Were being drained in nearby nightclubs
As the panic grew to terror.

Eucharia, Gonzaga, Edith,
Seraphia, Margaret, Rosario,
Six swallows of the veil
Have flown to the Gardens of Heaven.

They are the words of a song
That will never be forgotten,
Instruments that are now
In God's hands:

Eucharia, Gonzaga, Edith,
Seraphia, Margaret, Rosario,
Six swallows of the veil
Have flown to the Gardens of Heaven.

JOHN McNAMEE (*b.* 1946)

At the Shelbourne
Elizabeth Bowen, Nov., 1940

Sunrise in the Irish Sea, dawn over Dublin Bay
after a stormy night, one shivering star;
and I picture the harsh waking everywhere,
the devastations of a world at war,
airfields, radio silence, a darkened convoy
strung out in moonlight on a glittering sea.
Harsh the wide windows of the hotel at daybreak
as I light up the first ciggie of the day,
stormy the lake like the one in Regent's Park,
glittering the first snow on the Wicklow hills.
Out back, a precipitous glimpse of silent walls,
courtyards, skylights of kitchen and heating plant,
seagulls in rising steam; while at the front
I stand at ease to hear the kettle sing
in an upper room of the Kildare St. wing,
admiring the frosty housetops of my birthplace

miraculously immune (almost) to bomb damage.
Sun through south-facing windows lights again
on the oval portrait and the polished surface
where, at an Empire writing table, I set down
my situation reports for the Dominions Office,
pen-sketches of MacEntee, James Dillon and the rest,
letters to friends in Cork or in Gower St.,
— Virginia, Rosamond and the *Horizon* set —
bright novelistic stuff, a nation on the page:
' ... *deep, rather futile talks. It is hard afterwards*
to remember the drift, though I remember words,
that smoke-screen use of words! Mostly I meet
the political people; they are very religious.'

There's nothing heroic or 'patriotic' about this;
for here in this rentier heaven of racing chaps,
journalists, cipher clerks, even Abwehr types
and talkative day trippers down from Belfast,
I feel like a traitor spying on my own past.
It was here the ill-fate of cities happened first —
a cruiser in the Liffey, field guns trained on the GPO,
the kicking-in of doors, dances cancelled, revolvers
served with the morning tea on silver salvers,
a ghostly shipboard existence down below,
people asleep in corridors as now
in the London Underground, mysterious Kôr,
a change of uniforms in the cocktail bar
though the bronze slave girls still stand where they were,
Nubian in aspect, in manner art-nouveau.
This is home really, a place of warmth and light,
a house of artifice neither here nor there
between the patrician past and the egalitarian future,
tempting one always to prolong one's visit:
in war, peace, rain or fog you couldn't miss it
however late the hour, however dark the night.

DEREK MAHON (*b.* 1941)

Hopkins in Newman House

To its kitchen
from a cold room
you drift down to sit

in the warmth
of another corner,
rustling fifty papers

for correction before tea,
forbidding your fingers
to drum syllables

on the thick table or count
how many you can fit
into a five stress line.

But when did you write,
pale priest, a poem
about indoors,

you for whom
the wind is iambic,
every leaf's intricacy

a world? And why
do I find you here,
dulled by duty

in dark rooms, so removed
from the lovely fuss
of cloud and wind?

For you will die in Ireland,
your spirit chilled,
uncomforted,

unless you return
to the wild astonishments
of light,

the love light,
Christ light,
of your Welsh hills.

SHEILA O'HAGAN (*b*. 1933)

The Dolls Museum in Dublin

The wounds are terrible. The paint is old.
The cracks along the lips and on the cheeks
cannot be fixed. The cotton lawn is soiled.
The arms are ivory dissolved to wax.

Recall the quadrille. Hum the waltz.
Promenade on the yacht-club terraces.
Put back the lamps in their copper holders,
the carriage wheels on the cobbled quays.

And recreate Easter in Dublin.
Booted officers. Their mistresses.
Sunlight criss-crossing College Green.
Steam hissing from the flanks of horses.

Here they are. Cradled and cleaned,
Held close in the arms of their owners.
Their cold hands clasped by warm hands,
Their faces memorised like perfect manners.

The altars are mannerly with linen.
The lilies are whiter than surplices.
The candles are burning and warning:
Rejoice, they whisper. After sacrifice.

Horse chestnuts hold up their candles.
The Green is vivid with parasols.
Sunlight is pastel and windless.
The bar of the Shelbourne is full.

Laughter and gossip on the terraces.
Rumour and alarm at the barracks.
The Empire is summoning its officers.
The carriages are turning: they are turning back.

Past children walking with governesses,
Looking down, cossetting their dolls,
then looking up as the carriage passes,
the shadow chilling them. Twilight falls.

It is twilight in the dolls museum. Shadows
remain on the parchment-coloured waists,
are bruises on the stitched cotton clothes,
are hidden in the dimples on the wrists.

The eyes are wide. They cannot address
the helplessness which has lingered in
the airless peace of each glass case:
to have survived. To have been stronger than

a moment. To be the hostages ignorance
takes from time and ornament from destiny. Both.
To be the present of the past. To infer the difference
with a terrible stare. But not feel it. And not know it.

EAVAN BOLAND (*b.* 1944)

Three Paintings of York Street
for Ita Kelly

BEFORE THE PUBS CLOSE

Quick. Before the moon is eaten
by that cloud, rescue its dust,
sift it over the shopping centre,
the student hostel, that couple
hand in hand walking to the Green.
And quick. Before last orders and drunken cries
steal the breath the street is holding,
exhale it lovingly below each window
to reclaim from night the shadowy areas.

Salt your canvas with a woman
quietly weeping in a tenement room
until her tears become a blessing
sprinkled from your fingers,
those spatters of intense blue
beside the three black cats
who wait with … patience, is it?
on a granite step for you to find
the exact amber of their eyes
as they gaze at the moon.

WOMAN FOUND DEAD BEHIND SALVATION ARMY HOSTEL

You will have to go outside for this one.
The night is bitter cold
but you must go out,
you could not invent this.

You can make a quick sketch
and later, in your studio, mix the colours,
the purple, the eerie green of her bruises,
the garish crimson of her broken mouth.

For consolation there's the line
her spine makes as it remembers
its beginnings, as if at the very end
she turned foetal and knew again
the roar of her mother's blood in her ears,
the drum of her mother's heart
before she drowned in the seventh wave
beyond pain, or your pity.

Your hand will steady as you draw the cobbles.
They impose a discipline, the comfort of habit,
as does the symmetry of brick walls
which define the alley and whose very height
cut off the light and hid
the beast who maimed her.

CHILDREN OF YORK STREET AT PLAY IN THE COLLEGE OF SURGEONS' CARPARK

You worry given the subject
about sentimentality, about indulgence,
but as you work
the children turn to pattern
and you may as well be
weaving in a Turkish bazaar, one eye
on your son lest he topple to the tarmac.
And your fingers of their own volition
find the perfect stress between warp and weft.
Your mind can lope as loosely
as a gazelle through savannah
or nimble as a mountain goat,
attain an unexpected purchase on a sheer
cliff face, or you may be dolphin
and cavort the prismatic ranges
of the green sea's depth.
                              And after,
cleaning brushes, you will wonder
why no child can be discerned

on your canvas, why there is no bike,
no skateboard, no skipping rope,
no carpark, why your colours are
all primary, pure as you can make them,
why in your pattern the shapes keep shifting
like flighty spirits threatening
to burst into song.

PAULA MEEHAN (*b.* 1955)

Machines

One night in York Street
almost ten years back — so much
drink and junk around the place

it was hard to say
just who was us, or them — one night
as I lay down to sleep on my own

cold slab of light, it started up:
below in the street, a car alarm
wielding its terrible, surgical blade

of sound. Across the way,
the College of Surgeons grinned in the night
like a skull, like a stack of skulls,

but it was hard not to cheer
when someone from a few doors up
suddenly appeared. A yard brush

like a weapon in his hands, he climbed
onto the gleaming bonnet where he stood
and began to swing,

first with aim and intent, so that
one by one the front lights went in, then
the indicators, windscreen wipers, the windscreen itself ...

and then like some half-man, half-thing
swung, swung, swung, swung,
swung till his muscles must have ached,

till the mangled brush tumbled from his grip
and he stopped, turned, looked up at us and roared
as if his spirit could no longer be contained

by the silence, by the darkness,

by the slow-motion tragedy of
so much of Dublin back in those
and still in these dehumanising days.

PAT BORAN (*b.* 1963)

The National Museum of Ireland

In these evil days,
when the old wound of Ulster is a disease
suppurating in the heart of Europe
and in the heart of every Gael
who knows that he is a Gael,
I have done nothing but see
in the National Museum of Ireland
the rusty red spot of blood,
rather dirty, on the shirt
that was once on the hero
who is dearest to me of them all
who stood against bullet or bayonet,
or tanks or cavalry,
or the bursting of frightful bombs:

the shirt that was on Connolly
in the General Post Office of Ireland
while he was preparing the sacrifice
that put himself up on a chair
that is holier than the Lia Fáil
that is on the Hill of Tara in Ireland.

The great hero is still
sitting on the chair
fighting the battle in the Post Office
and cleaning streets in Edinburgh.

SORLEY MacLEAN (1911–1996)
Translated from the Scottish Gaelic by the author

In a Dublin Museum

No clue
About the use or name
Of these few
Bronze Age things,
Rare
And in gold,
Too wide for finger-rings.
Till some old epic came
To light, which told
Of a king's
Daughter: how she slid them on to hold
The tail ends of her plaited hair.

SHEILA WINGFIELD (1906-1992)

Frost Moving

In the long days between the anniversaries
of Little Bighorn and Bloomsday
what passes for the sun in these parts

beats down on the living and the dead.
A Santa Clara man
checks out of Finn's Hotel

and, just as it was
one hundred years ago to the day,
he seems to know something

we don't know. Wearing a kerchief
of dried tobacco leaves
tied loose on his throat,

braided hair like a tennis player
and the white profile badge of FDR,
he says we are all being assimilated

into the one race and, however far-fetched,
our smiles are coming together.
So when I check into Finn's Hotel

I stroke my yellow hair
and the maid in love with dew on the lens
carries my bags up a winding stair.

GERARD FANNING (*b.* 1952)

French Exam, Alliance Française

Elements of the épreuve écrite are difficult,
the sense of A-level déjà-vu complete.

My ballpoint hangs 4 cm above an untracked page,
long distance Manche I am no Biériot to cross.

I raise my eyes for inspiration — no hills there
but the wall's not blank, and mouldings bulk,
stucco covings and architrave protrude, bas-relief vines run riot
the room around, deep-cut, dark-creviced, dust-laired.

I'm in a small, square room on the top storey, a late partition
with floor so hung I am ascendant, closer now to vine leaves
than any member was of the Kildare Street Club,
vine leaves so laid, so pruned they could be crown of thorns.

Partition walls for this my cell, electric ducts and ventilators
are hacked across the bas-relief. I rest my wrist,
consider the vine leaves, masons' aprons and diversity,
and crossing the Sound of Tory, stomach lurching as in the TGV.

GRÉAGÓIR Ó DÚILL (*b.* 1946)

The Natural History Museum

The cold turnstiles creak with our passing out
from sunlight and the government buildings
— the glue-sniffers' convention we called it —
into the history of the species, the Darwin
chain unhooked by the Free State employee,
and all its missing links, I among them.

We block the entrance like excursion kids
just up for the day from Monasterboice
or Virginia, any provincial town.
My big-boned Dutch boy shines in the dark,
filling out the Continental denim
like taxidermy, all his tucks concealed.

I came here with my father years ago,
to see the lie of the land, its broad spectrum

184

from fossil to mammal, our chain of being.
Now with my son, the blond surrogate one
who's not on my passport, I catch me out
pointing and explaining, my father's role.

Who was it said we are poor forked creatures
risen from the slime? He leads me around
the showcases, all our banished reptiles,
the predatory birds, the small soft ones
he knows the names of in two languages
and cradled in the polders as a child.

I decipher the Latin roots, inked tags
fading behind the glass my boy mists up.
Their fixed habitats smell of old ether,
their eyes bright and hard as teddy bears'.
Our forked tongues move easily among them,
ornithologist, catcher in the rye.

All that moves is the thirties clock, ticking
our strange communion in this strange museum.
The noon sunlight comes through in blinding shafts
from the state buildings, the lie of the land.
We turnstile slowly back the way we came,
unhook the chain and vanish into light.

PADRAIG ROONEY (*b.* 1956)

A Child's Map of Dublin

I wanted to find you Connolly's Starry Plough,
the flag I have lived under since birth or since
I first scanned nightskies and learned the nature of work.
'That hasn't been on show in years,' the porter told us.
They're revising at the National Museum,
all hammers and drills and dust, converting to
an interpretive centre in the usual contemporary style.

The Natural History Museum: found poem
of oriole, kingfisher, sparrowhawk, nightjar,
but the gull drew me strongest — childhood guide
to the freedom and ecstasy of flight. Common
cacophonist, nothing romantic about that squabbler
of windowledges, invader of the one p.m. schoolyard,
wakefollower of sailors. But watch him on a clear ocean

and nothing reads the wind so well. In the updraught
of a sudden love, I walk the northside streets
that whelped me; not a brick remains
of the tenement I reached the age of reason in. Whole
streets are remade, the cranes erect over Eurocrat schemes
down the docks. There is nothing
to show you there, not a trace of a girl

in ankle socks and hand-me-downs, sulking
on a granite step when she can't raise the price of a film,
or a bus to the beach. The movie she ran in her head?
Africa — hostage slave to some Berber prince or, chainmailed,
she is heroine of a hopeless war
spurring her men to death, but honourable death.

Better I take you up Cumberland Street Saturday.
We'll hoke out something foreign and erotic,
from the mounds of cast-offs on the path.
And when the market's over we'll wander home,
only go the streets that are our fancy.
You'll ask me no questions. I'll tell you no lies.

Climb in here between the sheets
in the last light of this April evening. We'll trust
the charts of our bodies. They've brought us
safe to each other, battle-scarred and frayed
at the folds, they'll guide us to many wonders.
Come, let's play in the backstreets and tidal flats
till we fall off the edge of the known world,

and drown.

PAULA MEEHAN (*b.* 1955)

If Ever You Go to Dublin Town

If ever you go to Dublin town
In a hundred years or so
Inquire for me in Baggot Street
And what I was like to know.
O he was a queer one,
Fol dol the di do,
He was a queer one
I tell you.

My great-grandmother knew him well,
He asked her to come and call
On him in his flat and she giggled at the thought
Of a young girl's lovely fall.
O he was dangerous,
Fol dol the di do,
He was dangerous
I tell you.

On Pembroke Road look out for my ghost,
Dishevelled with shoes untied,
Playing through the railings with little children
Whose children have long since died.
O he was a nice man,
Fol dol the di do,
He was a nice man
I tell you.

Go into a pub and listen well
If my voice still echoes there,
Ask the men what their grandsires thought
And tell them to answer fair.
O he was eccentric,
Fol dol the di do,
He was eccentric
I tell you.

He had the knack of making men feel
As small as they really were
Which meant as great as God had made them
But as males they disliked his air;
O he was a proud one,
Fol dol the di do,
He was a proud one
I tell you.

If ever you go to Dublin town
In a hundred years or so
Sniff for my personality,
Is it Vanity's vapour now?
O he was a vain one,
Fol dol the di do,
He was a vain one
I tell you.

I saw his name with a hundred others
In a book in the library,
It said he had never fully achieved
His potentiality.
O he was slothful,
Fol dol the di do,
He was slothful
I tell you.

He knew that posterity has no use
For anything but the soul,
The lines that speak the passionate heart,
The spirit that lives alone.
O he was a lone one,
Fol dol the di do,
Yet he lived happily
I tell you.

PATRICK KAVANAGH (1904–1967)

Sketch of a Dubliner

Bearded bass boom
Slim-lined
Short-fused
Razor-sharp.

Centre-stage
Holding forth
Centre-bar
Toasting life.

Purveyor of street ballad
Crafter of story line
Disciple of Zozimus
Flirting with fame.

Imbiber of the black stuff
Epicentre of the craic
Master of retort
Outwitting the heckler.

Jovial raconteur
Conjuring with words
Precision timing
Knock-out punchline.

Grumpy at morning
Barbed wire vinegar
Convivial at evening
Rose without thorns.

Champion of the underdog
De-throning the haughty
Sounding uncomfortable truths
Uplifting the needy

Disenchanted
Weary of applause
Wary of patronage
Impatient for the wings

Distillation of the Liffey
Salt of the earth
Dublin personified —

Ronnie Drew.

JOHN SHEAHAN (*b.* 1939)
The Dubliners first played together in O'Donoghue's of Merrion Row.

Baggot Street Deserta

Lulled, at silence, the spent attack.
The will to work is laid aside.
The breaking-cry, the strain of the rack,
Yield, are at peace. The window is wide
On a crawling arch of stars, and the night
Reacts faintly to the mathematic
Passion of a cello suite
Plotting the quiet of my attic.

A mile away the river toils
Its buttressed fathoms out to sea;
Tucked in the mountains, many miles
Away from its roaring outcome, a shy
Gasp of waters in the gorse
Is sonneting origins. Dreamers' heads
Lie mesmerised in Dublin's beds
Flashing with images, Adam's morse.

A cigarette, the moon, a sigh
Of educated boredom, greet

A curlew's lingering threadbare cry
Of common loss. Compassionate,
I add my call of exile, half-
Buried longing, half-serious
Anger and the rueful laugh.
We fly into our risk, the spurious.

Versing, like an exile, makes
A virtuoso of the heart,
Interpreting the old mistakes
And discords in a work of Art
For the One, a private masterpiece
Of doctored recollections. Truth
Concedes, before the dew, its place
In the spray of dried forgettings Youth
Collected when they were a single
Furious undissected bloom.
A voice clarifies when the tingle
Dies out of the nerves of time:
Endure and let the present punish.
Looking backward, all is lost;
The Past becomes a fairy bog
Alive with fancies, double crossed
By pad of owl and hoot of dog,
Where shaven, serious-minded men
Appear with lucid theses, after
Which they don the mists again
With trackless, cotton-silly laughter;
Secretly a swollen Burke
Assists a decomposing Hare
To cart a body of good work
With midnight mutterings off somewhere;

The goddess who had light for thighs
Grows feet of dung and takes to bed,
Affronting horror-stricken eyes,
The marsh bird that children dread.

I nonetheless inflict, endure,
Tedium, intracordal hurt,
The sting of memory's quick, the drear
Uprooting, burying, prising apart
Of loves a strident adolescent
Spent in doubt and vanity.
All feed a single stream, impassioned
Now with obsessed honesty,
A tugging scruple that can keep
Clear eyes staring down the mile,
The thousand fathoms, into sleep.

Fingers cold against the sill
Feel, below the stress of flight,
The slow implosion of my pulse
In a wrist with poet's cramp, a tight
Beat tapping out endless calls
Into the dark, as the alien
Garrison in my own blood
Keeps constant contact with the main
Mystery, not to be understood.
Out where imagination arches
Chilly points of light transact
The business of the border-marches
Of the Real, and I — a fact
That may be countered or may not —
Find their privacy complete.

My quarter-inch of cigarette
Goes flaring down to Baggot Street.

THOMAS KINSELLA (*b.* 1928)

from **Merrion Square: A Descriptive Poem**

These clear November mornings light is kind:
The ebb of shadow like a slow-drawn blind
Retreats toward my point of view, and there,
Still touched with lingering mist, lies Merrion Square.
These hundred years, its builders in retreat
Have left square after square, street after street.
The buildings lasted longer than the lease:
The figures dwindle, and the frames increase;
And those who built this city for a few
Laid out the Wide Streets wider than they knew …

When evening draws the lengthening vistas out,
Distinguished spectres surely walk about
Under the trees: Yeats with his chin in air,
And Russell nestling in his beard, are there,
And spattering on his patent-leather toes
The drop still drips from Edward Martyn's nose
And Moore is fascinated still. Not I:
These, if they walk, have always passed me by.
Even the archetypal mage of all,
Sheridan Le Fanu, to whose least call
Unnumbered apparitions rose, can raise
No shadow of himself to haunt these ways …

And dark, indeed, is all that may be seen
At night in Merrion Square and Stephen's Green.
The crowded trams that lurch along the lines
To dim Dunleary and to raw Rathmines
Plough each their wake of light. From dim-lit verge
The drab and sluttish prostitutes emerge
Flaunting and cringing each alternate yard
For Civil Servant, or for Civic Guard;
Till midnight puts a hush on everything
And cats and drunken medicals may sing …

At last all's quiet; not a sound is heard
Save horn, like call of predatory bird

From far away, where carfuls of police
Patrol the empty streets to keep the peace.

A gentle mist may still caress at dawn
This bristle-tufted and unshaven lawn,
May still dissolve harsh lines, and so erase
The profile of each bush around the base,
That Leinster House, though just across the way,
Gleams faint beyond an acre of Cathay.
The lesser, too, that flank its grey with red,
Though ill-regarded, still remain well-bred
No rigid uniformity of edge
Binds all together, yet the coping-ledge
May mask a catwalk for a lonely gun,
Give cover for a tabby on the run,
And, in the dog-days, trap the throbbing sun.
Gentility and chastity of line,
Augustan principles of street design,
May warm no other heart, and yet warm mine.

But one by one the gentle and the chaste,
Damp-rotten, are repointed and refaced
And re-emerge, as though the brickwork bled,
Touched up with slabs of raw and glossy red.
And yet the light is kind even to these,
And through the screen, even of winter trees,
With time and weather, they contrive to please.

To please? No more? It's a time I should produce
Some colourable shadow of excuse
Why I, whose father in a country town
Kept, at my age, a watch on each half-crown,
Should snatch the past of others for my own,
Instal myself upon an empty throne,
And heir-presumptive, with presumptuous air,
Survey the monarchy of Merrion Square.

MAURICE CRAIG (1919–2011)

The Washing of Feet

It's the simplest form of healing:
late at night,
the washing of feet.

When the light called sky
is an absence,
when the traffic's asleep;

when song
is a physical thing
needing physical shape

but you're just so worn out
facing darkness again
and those brave

tulips and roses
in Merrion Square
have long since turned in

to the dark, cottony
breath that simmers
inside of them.

When the world
is a cave, is a dungeon,
when the angels retreat,

return to this tiny
pacific ocean,
to the washing of feet.

PAT BORAN (*b.* 1963)

The National Gallery Restaurant

One of the snags about the National Gallery Restaurant
Is that in order to gain access to it
One has to pass through the National Gallery.
I don't mind saying that at half-past twelve in the day,
In my handmade pigskin brogues and my pinstripe double-vent,
I don't feel like being looked at by persons in pictures
Or, worse, having to wax eloquent to a client's wife
About why it is that St Joseph is a black man
In Poussin's picture of *The Holy Family:*
The historical fact is that St Joseph was a white man.
I'd prefer to converse about her BMW — or my BMW —
Or the pros and cons of open-plan in office-block architecture.
I clench the handle of my briefcase
Wishing to Jesus Christ that I could strangle Homan Potterton
The new young dynamic whizz-kid Director.
Oh but he's a flash in the pan —
Otherwise he'd have the savvy to close the National Gallery
When the National Gallery Restaurant is open.
Who does Homan Potterton think he is — Homan Potterton?

PAUL DURCAN (*b.* 1944)

Merrion House Sestina

I live and work on the top floor at the back
of this four-storey building. Mostly I go
through the motions. Each morning as I watch
a gradual transformation take place
in these lanes and car-parks, the light
returning to a city that seemed lost

just hours before, it's the lost
I'm drawn to, those neighbours in the back
of my mind in a house where even daylight

no longer enters. While office workers go
about their business, taking their places
behind drawn blinds and screens, I watch

for things I can't explain to them: that swatch
of tarmac, now matt, now glossed
with a shower of rain; the commonplace
miracle of buddleia; and here, back
from her travels above the archipelago
of rooftops, that female gull, in flight

a creature without weight until she alights
with a thud in the nest above me to watch
over her young. And though it's not so long ago
since other families grew up here, felt lost
as they waited for a parent to come back
with food, or news, with proof of other places

beyond this house, that was another place,
another time. These days there's just my light-
sleeping beloved, myself, and gulls. And at the back
of this maze of lanes, late at night, the watching,
cautious eyes of an urban fox. Have the last
secretaries suffering from the vertigo

of computer screens not noticed her, not seen her go
down these same lanes, a shadow in a place
of shadows, a creature that has lost
one world and claimed another. Before the light
returns, she slips into the spaces no one watches,
no one remembers. And then I'm here, back

in the go-slow chair of poetry, the resident hunchback
of this haunted, haunting house where my wristwatch
like myself struggles out of loss and into light.

PAT BORAN (*b.* 1963)

Westland Row

We came to the outer light down a ramp in the dark
Through eddying cold gusts and grit, our ears
Stopped with noise. The hands of the station clock
Stopped, or another day vanished exactly.
The engine departing hammered slowly overhead.
Dust blowing under the bridge, we stooped slightly
With briefcases and books and entered the wind.

The savour of our days restored, dead
On nostril and tongue. Drowned in air,
We stepped on our own traces, not on stone,
Nodded and smiled distantly and followed
Our scattering paths, not stumbling, not touching.

Until, in a breath of benzine from a garage-mouth,
By the Academy of Music coming against us
She stopped an instant in her wrinkled coat
And ducked her childish cheek in the coat-collar
To light a cigarette: seeing nothing,
Thick-lipped, in her grim composure.

Daughterwife, look upon me.

THOMAS KINSELLA (*b*. 1928)

Holles Street

It sure was intimate.
I meet women I knew then
and we don't even say hello.
I knew when their bowels moved,
when their breasts leaked,
what and how much they liked to eat,
what sorts of husbands they had

and how often,
the stuff they were made of,
how much money they had in the bank,
but seldom their names.
I knew their babies —
they were gazed at, compared.
I swear that I thought
each one as amazing as mine.
I inspected the ranks —
the monkey-faced one incubated,
the twins, the red-headed guy with the scabs,
the feminine boys and my masculine girl,
my spanking-new fat-legged girl!
My next-door-bed-neighbour was deaf.
Her husband and children would visit:
stream in and spread out on her bed
a fiesta of rough diamond talk.
I knew the snobs,
the ones who cut off,
the women who'd been there before
and the ones who fell down adoringly before Christ
in thanks for their child,
the women lying in pain
the ones who were clipped
the big women who loved
who were wheeled in at night,
stunned and rekindled each time
they remembered their child.
There was no shortage of pain,
of loss, of silence, of death.
We were the elected,
the chosen few.
We were the crème de la crème.
My breasts spouted milk.
My whole body swaggered —
casual about its great coup.
It was so bloody glamorous!
My baby slept like a nun

in no rush to let the world in.
I outstared the night,
watched Dublin turn yellow and navy and pink,
and surging through me were giant peals of joy, joy, joy —
and I couldn't wait to get out.

MAIRÉAD BYRNE (*b.* 1957)

from **Home**

I gave her bread and bid her lead me home,
For kilt she was with standing in the cold,
An' she, the creature, not turned eight years old.
She went before me on her small bare feet,
Clutching some papers not yet sold,
Down Westland Row and up Great Brunswick Street.
Sometimes she'd turn and peer
Into my face with eyes of fear.
She'd hunch her rags in hope to find some heat,
And stare at shops where they sold things to eat.
Then suddenly she turned,
And where a street lamp burned
Led me along a narrow dirty lane;
Dim glass and broken pane
Stood for the windows. Every shadowed door
Held children of the poor
That sheltered from the rain.
Through one dark door she slipped and bid me come
For this was home.
A narrow stair we had to climb
To reach the topmost floor.
A hundred years of grime
Clung to the walls, and time
Had worked its will. Tenants the like o' these
The landlords don't be planning how they'll please.
A smell was in it made you hold your breath:

These dirty houses pay the tax to death
In babies' lives. But sure they swarm like bees,
Who'd wonder at disease?
The room held little but a depth o' dark;
A woman stirred and spoke the young one's name
The first showed no spark,
But presently there came
A slipeen of a girl who made a flame
By burning paper, holding it torch-fashion,
Thinking, maybe, the place would stir compassion.

WINIFRED M. LETTS (1881–1972)

The Impact

It is late evening when the shouts
of local boys and girls begin. Across this city
street they shoot footballs, bottle tops,
hot chips from the chip shop whose steadfast
neon light shines opposite my window,
more dependable than summer sun.
Car horns bleat intermittently, or tyres break
to a dead halt, and each time I look out
I expect to see some body flung
far from itself, broken to a new form —
but the cars only ever move on, trailing
coarse words that elicit appreciative roars.
As evening darkens and turns the windows
of vacant houses black, they gather under
the light of a lamppost, blow cigarette smoke
in fat rings that grow thin, imperfect halos.
As the smoke reaches a bouquet of flowers
tied above them on the lamppost,
I wonder if they know what misfortune
it marks — though wilting now, I often wake
to see them blooming. As they begin

to move on, a small boy flicks
the butt of his cigarette at the windscreen
of an oncoming car, his parting gesture.
For a moment the embers flare
magnificently, a cheer goes up
in recognition of the boy, his daring,
the unexpected beauty of the impact.

LEEANNE QUINN (*b.* 1978)
(Pearse Street)

A Reason for Walking

Words when I think,
thoughts when I word.
Hours with this thought only:
Only words,
not what I feel.

The streets offer
not promise, but escape.
Harmony Row, Misery Hill.
Any named place
better than this.

Back home, the summer sheets
an open book, if blank.
But then the light impression
of our bodies, curled up
in the hieroglyph for love.

PAT BORAN (*b.* 1963)

From Mount Street Bridge

That night three girls were swimming there
between the tall reeds

in the canal, bare arms and legs waving
palely in the dark water;

laughing, shaking their hair, tossing
an affectionate "fuck off"

to someone standing on the bank. We loitered
to breathe it in: soft skin

and loud voices, ambering in the dark water,
close to the road, the streetlights.

MARK GRANIER (*b.* 1957)

Waiting in the Eye and Ear Hospital on Christmas Eve

My eyes burn with atropine —
Hot drops
Pushed from a plastic point
Squeezed beneath my eyelids and left to simmer.

The nurse hands me a crumpled tissue.

In my stinging darkness
I lace it between my fingers
And hold it like a paper rosary.

Then a hand rests on my shoulder
And they promise it won't hurt for long.
I am a brave soldier who must keep his head back.
I am a big boy who must be strong.

And outside —
The sleigh bells
Throw wishes at the rain.
I am longing for the first light of Christmas —
I am burning to see again.

STEPHEN KENNEDY (*b.* 1971)

Trees that Lead to You

Sycamore, copper beech, oak,
steadfast on Adelaide Road
one winter afternoon —
these trees that lead to you

flinging your day into my arms,
your face at last close to mine,
the hour before tea and the night
that sneaks you away from me again.

In your bag a handmade mask
burns orange as the toppling sun,
You've been hours away from me
and your shirt is a muddy testament to fun.

At the steps of the church the rector
pins his dream to the notice board.
We stand beneath these trees.
Fear not. Only love can lead to You.

ENDA WYLEY (*b.* 1966)

from **The Undergraduate**

i.

A smell of burning leaves in the Green,
but scattered remnants lift and twirl beside the pond
as Martin hurries towards Earlsfort Terrace.
When he pushes through the double doors
noise assaults him, shouts, laughter,
footsteps clattering on black and white tiles.
Students are hurrying to classes,
ascending the stairs at either side.

A tall figure in black with a bald head
moves intently about,
singling out individual students.
Already questioned — name, place, school, subject —
Martin avoids the piercing blue eyes,
the womanish hands.
He'd had enough of that.

In a chalk-stained old gown
draped from his thin shoulders,
in a mournful voice the professor
paraphrases, explains hard words,
gives biographical information,
reads *Midsummer Night Madness* in a variety of voices,
speaks of Milton's *Paradise Lost*.
He strolls in the valleys of tradition,
at ease with what he knows.
Aloof in the corridors,
unapproachable.

x.

They met laughing on Nelson's Pillar,
went to the zoo where she clapped her hands
in merriment before the monkey's cage;
were silenced by the epitaph in St Patrick's Cathedral;

she felt the woman's breast in St Michan's,
he shook hands with the crusader.
They caught productions in the old Abbey.
Making the city theirs,
museums, galleries, river vistas
discovered together, built into them.

On St Patrick's Day or Easter Monday
they danced at the Crystal Ballroom,
to favourite songs,
Mona Lisa, Put another nickel in,
The Tennessee Waltz, Buttons and Bows.
They could enter the liveliness,
lost in the rhythms
she on her mettle,
he taken out of himself.
They kept their romance secret.
In a circle of privacy
protected what they had,
perfecting it.

MAURICE HARMON (*b.* 1930)

Ely Place

'Such a depth of charm here always ...'

In Mortuary Lane a gull
cried on one of the Hospital gutters
I.I.I. ... harsh in sadness
on and on, beak and gullet
open against the blue.

Darkness poured down indoors
through a half light stale as the grave
over plates and silver bowls
glimmering on a side table.

Down at the corner a flicker of sex
— a white dress — against the railings.

'This is where George Moore ...'
                                    rasps
his phantom walking stick
without a sound, toward the Post Office
where her slight body, in white, has disappeared.

A blood vision started out of the brick:
a flustered perfumey dress;
a mothering shocked smile;
live muscle startling in skin.
The box of keys in my pocket
— I am opening it, tongue-tied.
I unpick the little penknife
and dig it in her throat,
in her spirting gullet.

And they are on it in a flash,
tongues of movement feeding,
ravenous and burrowing,
up streaming through the sunlight with it
until it disappears, buried
in heaven, faint, far off.

'... with a wicked wit, but self-mocking;
and full of integrity behind it all ...'

A few beginnings, a few
tentative tired endings
over and over.
                        Memoirs, maggots.
After lunch a quarter of an hour,
at most, of empty understanding.

THOMAS KINSELLA (*b.* 1928)

Herbert Street Revisited

for Madeleine

I

A light is burning late
in this Georgian Dublin street:
someone is leading our old lives!

And our black cat scampers again
through the wet grass of the convent garden
upon his masculine errands.

The pubs shut: a released bull,
Behan shoulders up the street,
topples into our basement, roaring 'John!'

A pony and donkey cropped flank
by flank under the trees opposite;
short neck up, long neck down,

as Nurse Mullen knelt by her bedside
to pray for her lost Mayo hills,
the bruised bodies of Easter Volunteers.

Animals, neighbours, treading the pattern
of one time and place into history,
like our early marriage, while

tall windows looked down upon us
from walls flushed light pink or salmon
watching and enduring succession.

II

As I leave you whisper,
'Don't betray our truth,'
and, like a ghost dancer,
invoking a lost tribal strength,

I halt in tree-fed darkness
to summon back our past,
and celebrate a love that eased
so kindly, the dying bone,
enabling the spirit to sing
of old happiness, when alone.

III

So put the leaves back on the tree,
put the tree back in the ground,
let Brendan trundle his corpse down
the street singing, like Molly Malone.

Let the black cat, tiny emissary
of our happiness, streak again
through the darkness, to fall soft-
clawed into a landlord's dustbin.

Let Nurse Mullen take the last
train to Westport, and die upright
in her chair, facing a window
warm with the blue slopes of Nephin.

And let the pony and donkey come —
look, someone has left the gate open —
like hobbyhorses linked in
the slow motion of a dream

parading side by side, down
the length of Herbert Street,
rising and falling, lifting
their hooves through the moonlight.

JOHN MONTAGUE (*b.* 1929)

Dublin, Dublin

In the orange lights the shadows of your railings
draw letters on the steps up to silent Georgian doors

Pepe's gleaming juggernaut from Valencia
unloaded oranges near Beresford Street;
the hoarse-voiced streetboys watched and in the night
slashed at the lorry wheels; unused to dreams
they scutted the length of the Kimmage Road
till the driver studded the back with nails;
they're waiting now with bottles and with knives.

In the orange lights the shadows of your railings
draw letters on the steps up to silent Georgian doors

Ten years ago three schoolgirls skipped down Mespil Road,
three slender lollipop sticks peeping from bulging mouths,
their childhood vibrant as their bright-red tights;
now stand together in the night near Herbert Place
listening for a footfall, their lips, their clothes flash red
but eyes are murky as the blocked canal. They will not sit,
all furred, to chat in Bewley's over coffee and cream cakes.

In the orange lights the shadows of your railings
draw letters on the steps up to silent Georgian doors

JOHN F. DEANE (*b.* 1943)

You never saw a bed-end in a Protestant fence
for Leland Bardwell

There is a film of icy dew over
The spread pastures of Leeson Street.
The dandelions fringing the partitions,
The bunched underwear tossed and dangled
Across nine-bar gates, are flecked

With frost. The Jesuits
Behind walls of transparent mist
Move slowly to their prayers, steaming
And solid, like morning cattle.
Below the street the sleepers are herded
Horizontal in their sofa beds and horse boxes,
The fuzz of ice on their shoulders,
On their tossed hair, not bothering them
At all; the three children going out to school
Whisper and hop between them
In a chink of busfares.

The area is a breath of cold bright wind
As you climb, holding a child in each hand.
Across the street in 1968
The Garda is still protecting the frozen bus
That carries the strike-breakers to the ice-factory.
The sun lands on him before anything else in the street.
Every inch of his body is tired
As the melting drops on the railings,
On the telephone wires, on the Georgian weeds,
Each one sagging, reflecting the world upside down.

EILÉAN NÍ CHUILLEANÁIN (*b.* 1942)

The Huguenot Graveyard at the Heart of the City

It is the immodesty we bring to these
names which have eased into ours, and
their graves in the alcove of twilight,
which shadows their exile.

There is a flattery in being a destination.
There is a vanity in being the last resort.
They fled the Edict of Nantes —
hiding their shadows on the roads from France —

and now under brambles and granite
faith lies low with the lives it
dispossessed, and the hands it emptied out,
and the sombre dances they were joined in.

The buses turn right at Stephen's Green.
Car exhausts and sirens fill the air. See
the planted wildness of their rest and
grant to them the least love asks of

the living. Say: *they had another life once.*
And think of them as they first heard of us:
huddled around candles and words failing as
the stubborn tongue of the South put

oo and *an* to the sounds of Dublin,
and of their silver fingers at the window-sill
in the full moon as they leaned out
to breathe the sweet air of Nîmes

for the last time, and the flame
burned down in a dawn agreed upon
for their heart-broken leave-taking. And,
for their sakes, accept in that moment,

this city with its colours of sky and day —
and which is dear to us and particular —
was not a place to them: merely
the one witty step ahead of hate which

is all that they could keep. Or stay.

EAVAN BOLAND (*b.* 1944)

Camden St.

In Sunday's phone booth
A silver box:
Last night's sweet and sour.

TOM MATHEWS (*b.* 1952)

Mrs. Katherine Dunne, Street Trader, Camden Street, Dublin, Died March 1983

Three on the bottle! Just like me!
She gave me a pram then — did she remember?
Now I address her dignity — summer and winter,
On the pavements of time. One day, too,
And I cold, she gave me tea as she stood
With snow on her lips and the shyest of smiles.

But that was a while ago now and the children
Have plagued and played us, as tombola and fife.
The bingo of life picks the strangest numbers
And drums up tunes in the weirdest disarray.

In the lamplight of chat — how the country swings
(And not for us) — I'd finger the aubergines,
The wounded cabbages, the French Delicious,
Tasteless as electricity in their super-shine,
Happy to find an Irish Cox
Whose sweet juice runs on the tongue
And she'd say: Ah, I kept that one for you.

Not easy to be a trader all those years,
Summer and winter, watching the generations pass
Like camels on a video horizon,
And staying motionless as Asia, never growing old
Herself, just wiser and more beautiful.

Was she always waiting for that pain to come,
To call a taxi like a tumbril and say Cheerio
And see you soon. I wonder why I'm left
The simple pride of having known her.

If the Baby Powers we shared
In the rush and tinsel of one Christmas Eve
May not be drunk this year nor any future
Year, I'll gladly hold the gift-horse bridle reins
And wait for the pain to come to call a cab.

LELAND BARDWELL (*b.* 1922)

Construction

A. 1. I had just turned off from Stephen St.
        Into Great Ship St., was confronted
        By a massive grey stone wall.

        The late rain lay in patches
        On the pavements, shone
        Between the grey-green cobbles

        Of the roadway, throwing up
        Grey facets of built stone.

    2. The cobbles were enamel,
        Chipped away in places,
        Showing the basic texture
        Underneath; grey rock.

B. 1. This was suave ceramic
        Fired in the mind's furnace.
        I had to look again.

    2. Each individual limestone cuboid
        Chisel-squared and weathered

Rough and grimy, holding on its face
All its past history and the threat
Of its future. Streams
Of rust-brown rain had stained
The entire wall; each
Block realised its presence
In this pattern and the wider
Patterns of sunlight, shadows, tone
And the complete distributed
Weight of rock
Combined for the present.

C.   My brain had built
A scheme of echoes,
Of ancient meanings held
In rock, in sunlight on ice,
In the low beginnings of thunder

But this wall needed no exterior
Aid for its stability,
No echo in its circumstance.

TREVOR JOYCE (*b.* 1947)

Meeting at the Chester Beatty

We have only just met
Downstairs at the Chester Beatty Library
We have not touched each other yet

Upstairs Dürer's Adam and Eve are contemplating
Each other and the apple
The serpent is already waiting

Upstairs are jars older than Grecian urns
Where lover strains towards lover
Fragments assembled so the hero yearns

Towards a clear plastic mould
A stopgap in scuffed images
Whole stories cannot be told

We have not yet become curators of ourselves
Guiding each other through halls of memory
Reading the small notes by the shelves

You have still time to discover
There are whole sequences lost from mine
Here or there, a missing line or lover

Upstairs is story within silken story:
Silkworms who shot threads like tiny roads
Were miniature cartographers of glory
For emperors who mapped their own silk routes
To carry gleaming bolts of gossamer
In colours of dreamed forbidden fruits

And we have not yet
Set up paths to each other carrying bolts of brightness
We have only just met

Upstairs are fabulous creatures with horns
In Cantimpré's *On the Nature of Things*
Monsters with benign faces, unicorns

Upstairs Isabella's marriage contract has no seal
Though holes gape where a ribbon might thread through
Louis loved another and thought better of a deal
That would have sealed up a century of war
Blood ribboning between England and Flanders
Love pounded louder than a battle's roar

Everywhere there is love and contract
Upstairs in the Chester Beatty Library
Where we have not made contact

Downstairs only our eyes have met
Beneath the weight of silks and histories
We have not touched each other yet

CATHERINE ANN CULLEN (*b.* 1961)

Essex Street

They lived down there,
they lived in the cold winter of the past
in damp clothes and bad humour,
rubbish everywhere, skulls everywhere

or the summer had arrived, and dug in:
gaieties of the riverside, the plying of trades,
the comings and goings of ships, merchandise,
girls with braided hair, sensible matches

some lost their heads, descended to winter
but see how cleverly the dwellings,
with what intricacy the wattle, the gold clasps

far from us, in sunken houses, by the river
speaking, loving, by the fire
that rises towards us, hearth above hearth,
floor upon floor, stone, wattle, wood
till we stand beside them, till they look
blankly at us, unnamed

or we have fallen through
dragging our sun with us,
our bones settling in the pit,
our winters mingled

again and again the careful pencil
of the finds illustrator,
watches and ingots, an ash bowl, a remote control,

the roof beams tied together, the cloth drying,
standing at the door convincingly arrayed
to wonder who has called us from the fire

it was nothing, a wrong number, an invisible hand,
a freak of the wind or the land
yet still we stand frozen and exposed
waiting for you to reach down, observe the season,
how the rain falls, the walls blacken, the streetlamps shine,
how as we approach each other
our bodies slip their ropes and drift,
how lightly, without hesitation or inquiry,
one steps into another, and stays there

PETER SIRR (*b.* 1960)

The Ring

Coats nearly touching
in the movie queue
that gives me a place
on a Saturday night
along O'Connell Street,
then I have my plate
of chips at Beshoff's,
wait for the No. 8
by Eden Quay and break,
go over the wall,
down wet steps,
run on the Liffey
under its bridges
out to the bay
and the Baily Light,
my lost gold ring.

TED MCNULTY (1934–1998)

In The Brazen Head

Under the image of the rebel on the scaffold,
perhaps on the very spot where the plot was hatched,
we sat in a corner of The Brazen Head,
spent long evenings until we came to the dregs,
sharing the company of men of all trades,
fellow-travellers in from the cold, in from the rain,
from nights of frost and the four winds passing
through places soon to be rubble, sites of desecration.
We sat in a Cupid's corner, eavesdropping
on raw music in the backroom: banjo and whistle,
and the balladeers swilling songs
from the cup of tradition: *Boolavogue, The Foggy Dew*.
All the listeners keeping time, tapping the tunes.

GERARD SMYTH (*b.* 1951)

The Messiah

Listen! Rehearsals in the Musick Hall!
Mr. Handel's choir. Twenty tongues
By the gut-strewn Liffey. Immanuel
Gilds the June-lilied afternoon.

Hall windows are unpaned as belles
In carriage, chariot and landaus
Trundle past me, crunch cockle shells
Down the gabbard-swearing quays.

Pink lords on their sedan chairs go by,
Castle ladies peacocked with finery;
For it is the City's Second Messiah:
"Comfort Ye! Comfort Ye! Comfort Ye!"

O Dublin snares on as is normal
For any Christ or coney in the pot.
Hucksters haggle. Jobbers squabble.
Balladsingers lilt my Forget-Me-Not.

For 'the People that Walked in Darkness'
It's a tight squeeze! Cooped up like birds,
They may not wear their hoops, the ladies,
Or the powdered gentlemen, their swords!

Wheeling my ghostly barrow on by
I got an eyeful of the New Ladies' Room
Mirrored in gold. O just heavenly!
Cousin Mary Brown gave it the broom.

O to hear in the flesh, tall Susanna,
I'd trade all the fish in the sea!
And 'Woman, Be All thy Sins Forgiven!'
Ejaculate from bold Rector Delany!

And to see Mr. Handel who's recovered
Leap again to Mr. Dubourg's Band,
And Mr. Maclaine travel the organ
Keys with a laced sleight of hand!

"He was Despisèd
And Rejected of Men."
Listen! The weeping of prisoners is
Stilled in the Marshalsea. And the Christ Church dean

Rubs shoulders with the Newgate
Bribesmen and their ladies, out to be seen,
With fans. Glad of their dungeon respite
The chained sleep, fever-ridden.

"Surely He has Borne our Griefs,
Thy Rebuke hath Broken His Heart",
In these times there's brief tell of Him.
Look! He comes! A poor corpse on a cart!

"I know that my Redeemer Liveth
And though Worms Destroy this Body
Yet in my Flesh shall I see God." Give
Me His nets, it's there I'd lie

Like old Mary over from Smock Alley.
He cooked fish by the lake in His day.
And we are well stocked and stalled
Crying cockles all this Corpus Thursday.

"The Trumpet shall Sound
And the Dead shall be Raised."
All over so! Sister, hurry down to the Ormond,
Sell your fillets to be fried, boilt or braised.

JOHN ENNIS (*b.* 1944)

All That is Left

All that is left of the medieval wall stands over
the underground river that snakes beneath
Fishamble, Cornmarket, Winetavern Street
where we strolled together like the pair in the legend
of Diarmuid and Gráinne or stopped to stand in
from the rain that fell on the ghosts of Hibernia.
The orators and the uncrowned king: all the fallen
who rose again on the stonemason's plinth.

In the Castle yard a tourist camera clicks, makes an image
of the gates through which the English departed.
In Ship Street walls were built on the bones of men.
Walls that listen to what the grey gulls tell.
The tourist can smell the lapidary damp
and puddled rain behind the Centre of Administration.

GERARD SMYTH (*b.* 1951)

from **Sonnets to James Clarence Mangan**

1

Fishamble Street, the Civic Offices
turning the sky a bureaucratic grey
above a vacant lot's rent-free decay:
craters, glass, graffiti, vomit, faeces.
One last buttressed Georgian house holds out
precariously against the wreckers' ball
or simply lacks the energy to fall
and rise again as one more concrete blot.
Ghost harmonics of the first *Messiah*
echo round the Handel Hotel and mix
with bells long redeveloped out of use
at Saints Michael and John's, a ghostly choir
rising and falling until the daydream breaks ...
Silence. Of you, Mangan, not a trace.

12

A burger box and a burger too, a chipbox
and a milkshake bobbing in the fountain:
sustenance for your undernourished phantom.
Soapsud refill cans of Harp and Beck's.
The Eason's clock and Pro-Cathedral bells
chime a sacred-secular *Te deum*
on the hour to break the tedium
(real bells this time!) in busy streets and malls
Evening Herald! ... Roaring every word
a harmless case informs me Who is master,
and Who died for my sins to save the dayglo
giant foetus on his sandwich board.
Three for a pound, the cigarette lighters! ... The poster
for a clearance sale reads: ALL MUST GO.

DAVID WHEATLEY (*b.* 1970)

Viking Dublin: Trial Pieces

I

It could be a jaw-bone
or a rib or a portion cut
from something sturdier:
anyhow, a small outline

was incised, a cage
or trellis to conjure in.
Like a child's tongue
following the toils

of his calligraphy,
like an eel swallowed
in a basket of eels,
the line amazes itself

eluding the hand
that fed it,
a bill in flight,
a swimming nostril.

II

These are trial pieces,
the craft's mystery
improvised on bone:
foliage, bestiaries,

interlacings elaborate
as the netted routes
of ancestry and trade.
That have to be

magnified on display
so that the nostril
is a migrant prow
sniffing the Liffey,

swanning it up to the fold,
dissembling itself
in antler combs, bone pins,
coins, weights, scale-pans.

III

Like a long sword
sheathed in its moisting
burial clays,
the keel stuck fast

in the slip of the bank,
its clinker-built hull
spined and plosive
as *Dublin.*

And now we reach in
for shards of the vertebrae,
the ribs of hurdle,
the mother-wet caches —

and for this trial piece
incised by a child,
a longship, a buoyant
migrant line.

IV

That enters my longhand,
turns cursive, unscarfing
a zoomorphic wake,
a worm of thought

I follow into the mud.
I am Hamlet the Dane,
skull-handler, parablist,
smeller of rot

in the state, infused
with its poisons,
pinioned by ghosts
and affections,

murders and pieties,
coming to consciousness
by jumping in graves,
dithering, blathering.

V

Come fly with me,
come sniff the wind
with the expertise
of the Vikings —

neighbourly, scoretaking
killers, haggers
and hagglers, gombeen-men,
hoarders of grudges and gain.

With a butcher's aplomb
they spread out your lungs
and made you warm wings
for your shoulders.

Old fathers, be with us.
Old cunning assessors
of feuds and of sites
for ambush or town.

VI

'Did you ever hear tell,'
said Jimmy Farrell,
'of the skulls they have
in the city of Dublin?

White skulls and black skulls
and yellow skulls, and some
with full teeth, and some
haven't only but one,'

and compounded history
in the pan of 'an old Dane,
maybe, was drowned
in the Flood.'

My words lick around
cobbled quays, go hunting
lightly as pampooties
over the skull-capped ground.

SEAMUS HEANEY (1939–2013)

Clearing a Space

A man should clear a space for himself
Like Dublin city on a Sunday morning
About six o'clock.
Dublin and myself are rid of our traffic then
And I'm walking.

Houses are solitary and dignified
Streets are adventures
Twisting in and out and up and down my mind.
The river is talking to itself
And doesn't care if I eavesdrop.

No longer cluttered with purpose
The city turns to the mountains
And takes time to listen to the sea.
I witness all three communing in silence
Under a relaxed sky.

Bridges look aloof and protective.
The gates of the parks are closed
Green places must have their privacy too.
Office-blocks are empty, important and a bit
Pathetic, if they admitted it!

The small hills in this city are truly surprising
When they emerge in that early morning light.
Nobody has ever walked on them,
They are waiting for the first explorers
To straggle in from the needy north

And squat down here this minute
In weary legions
Between the cathedral and the river.
At the gates of conquest, they might enjoy a deep
Uninterrupted sleep.

To have been used so much, and without mercy,
And still to be capable of rediscovering
In itself the old nakedness
Is what makes a friend of the city
When sleep has failed.

I make through that nakedness to stumble on my own,
Surprised to find a city is so like a man.
Statues and monuments check me out as I pass
Clearing a space for myself the best I can,
One Sunday morning, in the original sun, in Dublin.

BRENDAN KENNELLY (*b.* 1936)

Dublin City (AKA The Spanish Lady)

As I walked out through Dublin City
At the hour of twelve o'clock at night
Who should I spy but a Spanish lady
Washing her feet by candlelight

First she washed them and then she dried them
Over a fire of ambry coals
In all my life I ne'er did see
A maid so sweet about the soles.

Whack fol the toor a loor a laddy
Whack fol the toor a loor a lay
Whack fol the toor a loor a laddy
Whack fol the toor a loor a lay

I stopped to look but the watchman passed
Says he, "Young fellow, the night is late.
Along with you home or I will wrestle you
Straight away through the Bridewell gate"
I threw a look to the Spanish lady
Hot as the fire of ambry coals —
In all my life I ne'er did see
A maid so sweet about the soles.

As I walked back through Dublin City
As the dawn of day was o'er
Who should I see but the Spanish lady
When I was weary and footsore.
She had a heart so filled with loving
And her love she longed to share —
In all my life I ne'er did meet
A maid who had so much to spare.

Now she's no mot for a puddle swaddy
With her ivory comb and her mantle so fine,
But she'd make a wife for the Provost Marshall
Drunk on brandy and claret wine.
I got a look from the Spanish lady
Hot as a fire of ambry coals —
In all my life I ne'er did meet
A maid so sweet about the soles.

I've wandered north and I've wandered south
By Stoneybatter and Patrick's Close,
Up and around by the Gloucester Diamond
And back by Napper Tandy's house.
Old age has laid her hands upon me
Cold as a fire of ashy coals —
But where is the lonely Spanish lady
Neat and sweet about the soles?

As I was leaving Dublin City
On that morning sad of heart,
Lonely was I for the Spanish lady
Now that forever we must part.
But still I always will remember
All the hours we did enjoy —
But then she left me sad at parting
Gone forever was my joy.

ANONYMOUS

A Son! A Son!

You around whom, at every hour,
The void thickens like an atmosphere
Rank with unsolved mystery, childish fears,

Go back now, through the Dublin lanes
To that very first year
Of malt and drayhorse, Francis Street, the Coombe.

Two women wait, in an ante-room.
A man who has crashed the lights
At Cuffe Street in the small hours, in the rain,

Chainsmokes endlessly — Players cigarettes.
Doctor Kidney, hedging his bets
And slapping nurses' bottoms, flashes through

In a white housecoat, the local deity,
Yes, we must all be patient,
Even you in the ageless womb,

In the shadow of Saint Nicholas of Myra,
Where salt waits, oil in its cruse.
You will find your own way out of this maze

Of headscarves, factory whistles, cheap red meat
And dark soutanes on Thomas Street —
The fifties ... Then as now,

To be hung upside down, on a brilliant scales,
A thumbprint on your brow,
Is all you know. And the old wives' tales

In the ante-room, the man dissolving in tears
Who has just become your father
Lost in a fog of years.

HARRY CLIFTON (*b*. 1952)

Madly Singing in the City
after Po Chü-i

And often, when I have finished a new poem,
I climb to the dark roof garden
and lean on a rail over an ocean of streets.
What news I have for the sleeping citizens
and these restless ones, still shouting their tune
in the small hours. Fumes rise from the chip-shop
and I am back at the counter, waiting my turn.
Cod, haddock, plaice, whiting.
The long queue moves closer;
men in white coats paint fish with batter,
chips leap in the drying tray.
There's a table reserved for salt and vinegar

where the hot package is unswaddled,
salted, drenched, wrapped again
and borne out into the darkness.
In darkness I lean out, the new words ready,
the spires attentive. St Werburgh's, St Patrick's, Nicholas
of Myra. Nearby, the Myra Glass Company
from where we carried the glass table-top.
In a second I will sing, it will be as if
a god has leaned with me, having strolled over
from either of the two cathedrals, or from the green
and godly domes of Iveagh Buildings.
Ever since I was banished from the mountains
I have lived here in the roar of the streets.
Each year more of it enters me, I am grown
populous and tangled. The thousand ties of life
I thought I had escaped have multiplied.
I stand in the dark roof garden, my lungs swelling
with the new poem, my eyes filled with buildings
and people. I let them fill, then,
without saying a word, I go back down.

PETER SIRR (*b.* 1960)

Eyrie, Christ Church Place

When we moved
to our high eyrie
overlooking the city
belled by cathedrals
we danced
on blonde floorboards
marvelled
at windows
best left undressed,
air, light,
light, air —
light-headed

even in sleep
we danced
in our blonde bed.

Now we are the roof
of our building,
not quite eyeball to eyeball
with the weathervane
on Christ Church Cathedral.
Waking at dawn
to re-discover
our newfound land,
alert to the silence
of the bells,
we looked towards
the parapeted bridge
to mark
the progress
of a lone
reveller.

CLAIRR O'CONNOR (*b.* 1951)

The View from St Augustine Street

And did you make the journey
to see the view from St Augustine Street,
where the factory horn went silent long ago?

Did you arrive somewhere between
a treasure trove of the city's corner stones
and junkyard debris from its broken homes?

There, a shadow might stab you in the back,
the vicious tongue had no kind words to speak.
There was a man who swept the street,

his brush kept finding things that people dropped,
and a man who thought he was a real gunslinger,
who aimed his front door key and shot

those who looked familiar and those who were not —
his life was one long cowboy film,
days crossing the frontier of his own Wild West.
He became a legend on St Augustine Street.

GERARD SMYTH (*b.* 1951)

The Fall

The Garden of Eden (described in the Bible)
Was Guinness's Brewery (mentioned by Joyce),
Where innocent Adam and Eve were created
And dwelt from necessity rather than choice;

For nothing existed but Guinness's Brewery,
Guinness's Brewery occupied all,
Guinness's Brewery everywhere, anywhere —
Woe the expulsion that succeeded the Fall!

The ignorant pair were encouraged in drinking
Whatever they fancied whenever they could,
Except for the porter or stout which embodied
Delectable knowledge of Evil and Good.

In Guinness's Brewery, innocent, happy,
They tended the silos and coppers and vats,
They polished the engines and coopered the barrels
And even made pets of the Brewery rats.

One morning while Adam was brooding and brewing
It happened that Eve had gone off on her own,
When a serpent like ivy slid up to her softly
And murmured seductively, Are we alone?

O Eve, said the serpent, I beg you to sample
A bottle of Guinness's excellent stout,
Whose nutritive qualities no one can question
And stimulant properties no one can doubt;

It's tonic, enlivening, strengthening, heartening,
Loaded with vitamins, straight from the wood,
And further enriched with the not undesirable
Lucrative knowledge of Evil and Good.

So Eve was persuaded and Adam was tempted,
They fell and they drank and continued to drink
(Their singing and dancing and shouting and prancing
Prevented the serpent from sleeping a wink).

Alas, when the couple had finished a barrel
And swallowed the final informative drops,
They looked at each other and knew they were naked
And covered their intimate bodies with hops.

The anger and rage of the Lord were appalling,
He wrathfully cursed them for taking to drink
And hounded them out of the Brewery, followed
By beetles (magenta) and elephants (pink).

The crapulous couple emerged to discover
A universe full of diseases and crimes,
Where porter could only be purchased for money
In specified places at specified times.

And now in this world of confusion and error
Our only salvation and hope is to try
To threaten and bargain our way into Heaven
By drinking the heavenly Brewery dry.

FERGUS ALLEN (*b.* 1921)

234

The Hot Bread of St Catherine's
for Irene and Michael Smith

From Mount Brown and Golden Lane
they come to these streets
that are like the streets in an old engraving.
They have finished
the rubbing of brass, the scrubbing of steps.

A window brought to a shine reflects
mid-morning, the routine
of tradesman and apprentice,
of women wearing headscarves out to replenish
the message bag, the pension purse.

It's an old parish, an inner-city labyrinth.
And there beyond the shine of glass
are ribbons of meat hanging on hooks,
eggs in a basket, the cures
concocted by Mushatt the chemist,
the hot bread of St Catherine's.

GERARD SMYTH (*b.* 1951)

Scene with Lights: Thomas Street

A darkening sky, six fellows with sticks
Can't manage to drive four black cows
Into Tyrell's Yard.

The skinheads outside the bookmaker's
Egg the animals on.

The lady in the fruitstall laughs
As the cows run towards the river.

A big car draws up;
A man gets out and buys bright oranges.

PÁDRAIG J. DALY (*b.* 1943)

Vicar Street Flats

On winter evenings
They stand, silent as mountains,
Against the sky

Until an unheard summoning
Brings the children
From door after door

Like the Hopi of legend,
Brought forth into light
Out of the belly of the world;

Or the people Signorelli saw,
With slow joy, tear themselves,
Limb after limb, from the earth.

They tie ropes around lamp-posts
And swing till nothing is solid
Or distant or fearful anymore.

PÁDRAIG J. DALY (*b.* 1943)

Dick King

In your ghost, Dick King, in your phantom vowels I read
That death roves our memories igniting
Love. Kind plague, low voice in a stubbled throat,

You haunt with the taint of age and of vanished good,
Fouling my thought with losses.

Clearly now I remember rain on the cobbles,
Ripples in the iron trough, and the horses' dipped
Faces under the Fountain in James's Street,
When I sheltered my nine years against your buttons
And your own dread years were to come:

And your voice, in a pause of softness, named the dead,
Hushed as though the city had died by fire,
Bemused, discovering ... discovering
A gate to enter temperate ghosthood by;
And I squeezed your fingers till you found again
My hand hidden in yours.

                                    I squeeze your fingers:

            Dick King was an upright man.
            Sixty years he trod
            The dull stations underfoot.
            Fifteen he lies with God.

            By the salt seaboard he grew up
            But left its rock and rain
            To bring a dying language east
            And dwell in Basin Lane.

            By the Southern Railway he increased:
            His second soul was born
            In the clangour of the iron sheds,
            The hush of the late horn.

            An invalid he took to wife.
            She prayed her life away;
            Her whisper filled the whitewashed yard
            Until her dying day.

And season in, season out,
He made his wintry bed.
He took the path to the turnstile
Morning and night till he was dead.

He clasped his hands in a Union ward
To hear St James's bell.
I searched his eyes though I was young,
The last to wish him well.

THOMAS KINSELLA (*b.* 1928)

Golden Lane

Born beneath cathedral bells,
he heard their morning and evening Pathétique.
The cheerfulness of their clanging metals
came gusting to his doorstep.

The boy from Golden Lane
with an ear for melancholy.
The idol of Paris, Vienna, St Petersburg.
The pensive maker of the transcendent nocturne.

Moscow congratulated him
for his lullabies to soothe the nineteenth century.
Night after night the privileged and prosperous
came to hear and applaud

John Field who made piano-chords
sound like the rise and fall of breath,
who when he played seemed to bend
and whisper to his easeful melody.

GERARD SMYTH (*b.* 1951)

Long Lane

Long Lane, one of Dublin's back-streets,
just such a street as Mangan struggled down,
the winter darkness and the pitchy dampness ...

Then, like some strange figure out of mythology —
a sphinx — the silhouette of this club-footed man
against the glaring yellow of the lamplight.

As the branch tip tapping on the window glass
in the snow-stormed night becomes the object,
to return always when a sense of loss occurs

so fear comes now with twisting twisted legs,
hobbling down Long Lane a winter's night,
climbing steps, then knocking at a door, and passing in.

MICHAEL SMITH (*b.* 1942)

Notebook Shop

All the poems we might write,
gather here in these blank books
made from vellum, soft Indian paper,
shelved in the corner shop on Francis Street.
But then a wind blows the door open,
the bell rings, and our thoughts float
out and up past the antique shops,
the Tivoli Theatre pounding its heart
of rehearsals, Oxfam's sofa graveyard
and the man from the Coombe
clattering by with his horse and cart —
our unmade poems coming alive,
flapping on the seagulls' wings,
peeping into the cages of Marsh's Library,

singing with St Patrick's choir,
lying down in St Werburgh's
with Edward Fitzgerald and Major Sirr.
There is no end to where our poems go —
anywhere to be free, not to be trapped
in these fine and beautiful books
that are hungry for a scribble,
a dream, the rush of a word.

ENDA WYLEY (*b.* 1966)

Houses off Francis Street

I have been four years away
From an Irish autumn
And had quite forgotten
How trees suddenly turn gold
And drop their beauty
Spendthrift to earth.

I had almost forgotten
The slanting passages
The sunlight makes through
The woods at evening time,
Clouds shapechanging
Continually, fields glowing orange.

I had forgotten too how
The houses off Francis Street
Cling for warmth together
Just as twilight comes
And the quiet smoke begins
To hide them from the stars.

PÁDRAIG J. DALY (*b.* 1943)

The Old Jockey

His last days linger in that low attic
That barely lets out the night,
With its gabled window on Knackers' Alley,
Just hoodwinking the light.

He comes and goes by that gabled window
And then on the window-pane
He leans, as thin as a bottled shadow —
A look and he's gone again:

Eyeing, maybe, some fine fish-women
In the best shawls of the Coombe
Or, maybe, the knife-grinder plying his treadle,
A run of sparks from his thumb!

But, O you should see his gazing, gazing,
When solemnly out on the road
The horse-drays pass overladen with grasses,
Each driver lost in his load;

Gazing until they return; and suddenly,
As galloping by they race,
From his pale eyes, like glass breaking,
Light leaps on his face.

FR HIGGINS (1896–1941)

The Song of Zozimus

Gather round me boys, will yez
Gather round me?
And hear what I have to say,
Before ould Sally brings me
My bread and jug of tay.

I live in Faddle Alley,
Off Blackpitts near the Coombe;
With my poor wife called Sally,
In a narrow, dirty room.

Gather round me, and stop yer noise,
Gather round me till my tale is told;
Gather round me, ye girls and ye boys,
Till I tell yez stories of the days of old;
Gather round me, all ye ladies fair,
And ye gentlemen of renown;
Listen, listen, and to me repair,
Whilst I sing of beauteous Dublin town.

MICHAEL J MORAN / ZOZIMUS (c. 1794–1846)

Night Walk (*from* 'City')

Out here you can breathe.
Between showers, the street
empty. Forget your lover
faithless in the chilly bed
who'll wake soon and wonder
if you've left for good.
Granite under your feet
glitters, nearby a siren. Threat

or a promise? You take Fumbally Lane
to the Blackpitts, cut back by the canal.
Hardly a sound you've made, creature
of night in grey jeans and desert boots,
familiar of shade. Listen.
                              The train
bearing chemicals to Mayo, a dog far off, the fall
of petals to the paths of the Square,
a child screaming in a third floor flat.

On Mount Street high heels clack,
stumble in their rhythm, resume.
Let her too get home safe, your prayer,
not like that poor woman last night
dragged down Glovers Alley, raped there,
battered to a pulp. Still unnamed.
Your key in the door, you've made it back,
a chorus of birds predicting light.

PAULA MEEHAN (*b.* 1955)

Walls: John's Lane 1978

I know where the walls should be;
When I go out, I pass under their towers;
I have measured their breadth with my arms.

At night I sleep in the house of Aelred,
Who found God old and ailing
In these shadow-ways and alley-ways;

By the garden of Elena, where friars
In lieu of rent, on the feast of Blessed John,
Cut their reddest rose.

Now it is open country again;
Delicate birches hold raindrops along the roadside,
Shrubs shock you with nursery brilliance;

Little of what was remains, but Audeon's tower
Standing like a corner of crumbling wedding cake
When the bubbles have died and the talk is elsewhere;

And they have lost the lay of the streets.
Dublin is buried forever
Under the great tar for Cork and Inchicore.

PÁDRAIG J. DALY (*b.* 1943)

Street Games

Unholy bits, ring, neck, of porter and Bass bottle
From the six public-houses at those four corners,
Nicholas St, Clanbrassil St, the Coombe
And Kevin St, shrine on high wall — fierce Spot —
Protecting the Sisters of the Holy Faith, warning
By sun and moon the ruffians in top-back room
Or cellar. Last week I saw a marching band,
Small Protestants in grey clothes, well-fed pairs
Led by a Bible teacher, heard the noise
Of boot-heel metal by bread-shop, sweet-shop, dairy,
Scrap, turf, wood, coal-blocks. Suddenly Catholic joylets
Darted from alleys, raggedy cherubs that dared them:
'Luk, feckin' bastards, swaddlers, feckin' bastards!'
Too well they knew the words their mothers, fathers,
Used. Silent, the foundlings marched along the street-path
With click of boot-heel metal. We have cast
Them out. Devotion, come to the man-hole at last,
Bawls: 'Feckin' bastards, swaddlers, feckin' bastards!'

AUSTIN CLARKE (1896–1974)

Peter Street

I'd grown almost to love this street,
each time I passed looking up
to pin my father's face to a window, feel myself

held in his gaze. Today there's a building site
where the hospital stood and I stop and stare
stupidly at the empty air, looking for him.

I'd almost pray some ache remain
like a flaw in the structure, something unappeasable
waiting in the fabric, between floors, in some

244

obstinate, secret room. A crane moves
delicately in the sky, in its own language.
Forget all that, I think as I pass, make it

a marvellous house; music should roam the corridors,
joy patrol the floors, St Valentine's
stubborn heart come floating from Whitefriar Street

to prevail, to undo injury, to lift my father from his bed,
let him climb down the dull red brick, effortlessly,
and run off with his life in his hands.

PETER SIRR (*b.* 1960)

Burial of an Irish President
(Dr Douglas Hyde)

The tolling from St Patrick's
Cathedral was brangled, repeating
Itself in top-back room
And alley of the Coombe,
Crowding the dirty streets,
Upbraiding all our pat tricks.
Tricoloured and beflowered,
Coffin of our President,
Where fifty mourners bowed,
Was trestled in the gloom
Of arch and monument,
Beyond the desperate tomb
Of Swift. Imperial flags,
Corunna, Quatre Bras,
Inkerman, Pretoria,
Their pride turning to rags,
Drooped, smoke-thin as the booming
Of cannon. The simple word
From heaven was vaulted, stirred
By candles. At the last bench

Two Catholics, the French
Ambassador and I, knelt down.
The vergers waited. Outside.
The hush of Dublin town,
Professors of cap and gown,
Costello, his Cabinet,
In Government cars, hiding
Around the corner, ready
Tall hat in hand dreading
Our Father in English. Better
Not hear that 'which' for 'who'
And risk eternal doom.

AUSTIN CLARKE (1896–1974)

Sráid na gCaorach

Ship Street deep
with the bells of two cathedrals

the day itself deepening
to that grey from which

suddenly, the city leans
as if it has remembered something

or woken again
to the wind on its face and the slow

geometry of light descending
and stretching towards them

with reluctance and strange joy
prepares to continue

a gull screeches over the castle
and Ship Street startled

rubs the wool from its eyes
and casts off ...

PETER SIRR (*b.* 1960)

Clanbrassil Street

Summer delivered before Easter,
of an evening walking up

Clanbrassil Street, I see a jet
above and am glad for once

not to be within its silver.
On past the house

that calls itself Hy-Brasil —
we substitute our own orients —

the Harold's Cross Halal
and the Bu Ali sending scents

of spices from its open green
door toward Emmet Bridge,

where a full moon rises on one side
and a sun sets on the other.

Over the canal where the mitred
swans graze underwater,

and beyond, amid all the asphalt,
a cherry blossom is beginning

its leap over a wall.

JOSEPH WOODS (*b.* 1966)

Heytesbury Lane

Waking at night
I hear a pig squeal.
My room is low-ceilinged
with half-moon windows.
Outside the front door
there is a courtyard.
On summer mornings
I can trap the sun.
Sometimes at night, though,
I wake to hear
the pitiable scream
of a trapped pig.
It is difficult to believe
I am not having a nightmare.
When I rise
in the late morning
there is a stillness
in the lane.
I stroll to the shops
past painted doors,
pointed facades,
ladies with toy dogs.
The lane hovers in the heat.
But it is not a nightmare,
this squealing of a pig.
Someone on this lane
is keeping a pig.
All that wealth,
that sobriety!
It is almost comic,
this strange hobby,
except that the animal
seems to be in terror,
bewilderment and outrage,
as if waiting

to be slaughtered,
and I cannot sleep.

JOHN BOLAND (*b.* 1946)

A Carol for Clare

whisper your name in Phibsboro
through prison yard and hospital

tiptoe through Portobello
assembling choir and canticle

pass on the grain of Rialto
where fog and snow are audible

still the hours in Pimlico
harmonise a madrigal

lie with your ghost in Marino
shepherd the final decibel

GERARD FANNING (*b.* 1952)

Pride of Pimlico

Come all ye broken hearted ones and listen to my lay
About a lovely damsel, as fair as any May,
Who's caused much tears and sorrow and grief and heartfelt woe
It's Kitty Flynn I'm speaking of, the Pride of Pimlico.

It's just about a month ago unto this place she came,
And set our hearts a blazing up in love's undying flame,
And made of every other lass about the place a foe,
Because she took their sweethearts, did the Pride of Pimlico.

Poor Paddy Burke the tailor now can't do a stroke of work,
Nor Billy Shee the handyman, nor steady Jack McGurk;
And if you ax the reason, all they'll answer you is: "O
'Tis all because of Kitty Quinn, the Pride of Pimlico."

Old Jimmy Kane the miser that no one could get round
And young Tom Ray who owns a forge and near a hundred pound
And Matt McCann whose father keeps the Irish Waxwork Show
Are raving night and day about the Pride of Pimlico.

It's time the polis saw to it. It soon will be too late
An divil a man in all the Coombe will have a solid pate,
Or soon beyond in Riley's, a sight of awful woe
You'll see ten thousand victims of the Pride of Pimlico!

ARTHUR GRIFFITH (1872–1922)

A Parable of Pimlico

A kind lady of poorish Pimlico,
Lonely, developed the unusual custom
Of feeding a rat that dared to her door.
Bread, mainly. The rat ate every crumb.
The kind lady relaxed into her chair
Feeling, almost, that she had found a friend.
The rat scoffed offerings with rattish care
Darting the odd glance at the lady's hand.
The lady sickened. The rat nipped to her door
And crossed the ready threshold for the bread
She owed him. But hunger owned the place.
Pimlico neighbours didn't visit her.
As she lay weak, weaker, and yet not dead
The rat sniffed at the hospitable face.

BRENDAN KENNELLY (*b.* 1936)

The Jewish Museum in Portobello

*Ireland, they say, has the honour of being the only country which never
persecuted the jews. Do you know that? No. And do you know why? ...
— Why, sir? Stephen asked, beginning to smile.
— Because she never let them in, Mr Deasy said solemnly.*
— James Joyce, *Ulysses*

Two candles on a kitchen table,
glazed bread beneath a cloth.
You lean against cool walls
as if to dodge a searchlight.

Edelstein? Your name's Edelstein?
Exile hovers around your name —
all that's left of your lost father
fleeing from Nazis in Dortmund.

Shreds of barbed wire from a camp,
a swastika on a polished badge.
Give me instead old Mushatt the chemist,
his balms and potions to ease a graze.

We stand before unrolled scrolls,
our fingers laced like plaited loaves.
I see you pleading behind camp gates,
your hair flung among the hair of thousands.

Your father is a quiet ghost moving
in the sealed ghetto of childhood.
The souvenir mug he gave you survives,
an ark of memory you never forsake.

In Fine's shop in Terenure I buy
rye bread, chunks of kosher cheese.
Streetlights are a bright menorah
lit with singing for our feast.

Your father lacked Abraham's luck,
abandoned by angels on the Sabbath.
His loss is a closing of synagogues,
the fading of black from prayer-straps.

We kiss under a canopy of clouds,
closer than a skull-cap to its skull.
Loss is a covenant between us,
the burnt bread of your father's exile.

SEÁN DUNNE (1956–1995)

On the Crest of the Bridge at Portobello

When on the crest of the bridge at Portobello
the doubledecker bus paused, for a minute,
and you — child, boy, youth, young man —
sitting in the front seat left on the top deck
had all Rathmines spread out before you
the sweep of the road as the bus swooped down again
your whole being through your eyes feasting
now rapturous now serene
on the red sandstone town-hall tower
crowned by cool green copper
and the blue hills beyond
and the green hills beyond —

it wasn't the centre of Geneva
but how could you know that then?
for it might have been the centre of the whole world —
it *was* the centre of the young world —
when the doubledecker paused on the crest of the bridge
over the canal at Portobello

PEARSE HUTCHINSON (1927–2012)

Enueg I

Exeo in a spasm
tired of my darling's red sputum
from the Portobello Private Nursing Home
its secret things
and toil to the crest of the surge of the steep perilous bridge
and lapse down blankly under the scream of the hoarding
round the bright stiff banner of the hoarding
into a black west
throttled with clouds.

Above the mansions the algum-trees
the mountains
my skull sullenly
clot of anger
skewered aloft strangled in the cang of the wind
bites like a dog against its chastisement.

I trundle along rapidly now on my ruined feet
Hush with the livid canal;
at Parnell Bridge a dying barge
carrying a cargo of nails and timber
rocks itself softly in the foaming cloister of the lock;
on the far bank a gang of down and outs would seem to be
        mending a beam.

Then for miles only wind
and the weals creeping alongside on the water
and the world opening up to the south
across a travesty of champaign to the mountains
and the stillborn evening turning a filthy green
manuring the night fungus
and the mind annulled
wrecked in wind.

I splashed past a little wearish old man,
Democritus,

scuttling along between a crutch and a stick,
his stump caught up horribly, like a claw, under his breech,
    smoking.
Then because a field on the left went up in a sudden blaze
of shouting and urgent whistling and scarlet and blue ganzies
I stopped and climbed the bank to see the game.
A child fidgeting at the gate called up:
'Would we be let in Mister?'
'Certainly' I said 'you would.'
But, afraid, he set off down the road.
'Well' I called after him 'why wouldn't you go on in?'
'Oh' he said, knowingly,
'I was in that field before and I got put out.'
So on,
derelict,
as from a bush of gorse on fire in the mountain after dark,
or in Sumatra the jungle hymen,
the still flagrant rafflesia.

Next:
a lamentable family of grey verminous hens,
perishing out in the sunk field,
trembling, half asleep, against the closed door of a shed,
with no means of roosting.
The great mushy toadstool,
green-black,
oozing up after me,
soaking up the tattered sky like an ink of pestilence,
in my skull the wind going fetid,
the water ...

Next:
on the hill down from the Fox and Geese into Chapelizod
a small malevolent goat, exiled on the road,
remotely pucking the gate of his field;
the Isolde Stores a great perturbation of sweaty heroes,
in their Sunday best,
come hastening down for a pint of nepenthe or moly or half

and half
from watching the hurlers above in Kilmainham.

Blotches of doomed yellow in the pit of the Liffey;
the fingers of the ladders hooked over the parapet,
soliciting;
a slush of vigilant gulls in the grey spew of the sewer.

Ah the banner
the banner of meat bleeding
on the silk of the seas and the arctic flowers
that do not exist.

SAMUEL BECKETT (1906–1989)

Madman. Twilight. Portobello Bridge

He rests.
He's had a busy afternoon.
Sixteen swans to say hello to.
And the man in the moon.

TOM MATHEWS (*b.* 1952)

Black Ball Gown

It's Wednesday, that in-between day.
I buy milk, bread, ham (enough for two)
and a black ball gown.

Black skirts billow swan feathers,
a black swan. Rare sighting among
old jumpers, reeds of widows' weeds
in the second-hand clothes shop.

Old shoes with loose tongues bring to mind
gossiping women in Mr. Bohannan's
(at least that's how the name sounded to a child)
sorting through the rubble of others' leavings,
searching out what was worth keeping,
the way Mr. Bohannan must have sorted
through the rubble of Europe.

I want to bury my head in its folds,
smell the smell of tulle.
I carry it back to the bedsit
beyond Leonard's Corner. A stream of black
flows through my arms, through the mouth
of a paint peeling front door (No. 8)
up the stairs into the one room
where my sister and I sleep and cook and dream
(the ceiling has a black disc of smoke
we burn so many meals, smoke so many cigarettes).

My black ball gown hangs across the wardrobe
for the whole of the year
I stay in that flat. I am barely eighteen,
not wanting to leave the nest of my Midland home.

There is no work there and besides
I have learned to type and take shorthand.

I walk to work each day, down Clanbrassil Street
down the diving dip at Christ Church onto the quays;

screams of gulls skim beneath black cloud balloons
bounce off Liffey waters, summer smell of the river
wending me towards Heuston Station,

to the typing pool, no place for swans.

My black ball gown,
how it lifts those black balloons
softens black discs on smoky ceilings.

While my fingers stammer over the typewriter
strange Van Hool McArdle words
it keeps its shape, is always
exactly as I left it.

EILEEN CASEY (*b.* 1956)

Little Back Streets of Dublin

The little houses near Greenville Avenue huddle
together in the stillness of the evening.
Sunday evening hangs somewhere far up
on a huge guilt of calmness trailing long
plumes of smoke into the hearths of the houses.
My lanky figure runs ahead disfiguring
itself in the windows where I peer
into kitchens knotted with neatness.
Carpets with prams and coffee tables,
sit around coal fires watching
television sets dreaming in the corners:
black and white cowboys staging a siege;
red and green jerseys thumping sweat
after a brown ball to coloured cheers.
Behind a red door buckets of music
rattling like mad, pop music falling
down a stairs with furious kicks and screams,
A mother waits in her apron at a door
her voice rocking along the cobbles of her accent
as she ushers her two dufflecoated
little boys into their warm kitchen, leaving
the streets as empty as a Christmas morning.
A few steel-blue clouds huddle together
smothering their huge binge of light
drunk on the thick taste of coal smoke.
Further down past the dour face
of the boys' and girls' National School,

past the back of the big coal yard,
two young men with moustaches
sitting back in a car bursting with music,
chatting up two girls standing by the wall,
their cigarettes glowing red as the car
moves off and they stroll home,
their heels clattering up along the street.
Trees would listen, if there were any here.
A song whispering across a pile of scrap
cars overflowing onto the street.
Crazy ... crazy for your love ... for your love.
A man with a cap pulled across his head
and a woman with a dirty blanket around her
shoulders sit in the shadow of the cars,
staring at their one solitary bottle;
it stands there, listening to the few scraps
of words they might throw at each other.
The church on Donore Avenue clamps down
on aisles and pews of light, squirting it out
through the windows into the face of the evening.
A Sunday evening that hangs around outside
listening to the hushed cloud of calmness flooding
through the little back streets of Dublin.

LIAM RYAN (*b.* 1955)

A Writer's Farewell

Bury me at Fatima Mansions
Between the wire and the wall
Within sound of the children's yelling
And their mothers' frantic call.

Encased beneath wet concrete
With nothing more to say,
My feet in ancient litter
And my head in Dublin clay.

As the washing waves above me
And the coal carts trundle by,
Unmarked and unremembered,
Safe at last I'd lie.

FRANCIS STUART (1902–2000)

Islandbridge

The river heron and the young canoeist rowing
past the picnic tables and war memorial
go by with the speed of those in a hurry.

In less than a moment they are gone
just like the men who wore grey beards when I was young,
stoic and silent when their wars were over,

their medals lost among the knick-knacks
of cottages on Long Lane
or sold to the moneylender who knew they'd never

be reclaimed or worn on Poppy Day.
Theirs was a new nation without a guiding star,
those men who lived on to know their day was gone

and in the dreams of afternoon sleep
feel again the itch of a Tommy's uniform
and the blast that threw them into the arms of mercy

when the big guns opened fire.

GERARD SMYTH (*b.* 1951)

from Mnemosyne Lay in Dust

Past the house where he was got
In darkness, terrace, provision shop,
Wing-hidden convent opposite,
Past public-houses at lighting-up
Time, crowds outside them — Maurice Devane
Watched from the taxi window in vain
National stir and gaiety
Beyond himself: St Patrick's Day,
The spike-ends of the Blue Coat school,
Georgian houses, ribald gloom
Rag-shadowed by gaslight, quiet pavements
    Moon-waiting in Blackhall Place ….

Cabs ranked at Kingsbridge Station, Guinness
Tugs moored at their wooden quay, glinting
Of Liffey mudbank; hidden vats
Brewing intoxication, potstill,
Laddering of distilleries
Ready to sell their jollities,
Delirium tremens. Dublin swayed,
Drenching, drowning the shamrock: unsaintly
Mirth. The high departments were filed,
Yard, store, unlit. Whiskey-all-round,
Beyond the wealth of that square mile,
    Was healthing every round.

AUSTIN CLARKE (1896–1974)

The Hunt

Where were we? As if we had dived
into the city's dreaming, tumbled
from strange nook to stranger cranny
as the year darkened

Mount Brown, Old Kilmainham
adrift in a hollow, gaunt stone
above the Camac, Lady's Lane
a murky glamour, cottages out of nowhere

We crossed a threshold
Rivals in the bedroom sniffed the air
investors in the kitchen
calculated rental income

We stayed a little, out of sight
melting into the furniture
we were pioneers in a deep interior
hungry ghosts among the Horlicks jars

We drifted through the intimate city
like dust, like light
settling briefly, silent but alert
looking for an opening

What relief to be out
in sun and early dark
greeting the brickwork
of Sitric street and Ivar street

or plunging eastward
canal water and stadium dusk
a shine of swans on the bank
the grey gash of a railway bridge

At 4.30 pm, the light withdrawn
the whole place pulled its chair
closer to the table
muttering secrets of itself

Skaldbrother
loped home with the booty
a crowd shifted outside the jail
old bones stirred

The poor, the triumphant
the pigkiller, the hanged
came out. We returned late
dust of centuries in our hair

old coins in our pockets
Tomorrow we'll spend them
A light long handled
will warm the brick again

PETER SIRR (*b.* 1960)

Kilmainham Gaol, Dublin, Easter 1991
for Frank Harte

Roadies in ponytails stringing lights and cables,
a beer can popped in the corner, echo of sound check.
Outside in the filling yard, hum of expectation.

We pour through the narrow gate under the gallows hook
in twos and threes, becoming an audience.
Before the lights go down we examine each other shyly.

The singer surveys his audience, heat rising
to the tricolour and Plough overhead.
As the first words of Galvin's lament climb to invoke
James Connolly's ghost, we are joined by the dead.

I say this as calmly as I can. The gaunt dead
crowded the catwalks, shirtsleeved, disbelieving.
The guards had long since vanished, but these
looked down on us, their faces pale.

I saw men there who had never made their peace,
men who had failed these many years to accept their fate,
still stunned by gunfire, wounds, fear for their families;
paralysed until now by the long volleys of May so long ago.

I think that we all felt it, their doubt and their new fear,
the emblems so familiar, the setting, our upturned faces,
so unreal. Only the dignity of the singer's art
had power to release them. I felt it, I say this calmly.

I saw them leave, in twos and threes, as the song ended.
I do not know that there is a heaven but I saw their souls
fan upward like leaves from a dry book, sped out into the night
by volleys of applause; sped out, I hope, into some light at last.

I do not know that I will ever be the same again.
That soft-footed gathering of the dead into their peace
was like something out of a book. In Kilmainham Gaol
I saw this. I felt this. I say this as calmly and as lovingly as I can.

THEO DORGAN (*b.* 1953)

Rehearsal for a Presidential Salute at the Irish Museum of Modern Art (IMMA), Royal Hospital, Kilmainham

Easy to imagine an army regiment
rehearsing over a cobbled square, the brass
urging them on with marching tunes
and a big-voiced soldier shouting —

and later, their return from a just war,
ghostly now, listless, faltering as they pass
through a group of tourists off the bus,
tour-weary, camera-shy, with another capital

crossed off their map; on past a class
of eight year olds in school uniform,
some holding hands, and past two women
not long retired from state jobs

who want to forget the parade of shadows
that passed for a life, forebodings
they swept off the desk each evening,
work they brought home.

HUGH O'DONNELL (*b.* 1951)

Bully's Acre
Royal Hospital, Kilmainham

We stand at Bully's Acre,
the old gates chained.
Beyond, the trees are vast,
the gardener's work
a full circle of cut grass
smooth as a blanket,
around the trunks' base.

At evening
the snatched bodies
from centuries ago
will rise from the surgeons'
ancient slabs,
retreat to their graves again
and we will find home in each other —
Bully's Acre with gates thrown wide.

ENDA WYLEY (*b.* 1966)

Inchicore, Early Autumn, 1986
for Evanna

There is a mist over the roofscape of Inchicore,
and there are sun-tinted clouds heading quickly to the south-
    west
in two layers parted by a dark grey strip. The sun suddenly
    disappears
and the pink strips slip away and appear elsewhere.
I can just make out the Dublin mountains over the technical
    school.
If I look at the roofs and spires long enough they seem to move.
I think this is because the eye is drawn towards the four blocks
    of flats
beyond them, and the roofs bend to the curve of the eye.
To the right of my window, my frame, there is a smoke stack.
which is in the direct line of my vision with the distant spires.
To the left of the stack is a row of trees along the river
and the one nearest to me is spectacular, very leafy.
predominantly green but with a horizontal cross of golden
    yellow.
A seagull is continuously flying towards it and then at the last
    moment
flies back upriver again. Its whiteness stands out in the
    enriched light.
The derelict factory, with its rhythmically placed girders,
    balances the picture
especially as, just above it, there is a yellow house.
Rows of small trees bordering two gardens fill out the
    foreground
until just below me my breath flows towards the dying
    splendour
of the Virginia creeper with its rich reds and yellows and
    fading greens.

PHILIP CASEY (*b.* 1950)

from **Inchicore Haiku**

Now, in Inchicore
my cigarette-smoke rises
— like lonesome pub-talk.

Along Emmet Road
politicians' promises
blow like plastic bags.

In St Michael's church
a plush bishop in his frock
confirms poverty.

On Tyrconnell Road,
Catholic Emancipation
— thirteen milk-bottles.

MICHAEL HARTNETT (1941–1999)

The House on Jamestown Road

Up to Dublin, for two westerns a day,
Theatre Royal then race to the Carlton,
at 5 my father collects me at Eason's,
my mind in Tucson, Arizona or some town
like Wichita Falls.

We stop at Mrs Sweeney's,
Jamestown Road, Inchicore —
cups of tea, let the traffic pass before
the long long road to Tullamore.

Mrs Sweeney's eldest daughter
enters with a tray,
swiz swiz of her stockings
loudest sound to my ear,
her suspender clip strokes my thigh
as she slides in beside me on the settee,
oh, so near.

I forget Randolph Scott, Audie Murphy too,
hope they don't notice the change in me;
a fast munch on a ham sandwich
I stare hard at Harry Worth
on the black and white TV

As the adults talk of Lynally, Mucklagh,
Rahan, an execution long ago
the Kirwin murder
that awful crime
and the secrets

And what a great dancer Barney was,
skillful, stylish, so full of charm,
then after dances he'd hitch home,
dancing shoes in brown paper
under one arm.

Then the tension between him
and his brother Larry,
no one knows why,
then despite a clemency petition
Barney waited four long months to die.

2nd June 1943, they swung him,
Mrs Sweeney grinned and winked at me.
Deirdre squeezed up from the sofa,
straightened her skirt,
topped up our cups with strong tan tea.

In darkness we travelled home
my father and I
the long long road to Tullamore,
Mrs Sweeney's daughter, the Kirwin brothers, that murder,
my head tumbling all that had gone before.

NEIL DONNELLY (*b.* 1946)

38 Phoenix Street

Look.
       I was lifted up
past rotten bricks weeds
to look over the wall.
A mammy lifted up a baby on the other side.
Dusty smells. Cat. Flower bells
hanging down purple red.

Look.
       The other. Looking.
My finger picked at a bit of dirt
on top of the wall and a quick
wiry redgolden thing
ran back down a little hole.

       *

We knelt up on our chairs in the lamplight
and leaned on the brown plush, watching the gramophone.
The turning record shone and hissed
under the needle, liftfalling, liftfalling.
John McCormack chattered in his box.

Two little tongues of flame burned
in the lamp chimney, wavering
their tips. On the glass belly
little drawnout images quivered.
Jimmy's mammy was drying the delph in the shadows.

*

Mister Cummins always hunched down
sad and still beside the stove,
with his face turned away toward the bars.
His mouth so calm, and always set so sadly.
A black rubbery scar stuck on his white forehead.

Sealed in his sad cave. Hisshorror erecting
slowly out of its rock nests, nosing the air.
He was buried for three days under a hill of dead,
the faces congested down all round him
grinning *Dardanelles!* in the dark.

They noticed him by a thread of blood
glistening among the black crusts on his forehead.
His heart gathered all its weakness, to beat.

A worm hanging down, its little round
black mouth open. Sad father.

*

I spent the night there once
in a strange room, tucked in against the wallpaper
on the other side of our own bedroom wall.

Up in the corner of the darkness the Sacred Heart
leaned down in his long clothes over a red oil lamp
with his women's black hair and his eyes lit up in red,
hurt and blaming. He held out the Heart
with his women's fingers, like a toy.

The lamp-wick, with a tiny head
of red fire, wriggled in its pool.
The shadows flickered: the Heart beat!

THOMAS KINSELLA (*b.* 1928)

Paper Mill Heartland

Over Ballyfermot's humpbacked bridge
the paper mill siren called my name
come dance for me the banshee wailed,
skip to the beat of a cardboard drum
in my print and pack auditorium.
Making elbow room twixt maidens and men
I blazed a trail down Killeen's river road
setting my pace at pushbike speed
along stony rites of passing tracks
amid rising pylons and smoking stacks.
While a tarp wrapped barge, morning pale,
slipped the lock gate's damp embrace
to follow the reed-decked waterways,
I punched my card and when properly shod
danced to the tune of a make-paper god.
Mid hissing steam, true grit and sweat,
I served those hungry mouth machines
with manual skills and diverse codes
along the yellow brick road of the union man
towards mill workers in New Jerusalem.
While baffles trashed and ground stuff down
and man-sized cogs made demonic sound,
I wondered where that canal barge might be,
perhaps like a swan she's paddling free
where water and wings are the powers that be.

PAUL MURRAY (*b.* 1935)

Procession

Ballyfermot: houses decked with streamers,
Reds, yellows, greens, strung from windows
To garden fences pocked with hedges.

And leaning out, women wave
To children representing roads and schools,
And men in doorways shuffle cigarettes

And wear their cotton shirts open-necked,
Scratched in summer … Doorsteps washed
clean of dog piss, house insects

Dead from turpentine;
Disinfectants mix with odours
Of the long-breathing space of ease,

Of Ballyfermot at the doors
And neighbours
Talking over fences.

The day is mild. Our Lady
Is walked, head nodding, in step
With sombre bearers, under

Clouds far up and floating
Above children of the host;
A priest leads her

In procession down Ballyfermot Road,
The less involved stood idle,
Watching with their hands in pockets

Those convinced the poor
Are heavenly bodies,
Vociferous in prayer and bowed

To elders of the Church and State.

The pews are ancient, hollow,
Muffled underfoot as congregants
Go silent to the altar steps,

Genuflecting
Under power of sin
Or acquiescence

To the host within the Tabernacle.
Christ have Mercy, Lord have Mercy,
Lips intone the rites of Benediction

Under incense and the priest in robes ...

And May knows no dark nights,
Processionists in Lady Blue
Caught in minor spotlight,

Sun rays
Highlighting dust through
Stained glass windows.

KEVIN BYRNE (*b.* 1953)

Opening the Door
i.m. Beatrice Behan

I knock, I knock.
I challenge the silence.
Knock! Knock! Knock!
I open the door into the room.
The blinds are drawn.
A bedside light is burning.
A glass of water stands on the table.
It's exactly 11.22 a.m.
She's in her bed, decently covered,
Her right hand outstretched,
A ring on her finger.
But she does not speak —
Ah, Beatrice was always the quiet one,
Walking her dogs Klaus and Karla

Beside the Dodder river,
Cycling home on the footpath
Noiselessly, with a Mona Lisa smile.
Upstairs I dial a number
While down in the street
People drift towards the Angelus
And across the way a honeyed wall
Is neutral under a March sky.

ROBERT GREACEN (1920–2008)

DART Journey

On a homeward journey.
Hear songbirds
Whistle down the line,
And a breeze singing
In wild columbine.

Look
On a platform
Flowers are dreams.
Young faces flashing by.

Quiet in Booterstown
A heron stands sentry.
Then Merrion Strand
Where on the far shore
The sea laps a hill.

And on the wayside
The heart flies
From wild Iris to bird,
From bird to a distant star,
And from star to home.

PADDY GLAVIN (*b*. 1934)

An Evening in Booterstown

After cold days taking photographs
confirming the nearest coastline,
I look from your window
and see how the tramp fields
have turned to a wax impression
of the sea's other shores. Reclining
like a folded mirror, or growing
in detail just as these blank papers
on the tray near the alcove
swim in their blue chemicals,
they gather the last of Dublin's
refracted light. See there
emerging from the covering darkness
of lintels, bay-windows and shut
doors, another circle of light corrects
the skyline. Like any brief town
time has polished it, with
the sea-marsh and the harbour wall,
to a pale permanence.

GERARD FANNING (*b.* 1952)

Booterstown

in memory of Gregory Lysaght

1

Beneath my house a smugglers' tunnel carves
Its way from a cave that looks into the Irish Sea
And ends outside the Catholic Church in Booterstown.
Was it there I heard, as a student, a drunk priest
Sermonize in screams against Friedrich Nietzsche
And defy the death of God? Is Death a smuggler
And God the precious object that the citizens

Of Death's own country coveted above all worldly goods?
I can believe in a dying country, in the citizens
Who are God-fearing and who have tempers that rise
Like high tide to break and furrow the rocky walls
Of the white railway station at Booterstown:
There the birds scream like mad priests
And the sea is offering its consecrated wines.
I can believe the birds in Booterstown Sanctuary
Finding their way to this house through the tunnel,
Deserting the fresh air, preferring to breed underground.
This is what they did on the day of a death,
A young man whose heart stopped in its second decade,
Whom we called Gregory. The neighbourhood mourned.
I saw the women's hair grow long in mourning
In this avenue of holy places and sacred names,
For sacred be the willows of Willow Place that weep
For Gregory. Go search through McCabe Villas,
St Helens Road, can you find him in Cross Avenue?
These are the places of his childhood, children hide.
Ah, you have found him in the Catholic Church,
His body laid out, his sister weeping,
As a donkey in the field outside starts to bray.
They played there, a boy and girl, discovering
The wheel. It is the wheel of fortune.
The wheel of fortune turns for good and ill.

2

In the living-room where I write, Gregory,
Above the mess of books and papers on the table,
There hangs a painting. It is red and orange
And gold and black. It is a flower on fire.
It is light itself. Do you remember light?
The light you would love is a gold medal
Picked up at the Olympics or at Wembley.
I would turn all of Booterstown Avenue
Into a football pitch, kick the fearless ball
With pleasure, break all the respectable windows.
Or you could sprint to win — I estimate the distance

To be covered in ten seconds as that between
The Punch Bowl and the Nook. I can see you
Race it in ten seconds. Blink and you'd miss it.
Like a flower's life. Blink and you miss it.
Do you remember flowers? Do you remember life?
Has it turned into a wax museum? History?
Wax moulds and melts, breaks and is found
In the ears of the living to block the sound
Of birds singing in the Booterstown trees
On the autumn morning of your death.
We wash the dead, we wash our ears and hear
What it is the birds sing about your life.
They remember you, one Saturday, in your mother's
Post office, working, and a gang attacked you,
Pulling a gun, wanting money. You gave it,
Knowing that money should give way to the gun
For it is only money, and life is more lovely

Than the gun and the gang. Well done, well done.
Gregory, that day you defied death.
You praised this life. But the good die young,
The rest of us reside in Booterstown Avenue,
Hostages to fortune in Booterstown Avenue,
Living where we live in Booterstown Avenue.

FRANK MCGUINNESS (*b.* 1953)

He tells me I have a strange relationship

with my city. As though I were something divorced
from the skin I'm in, could scrap or elope with
my own tattooed scapula, pouting belly, saddle curve
of his palm's kiss.

But here's the vein on my left wrist
fat as Liffey, my right skinny

lost Dodder; slit,
they run murky and thick
with city. My left breast
thingmote, my right sugarloaf,
my throat a high and narrow pane, frogged
and pointed like a lancet.

My country stretches from a ham's span
outside the pale to the top
of Parnell Street. I cannot leave.
It is a narrow, self-effacing swathe,
the shape of me —
enough scar to fret at, too close to desire or despise.
If Dublin is kicks in the shins, my shin
is its sweet spot, summer lunchtime Stephen's Green.

AILBHE DARCY (*b.* 1981)

The Humours of Donnybrook Fair

To Donnybrook steer, all you sons of Parnassus —
  Poor painters, poor poets, poor newsmen, and knaves,
To see what the fun is, that all fun surpasses —
  The sorrow and sadness of green Erin's slaves.
Oh, Donnybrook, jewel! full of mirth is your quiver,
  Where all flock from Dublin to gape and to stare
At two elegant bridges, without e'er a river:
  So, success to the humours of Donnybrook Fair!

O you lads that are witty, from famed Dublin city,
  And you that in pastime take any delight,
To Donnybrook fly, for the time's drawing nigh
  When fat pigs are hunted, and lean cobblers fight;
When maidens, so swift, run for a new shift;
  Men, muffled in sacks, for a shirt they race there;
There jockeys well booted, and horses sure-footed,
  All keep up the humours of Donnybrook Fair.

The mason does come, with his line and his plumb;
　The sawyer and carpenter, brothers in chips;
There are carvers and gilders, and all sort of builders,
　With soldiers from barracks and sailors from ships.
There confectioners, cooks, and printers of books,
　There stampers of linen, and weavers, repair;
There widows and maids, and all sort of trades,
　Go join in the humours of Donnybrook Fair.

There tinkers and nailers, and beggars and tailors,
　And singers of ballads, and girls of the sieve;
With Barrack Street rangers, the known ones and strangers,
　And many that no one can tell how they live:
There horsemen and walkers, and likewise fruit-hawkers,
　And swindlers, the devil himself that would dare;
With pipers and fiddlers, and dandies and diddlers,
　All meet in the humours of Donnybrook Fair.

'Tis there are dogs dancing, and wild beasts a-prancing,
　With neat bits of painting in red, yellow, and gold;
Toss-players and scramblers, and showmen and gamblers,
　Pickpockets in plenty, both of young and of old.
There are brewers, and bakers, and jolly shoemakers,
　With butchers, and porters, and men that cut hair;
There are mountebanks grinning, while others are sinning,
　To keep up the humours of Donnybrook Fair.

Brisk lads and young lasses can there fill their glasses
　With whisky, and send a full bumper around;
Jig it off in a tent till their money's all spent,
And spin like a top till they rest on the ground.
　Oh, Donnybrook capers, to sweet catgut-scrapers,
They bother the vapours, and drive away care;
　And what is more glorious — there's naught more
　　uproarious —
Hurrah for the humours of Donnybrook Fair!

ANONYMOUS (18th century)

Dublin 4

Lit carriages ran through our fields at night
Like promises being speedily withdrawn.
Awakened by train-noise, well-placed, suburban,
I ask myself is this where they were going.

SEAMUS HEANEY (1939–2013)

Lines Written on a Seat on the Grand Canal, Dublin
'Erected to the Memory of Mrs. Dermot O'Brien'

O commemorate me where there is water,
Canal water preferably, so stilly
Greeny at the heart of summer. Brother,
Commemorate me thus beautifully.
Where by a lock Niagarously roars
The falls for those who sit in the tremendous silence
Of mid-July. No one will speak in prose
Who finds his way to these Parnassian islands.
A swan goes by head low with many apologies,
Fantastic light looks through the eyes of bridges —
And look! a barge comes bringing from Athy
And other far-flung towns mythologies.
O commemorate me with no hero-courageous
Tomb — just a canal-bank seat for the passer-by.

PATRICK KAVANAGH (1904–1967)

In Vavasour Square

Almost a tramp, the man who wears a flower
Always in his lapel fell down the stair,
The single step, into his rank parlour.

Luckily he'd left open the hall door
So he was seen down the long corridor
And rescued by some young men passing there.
No one had any idea who they were,
It being midnight, a cul-de-sac, and rare
To see strangers out in Vavasour Square
At that or indeed at any other hour.

Earlier his lodger, a young mother,
Was hit by her husband with an armchair
And ran crying and bleeding from the ear
To the kind people in the house next door.
Their son, on crutches, his leg in plaster,
Brought her off to hospital in his car.

In the narrow front gardens of the square
Rose bushes thrive and, cut straight as a ruler,
The hedges grow higher. It's lonely here.
There's no traffic, no other traffic, near.
But what an old, old mistake is the air,
Exhaling the day's heat when it's cooler
So that the roses bend then slowly rear
Their blued pink heads, as is the night's desire.

BRIAN LYNCH (*b*. 1945)

Marlborough Road

On Marlborough Road
the houses have names —
Aclare, Larnaca, Ardeevin,
Shalamar, Woodstock, Hazelhurst
and St Elmo on the way to the station
where the ghost creaked the gate long ago
one early winter morning

and became a wide-eyed Red Setter before me,
as frightened of a girl as I was of him,
our still worlds interrupted.

Going home up Marlborough Road,
I see the garden boats covered in canvas,
the spiked green railings
darker than the hedges
and the copper beech and monkey trees.
The old black Morris Minor is still there
and the domes of the many glass houses.
I hear the shunting of an approaching train
bringing more people home
to this safe, quiet suburb.

And just for this fifteen minute stretch
of house-lined road and hill,
there is peace on Marlborough Road to remember.
I am five years old again, opening our front door,
shocked to see your handkerchief
wave like a flag of blood on your forehead,
and to hear you call my mother's name for help,
your footprints large red accident marks
stronger than the trails left behind you
by birds on our snow-filled drive.

You were my father who growled at nurses —
God almighty, how can a child be expected to eat that on her
     own? —
when, sick in my second year of life, nurses left me
jam sandwiches and a mug of hospital tea.
You were my father who appeared
at the top of Keem Bay, unexpected to us as the thunder storm,
with coats and hats, umbrellas and warm rugs
pulling us safely up the cliff edge and home to holiday beds,
wind and the gulls crying out in joy
Abba, Abba, Abba.

You were our father
my mother watched the kitchen clock for,
climbing up the stairs at five thirty
to make her red lips redder, her bright face brighter
just before we shouted *He's home, he's home!*
leaving behind our laundry-bin lid and kitchen-pot toys
racing each other to open the door to you
and tell of our day's hard work —
of our tree house creations and go-cart inventions,
of the apples and pears we'd stolen from next door's garden.

I have never seen you fall since
but that day your head fell
in tiredness against the train window
just before the flash of Sandymount Strand outside,
then later fell harder onto concrete
halfway along that snowy January road.
And coming home again now, I remember how
you must have slipped, then bled, unfairly vulnerable —
and in my head I want to help you up, brush you clean.
But Marlborough Road's icy beauty keeps pulling my father down.

ENDA WYLEY (*b.* 1966)

Morehampton Road

I defend myself on Morehampton Road
from ghosts and griefs, from inexplicable
sorrows that take their toll. My sofa bed
too short for my body, a Book of Kells
contorted letter painted blue on black,
sleepless, that's where I slept, glad of shelter —
the girls enduring the sweat of my shoes
souring the flat with their rancid leather.
Herbert Park, the tennis courts, the railings.

Refuge I fled to when breakfast erupted —
forks in the ceiling, spoons in the ceiling.
Live and let live, or you're out on your tod.
Joining the dole queues, feeding hand to mouth,
you walk the streets of seventies Dublin,
the city's manners neither graceful nor couth —
stop to your gallop and clip to your wings.
Back in Donnybrook it's changed times indeed —
meeting bank managers giving advice
why I should decamp to where profits lead,
following fashion, losing a fortune.
I order a decaf in McCloskey's.
Down in one go, no sugar to sweeten
the ghosts, the griefs, inexplicable wherefores,
trillions of reasons to love the heathen —
seductive the kiss between man and man.
X marks the spot where I learned secret codes,
sweet as Sunday missing every Mass.
I defend myself on Morehampton Road.

FRANK McGUINNESS (*b.* 1953)

Begin

Begin again to the summoning birds
to the sight of light at the window,
begin to the roar of morning traffic
all along Pembroke Road.
Every beginning is a promise
born in light and dying in dark
determination and exaltation of springtime
flowering the way to work.
Begin to the pageant of queuing girls
the arrogant loneliness of swans in the canal
bridges linking the past and future
old friends passing through with us still.

Begin to the loneliness that cannot end
since it perhaps is what makes us begin,
begin to wonder at unknown faces
at crying birds in the sudden rain
at branches stark in the willing sunlight
at seagulls foraging for bread
at couples sharing a sunny secret
alone together while making good.
Though we live in a world that dreams of ending
that always seems about to give in
something that will not acknowledge conclusion
insists that we forever begin.

BRENDAN KENNELLY (*b.* 1936)

On Raglan Road

(Air: The Dawning of the Day)

On Raglan Road on an autumn day I met her first and knew
That her dark hair would weave a snare that I might one day rue;
I saw the danger, yet I walked along the enchanted way,
And I said, let grief be a fallen leaf at the dawning of the day.

On Grafton Street in November we tripped lightly along the ledge
Of the deep ravine where can be seen the worth of passion's pledge,
The Queen of Hearts still making tarts and I not making hay —
O I loved too much and by such by such is happiness thrown away.

I gave her gifts of the mind I gave her the secret sign that's known
To the artists who have known the true gods of sound and stone
And word and tint. I did not stint for I gave her poems to say.
With her own name there and her own dark hair like clouds
     over fields of May.

On a quiet street where old ghosts meet I see her walking now
Away from me so hurriedly my reason must allow
That I had wooed not as I should a creature made of clay
When the angel woos the clay he'd lose his wings at the dawn
    of day.

Patrick Kavanagh (*b.* 1904–1967)

Raglan Lane
after Patrick Kavanagh

In Raglan Lane, in the gentle rain, I saw dark love again,
Beyond belief, beyond all grief, I felt the ancient pain,
The joyful thrust of holy lust, I stretched on heaven's floor,
One moment burned what the years had learned and I was
    wild once more.

The years' deep cries in her sad eyes became a source of light,
The heavy gloom and sense of doom changed to pure delight.
And as we walked in joy and talked we knew one thing for sure,
That love is blessed togetherness and loneliness is poor.

Then I grew rich with every touch, we loved the whole night long
Her midnight hair on the pillow there became an angel's song,
Her happy skin, beyond all sin, was heaven opened wide
But as the dawn came shyly on, I slept, and she left my side.

Why did she go? I'll never know, nor will the gentle rain,
Her up and go was a cruel blow, and yet I felt no pain
For I had known her body and soul in my own loving way,
So I lay and thanked the God of love at the dawning of the day.

BRENDAN KENNELLY (*b.* 1936)

Ringsend

'The Gaelic language was prohibited along with Gaelic dress —
saffron-dyed clothing, moustaches, long hair and forelocks'
    — John O'Beirne Ranelagh, *A Short History of Ireland*

Point of the tide, spit of land, An Rinn
where you spoke the tongue, rode bareback, lay
low, outside the city walls; The Green
Patch where The Dodder and The Liffey

bled into the sea's industry — air
briny and clean off the wrinkled sand or it swings
from the lower circles, sulphur —
end of the moorings, iron rings

threaded with ropes, the crew ashore
drinking at the sign of The Good Woman,
a fanlight intact or gone in above the hall door,
rum, cotton, coffee, tobacco, resin …

the city dump smoothing its dunes
shaken by raucous gulls to a snow-globe
where hand-to-mouth, ragged platoons
stumble, stoop, probe

for anything, a gleam like a ring in barmbrack,
the recycled riddle
crunching a razor-shell — container ships, stacks
of bibles and ironsides, landfill —

name that reclaims itself, sings, begets
lorries, caravans, tidal traffic —
from The Salmon Pool to the light on Poolbeg — nets
and net curtains, shipshape village of red brick,

Quality Row, Whiskey Row, drone
of dirt bikes revving near the Waste Water Treatment Plant

buffered by the bird sanctuary's green zone —
a Brent Goose, a wing-stretching cormorant —

ebbing bay-wide emptiness, the bare scroll
cloud-lit, in a steady state
of arrival / departure where a solitary soul
with bucket and spade, digging for bait,

pauses, as a Sealink ferry slides out
past the Pigeon House, landmark
chimneys ringed red & white,
giant goalposts, funnels — the land an ark

with washing strung on a high-
security fence (her blouse the forbidden saffron):
what a grey or blue or green or brown eye,
departing, will look back on.

MARK GRANIER (*b.* 1957)

Ringsend
after reading Tolstoy

I will live in Ringsend
With a red-headed whore,
And the fan-light gone in
Where it lights the hall-door,
And listen each night
For her querulous shout,
As at last she streels in
And the pubs empty out.
To soothe that wild breast
With my old-fangled songs,
Till she feels it redressed
From inordinate wrongs,
Imagined, outrageous,

Preposterous wrongs,
Till peace at last comes,
Shall be all I will do,
Where the little lamp blooms
Like a rose in the stew;
And up the back garden
The sound comes to me
Of the lapsing, unsoilable,
Whispering sea.

OLIVER ST JOHN GOGARTY (1878–1957)

Haiku

heading towards
the twin chimneys,
a two-horned snail

ANATOLY KUDRYAVITSKY (*b.* 1954)

The Ringsend Ferry
i.m. Frank Harte

Have you been on the Ringsend Ferry?
Have you been carried on the billowy waves
In the Liffey Harbour with two hefty navvies
Pulling the oars with long smooth strokes
From the slippy steps near the old Pigeon House
All the way over to the North Wall docks
Heaving and swaying in the keel-tar whiff
And the taste of salt on the wind off the bay.
The cap pulled down and a smoke on the way
Cupped in your hand like a little lighthouse.

The Baily blinking on the Hill of Howth —
Then the ganger's shouting in the early mist
And your back's bent under a five-stone bale
For a ten-hour shift with your guts held together
By a big leather belt and nothing in the belly
But a bit of bread and lard and a mouthful of tea
From the old billycan till the sun goes down
Behind the chimney pots at the other end of town
And you pay your tanner for the ferry back
Then it's up the slippy steps and you're nearly home.

JAMES J. MCAULEY (*b.* 1936)

Gas Light & Coke

It was after we'd crossed the Royal Canal
that we got the feel of the country's otherness,
people so chilly they were forced to burn
the land they lived on, chopped up into sods,
which they had to dry in the dark wet summers.
One day they would have consumed their smallholdings.

We by contrast were always warm and comfortable,
looked after by the Gas Light & Coke Company
(whose works on Misery Hill we avoided,
not liking the dust and the smell of sulphur).
As we walked our setter along the front,
discussing the heavy going at Leopardstown,

newsmen's flashes flickered across the sky,
as though triggered by angels on the prowl
for evidence to aid the prosecution.
A bolt stabbed the West Pier's finger tip, dousing
the light, while boulders rolled above our heads
and downpours soaked us, clad in tweed and voile.

Once home, the Gas Light & Coke Co took charge,
heated the baths, warmed up the Turkish towels
and made ice for our preprandial drinks.
Not that we took it for granted. Pathetic
turf-cutters were ever in our thoughts, as
were the confessors who kept them in order.

And the Pigeon House raised a smoky finger,
as though advising us against disdain.
Meantime Bray Head with a chip on its shoulder
frowned its Pre-Cambrian frown, while it tolerated
the chairoplanes and the side-show of freaks.
Where in the compass would salvation come from?

Round the horizon, north, south, east and west,
the band of sky was theatrically bright
with the cheerfulness of departing guests,
while overhead the clouds were like a lid
under which we citizens, rich or shabby,
waited with disquiet, as in a stockyard.

FERGUS ALLEN (*b.* 1921)

At the Irishtown Dump

A blizzard of seagulls. Wind whips in
The Irish Sea that is acrid with winter.
Garbage bellies out to froth-ridden waves.
Earning my bread with Stone & Son, I drive
Deep into this winged madhouse, empty
A transit of builders' debris. From the sky
The yellow beaks harry me. The seething
White craws are sufflated with sweepings.

Cocooned against the filthy storm of shit
Droppings, I'm loath in my cab to alight
Mingle with the foul birdbicker and swoop.
Lava of concrete spews the salty rocks. I stop,
Carry nothing of husks, crumbs or the rich offal
The waste fleets of the capital offer.
Waving me on toward the heartland, the attendant,
Reflective in his orange skins, is almost resplendent.

An aged tramp scavenges my path to the vermin cradle.
His old catechetical nose sniffs for the edible.
He grills the bric-à-brac of the functionless
Where Joyce once walked off into his conscience.
As I swerve to pass him, he laughs and spits.
Clothes and the next bite eat into his wits.
He lifts up a flower-torn panties to the breeze.
His porcupine head is grey, matted, contemptuous.

Gulls sheer off the glass. If for all their cries I had words,
My lips, too, could flabbergast the blue fictive crowds.
I petrify weekly to the core with Ringsend Stone & Son,
Vacate the warm cab seat now, taste on my own tongue
The true proclamation on this shore of rag and bone.
Corporation drivers revictual down town. I'm marooned,
Dizzy with no tip-up and wing-taunted by the gulls.
Vertiginous with their gold beaks my world wheels.

I hear the pentecostal jibe of my life's other heaven
From these char-throats raucous with hunger, intent
On real innards. You buffet me with another trajectory.
Lowering the cab glass, I accept this loud offertory
Of doves, delicate-feathered, off-white, food-crazy,
Find, in your stench, communion with a city sky
Where high voices are circling, cold and luminous,
Silvered with bodies, round a darkening unison.

JOHN ENNIS (*b.* 1944)

Scything Nettles in Churchyards

Scuffed with dust and rank with disinterest,
a brush of tortured badger's hair
carefully removes the mouse droppings
from copperplate, leather-bound minute books
to disclose the names of benefit masons
who dressed the stone that faces Ringsend Tech,
who tiered the terraces of Ballyfermot,
who built the Seven Gates of Thebes.

O'Brien's election posters,
once ripped from crossroads ashes in Tipperary,
are ironed out for fresh display and hang
beside the rescued Kernoff woodcut of Connolly,
his evil eye like some Labour Sacred Heart
unfairly following those who now re-enter
the long abandoned catacombs.
An old woman's cupped hands
contain neither yellow mule nor daddy-longlegs,
but a brass quarterly control button,
its carter's nagshead worn to a shine,
and a red hand badge that once truly dared
upon the only manly chest she ever knew.
The trust inherent in that gift
has lain dormant since she stood in the snow,
a year after her husband's accident,
to watch Larkin on his way to Glasnevin.

Membership cards, dog-eared or perfect;
rule books, scored or unconsulted;
photographs and scraps of rebel papers;
a candlestick and funereal drum
emblazoned with the arms of the Bakers' Guild;
even a Marian standard, green and brocaded,
from the House and Ship Painters:
they are all pieces saved from Dublin's ragged
terracotta soldiers that guard the memory
deadened by the success of our failure.

Watching the young workers,
deposited from the Dole into dingy basements,
painstakingly raising back the banners,
splinter by splinter, stitch by stitch,
is like the thrill of the first coppery godwit
skimming the rickety Bull Wall bridge in spring.
Scything nettles in churchyards
they have let stone legends roar
and made puny tribute of red roses.

FRANCIS DEVINE (*b.* 1949)

The Shellybanks
for Ulick O'Connor

Long-distance trucks have shaken the genteel terraces
For far too long, lugging their deep-frozen innards
Towards Hamburg or Milan past neat bow windows
Where brass telescopes once traced the horizon's
Receding hairline for a tuft of sail. On past
The smart new housing for the unemployed the diesels
Churn and hiss, trailing a dragon tang out to
The crane-forested docks and the ferry's leviathan jaw.

Needing a shield of silence I stride the beach,
Its lined brow gathered at the crowsfeet of pools,
And make for a fringe of tide, the limbs of the bay
Braced to bear the shifting ballast of the city.
Steps squelch in the coiled moulds of worms
I once mined for bait when what preoccupied
Was more innocuous. Far back a heap of bikes
Memorials boyhood like a maritime mark.

Reclaimed land — the very metaphor of memory.
Once all this was something, somewhere else.
The chemical mix of a million households

Is alive to its trove of trinkets and tokens —
Loveletter, prayerbook, photograph, toy, doll, sketch —
Interred like a ring for luck, a key for a prisoner.
What spells ferment under this skim of earth?
The unsettled ground refuses to rest in peace.

I catch myself glancing round yet again at the town
That exerts some tidal pull on the sargasso weed
That tangles the heart's arteries — or draws it on the rocks.
What stirs in the dark folds of the cauldron of currents?
Love and delight are swept in and out on the ribbed sand
And love's truces are sanctioned in the clasp of hills,
From the slumbering shoulder of Howth to the blunt nipple
Of the Martello tower on the fallen breast of Dalkey Island.

I need no wind at my back to hurry me on,
On towards the spur of beach and the granite ashlars
Of the breakwater, its slabs locking like giant vertebrae,
An uprisen Cyclopean road faring out to the lighthouse.
Here are the Shellybanks and here there are still shells —
Fans, blades, scallops, razors — flecked and spilt
Like sodden confetti in an apse of sand,
Under the scrollwork and tracery of the sky.

Out on the seawall there are gusts and cuffs,
Two centuries of the waves' swell have curved its spine.
On one side the surface is all shot silk,
The other a rag rug. Nightfall footpads the pier.
Here is the aloneness before homecomings,
Moments when the self is braced once more
For the brunt of love and its broken turnings.
The lighthouse wraps its scarf around the shore.

RORY BRENNAN (*b.* 1945)

The Waxies Dargle

The annual outing of Dublin's cobblers (or 'waxies') to the Dargle River at Irishtown was marked by the enthusiastic consumption of 'refreshments'.

Says my aul' one to your aul' one
"Will ye come to the Waxies' Dargle?"
Says your aul' one to my aul' one,
"Sure, I haven't got a farthin'.
I've just been down to Monto town
To see old Bill McArdle
But he wouldn't give me a half a crown
For to go to the Waxies' Dargle."

Chorus
"What'll ye have? Will ye have a pint?"
"I'll have a pint with you, sir."
And if one of us doesn't order soon
We'll be thrown out of the boozer.

Says my aul' one to your aul' one
"Will ye come to the Galway Races?"
Says your aul' one to my aul' one,
"With the price of me aul' lad's braces.
I went down to Capel Street
To the Jew-man moneylenders
But they wouldn't give me a couple of bob
On me aul' lad's red suspenders."

Says my aul' one to your aul' one,
"We have no beef nor mutton
But if we go down to Monto town
We might get a drink for nothin'."
Here's a nice piece of advice
I got from an aul' fishmonger:
"When food is scarce and you see the hearse
You'll know you've died of hunger."

ANONYMOUS (mid 19th century)

Sketch from the Great Bull Wall

In memory of my grandfather

He paints the sand when a tide has gone
and an arm of pier as ever out in water
lit clean yellow by a late-going sun.
His hand runs and taps at the rim of his hat
with a long-sticked brush among his fingers.
Green time sits on the tips of stakes
stiff to a hundred tides. Lined and
lined to the lighthouse at the end
cut stone goes in sleepered shape all warm with day
even in stretching shadow where the sun at some hour lay.

He paints a thin shimmer of the backing sea,
a dull fire tracing four serpent miles
from Bull Wall to Monkstown. Bulls
thud in herds along its back in autumn,
they spring like waves from the open sea
on leafless mornings. Tonight,
a tide will slop over the smooth wall
with water from the inner bay
oiled by entered ships.

            O sweet
is the oil in Dublin harbour,
sweet is the song of the sewerage plant,
sweet O sweeter is the fine dust of coalyards,
but sweetest of all the tall wind
ruffling buds of the heavy seaweed
near where he paints the untided sand.

SEBASTIAN BARRY (*b.* 1955)

from **The End of the Modern World**

116

There was supposed to be a Stella Gardens sequence
To put Yeats and his tower in their place,
For, after all, a visitor I had
Opined our little quarter had been built
For the aristocracy of labour — dockers,
Violent and bitter men perhaps when drinking.
The master bedroom measured twelve by six,
The other, square but smaller had no window
Since someone built the kitchen up against it.
The loo was out of doors. I don't complain.
In fact the Stella poems, like extensions
Projected, never started for the want
Of money, time and energy, were meant
To celebrate, as he did, rootedness.

117

Or anyway a roofing. 51
Stella Gardens, Dublin, was the first
House that I ever owned, almost the first
Object of any kind except for books
And, once, a car, although I was a bit
Past what old Dante called the middle of
The path which is our life. Am past it still.
So here I settled down in seventy-two
With wife and children, Iseult seventeen
And Sarah almost eight. I managed two
And sometimes up to four effusions weekly,
Facing the bedroom wall, my papers strewn
Behind me on the bed. There were no stairs
Or battlements to pace upon in Stella.

ANTHONY CRONIN (*b.* 1928)

Sandymount Now
for Frank Biggar

No one should go
Back to the old places.
Too many one knew
Are dead,
Old slow remembered customs
Gone with them.

And the streets, besides,
Seem narrower
In any event.
The Green tidied up
By the Municipal Council,
The rough fields covered
By semi-detacheds
With tiny gardens,
The teeming tumultuous sea
Pushed further back
By a new wall;
All disturbing elements
Pretty nearly
Accounted for

— Including, alas,
Regret,
Which, at any time,
Is irrelevant.

VALENTIN IREMONGER (1918–1991)

When the Dust Settles

On Lansdowne Road, right by the new stadium,
cherry trees still bloom. The monumental tiffany dome
refracts the heat of the sun, broods
over a street of Victorian redbricks

where old gardens flourish. Mature trees
defy wonders of the boom, promise irretrievable Dublin.
As if this were a first spring, damson, malus, plum,
pink heads reach past the builders' veneer.

CATHERINE PHIL MACCARTHY (b. 1954)

The Strand

The dotted line my father's ashplant made
On Sandymount Strand
Is something else the tide won't wash away.

SEAMUS HEANEY (1939–2013)

Dumhach Thrá

Gaineamhlach síoraí soir
go huiscí farraige i bhfad uaim
imeallbhord geal Bhleá Cliath
ag nochtadh pobal gréine.

MARCUS MAC CONGHAIL (b. 1970)

Sandymount

To the east sand shimmers
infinitely towards the distant sea
Dublin's light-soaked coastline
lays bare the people of the sun

MARCUS MAC CONGHAIL (b. 1970)
Translated from the Irish by Paddy Bushe

Doctors, Daughters

My mother's small face is wreathed
and criss-crossed by fear. She has
no time for food or sleep.

Away from the hospital
she rails at us her daughters,
who can do nothing,

her days layered with quests for solutions.
This man, whose pyjamas she irons
and re-buttons, which she brings to him

laundered and crisp, to whom she carries
perfect nectarines, cranberry juice,
is failing her. She wards off visitors

lest they witness his decline,
frantic to capture an antidote,
that special inscribed phial,

to bear it back in her hands
from monstrous caves like a magical gift,
past nurses, past mulling consultants

and, having fought, to shout in scorn:
"See? Fools?" Her every word
attests to the uselessness of doctors

and daughters, who cannot heal.

MARY O'DONNELL (*b.* 1954)
(St Vincent's Hospital, Elm Park)

The Stillorgan Road

Years ago a girl took flight,
imagining her skylark wings,
into the mountainous air
above the Stillorgan Road.
Or did she glimpse a hummingbird,
flamboyant plumage of the male,
alien to Donnybrook,
seeking passage to go home?

Cars beneath the Belfield bridge,
they sway like silver birch in winds
that purify the hard of heart
along the Stillorgan Road.
Athletes race and chase the time —
faster, fast, a second off.
They do not nod; they do not wave;
they know the direction home.

It may be they've been here before,
transmigrant souls just passing through —
halting site for next to nothing
beside the Stillorgan Road.
The week's wages I would spend
to raise the dead and stir the blood
tasting of wine from hummingbirds,
their plumage and the skylark's bones.

FRANK MCGUINNESS (*b.* 1953)

Refusals
for Benedict Ryan

The bus poised a-crest the bridge —
a traffic-light severe — some passengers

turned, waiting, from watching red sandstone
and cool green copper on the town-hall tower,
and looking right or left grasped a brief glance
at nature's light so grudging this late autumn
on the blue calm water in the Grand Canal;
that halt by water and its unsurpassed
capacity to welcome light consoling,
like many times in other broken weathers,
for stone-trapped Richmond Street and Rathmines Road.

But now the lookers-right saw only light on water —
leading to patriot-plaque and playing-pitch,
and purchase-homes in acres of slum-clearance —
while we who turned our rain-soiled eyesight left,
towards Ultan's hospital, the sunlit babies,
the locks where boys would bathe in better summers,
the film-censor's office, and green trees down
the Leeson-Baggot vista proud as Europe,
saw the familiar barge not level-changing
but stopped (they never stop), and a man bending
in soiled white overalls from blunted prow
to root with a long stick among the reeds,
half-heartedly encouraged by three boys,
his back to the hoarse hoardings, no swans breeding;
and as the red light ambered into green
I grew so curious about him
I felt I must get off and watch
till he found whatever he was seeking;
though even then I mightn't have been able
to tell what he'd found, and certainly
would not have dared to shout down from the bridge,
before those three brash gawpers, to enquire.

So gazing back till houses killed the view,
and one behind me thought I wanted her,
I rode on homeward half-an-hour too early
for lunch, and realised,
watching for six more stops the head in front,
it owned the first bald patch I'd ever noticed

with dandruff round the edge; and feared that feeling
had come too close to utterance,
the way the man just then looked out, back, down,
his nose grazing the window, his eye mine,
as young and old may do from pleasanter motives.

I rode on homeward, feeling well defeated,
I should have clambered down at the traffic-lights
to watch the man poking among the reeds:
to keep down curiosity seemed as grim
a crime, that day, as rancid a refusal
as when, last year, the girl in front
(met five years earlier) turned half-round,
glanced briefly, smiled briefly, and I —
got off three stops too early, knowing fear
too sensible for her
twenty-three years and yellow hair. That famous
Bolivian-Indian bracelet of beaten silver
still clasped her brown-gold arm, but could not force,
for all its magic glitter, better than refusal
out of me: no more than could
a long, unpolished, grey-black stick
searching the reeds that verge a dying canal.

PEARSE HUTCHINSON (1927–2012)

Shades of Ranelagh: 1984

As I came in from Drown Lake Mountain
Starved of money and dry to the bone
Where many long years back all burned out
Another exploded sixties myth I was
Caught good & proper on a judge's ruling
And my schooldays wheeled up Ranelagh Road.
As always in discipline I found me walking,
Before and after, all along Vergemount,

Where the Muckross girls drift by like clouds.
Is original sin still alive and well
On the shaded paths of the Dodder?
Does the fashion parade throw a daily shape
To the Bridge and Portobello,
Does everything stop at the Grand Canal
Including the four ten bus to Yuma?
Do the celluloid cowboys up in the Sandford
Still yodel the blues in pure valerian,
Taking tokes and pulling strokes
On the high chaparral of the fire escape
Where Homer nods to Rowdy Yates?
As I sail in from Drown Lake Mountain
On a nineteen forties turf-boat order
I sight my barge on the filled-in harbour
And dance my jigs without embargo,
By the Grand Canal where all things stop
My ballast is weight of Selskar Rock

MACDARA WOODS (*b.* 1942)

47 Sandford Road

for Mary Ellen Fox and Anne Kelly

I came back to the insanity of roses
unfolding at the sun's sole behest
in a space designed to reflect reason.

Everything was in proportion. A calm
facade. Minimal embellishment. Colour
serene and fresh, lemon, celadon.

An agitated guest, I was the ghost
who, when the living were out
and about, had the run of the place.

Random as dust motes, I would settle
on this and that, a painting in a reassuring
frame, silk too fine to touch,

photographs of strong-boned boys
growing up and up without a hitch,
handsome men mounting the staircase.

That house, a class set apart for salvation,
sat back from the road, insulated
from its roar by absorbent trees and grass.

And I was free to choose my window
by my mood. The world was not
about to change, just my view of it.

Now, all the houses on that fortunate
terrace like lounge chairs in the sun
relax at the back into long gardens.

The oblong frame I looked through shaped
the sense of what I saw, each pane
the sovereign facet of a crystal.

More than ever I hovered between
stories on that return, looking out
and over into Helen Dillon's garden.

I studied that gardener's studiously
artless art, how she could tempt
wild roses to trust a trellis,

make radically opposed flowers,
the easy-going daisy and tetchy
iris, just got on with the plan,

a place for every kind of display,
the needy vine, wildly clashing
colours revealing more of each other.

I had the thought that I could float
through glass without breaking it, adored
the sun so much I was the light.

The house returned me to the sanity
of building walls to last, block
upon block until the job is done.

PEGGY O'BRIEN (*b.* 1945)

Cinéma Vérité

The Rathmines Stella, completely shot of its twinkle, is inherited,
now that we've done with it, by the meek — our 'feathered
    street rats' —
who rise flurrying from their pink-toed prance, to the grid
of rectangular spaces high in the granite brickwork, their very
    own loft.
We imagine them as the brains of the edifice, hatching movie
    plots —
cinéma vérité, not fluffy romance — in that stony cerebrum.
And the doubtful delights of mould and fleapit itch come
    scurrying back
from years ago, the moral guardianship of the usherette
shining her torch among our kisses and gropes. Pigeon love,
dare we say this doesn't exist? — for look, they increase and
    multiply,
coo and preen, while their shelter, our forsaken den of dreams,
stays in the dark, no sunshine or exotic locations imaginable
    on-screen,
only dirt-stains and flimsy hammocks of spider-web hanging
where we watched the outlaw dismount from his het-up horse,
    the nurse
who'd seen too much of suffering administer a lethal dose,
the two soldiers play Russian roulette; — well, this audience
    roosts

unconcerned. The rumour of the street, a filtered whoosh, a
    beeping
car-horn, a gabble of voices behind us, won't stop them
settling for the night. And the plotlines of our lives —
    seemingly shapeless,
certainly untellable — move as we move, past steel-shuttered
    shop
and railing-rounded park, our prospects inauspicious, more
a case of earning the next crust than gazing at stardust, less
    intrigue
on the Orient Express than finding change for the last bus, yet
    somehow
to do with love even to the grand, impossibly heroic gesture
we promise ourselves we would rise to in face of impending
    catastrophe.

PATRICK DEELEY (*b.* 1953)

The Leinster Road

I have no idea what we talked about
that midsummer bank holiday evening
at the corner of the Leinster Road,

two students circling each other
by the side wall of Rathmines library
and jabbering on as if our lives depended

on it. We didn't know each other then,
and a lifetime later, as I watch you
in the garden from this bedroom window,

I'm only too aware that we still don't.
This, though, was where it all began,
among the sun-specked leaves and shadows

of the Leinster Road, that long journey
towards an accommodation destined to be
always inscrutable, if no longer unfamiliar.

JOHN BOLAND (*b.* 1946)

A Short Walk

On the old stone wall in the yard of the school
half the alphabet painted in white letters,
half a language frowning on playtime.
What happened? The paint ran out, the painter

wearied of instruction or was caught
whitehanded: mystified they shone their torches
a long time on the letters before shrugging home,
leaving the code; guided by it strange craft

arrive: an anxious people freighted with notebooks,
a lust for detail, descending to capture
for council elders the slate-pared light of Moyne Road,
its shifting mountain and houses squat, low-set

startled by the weight of light, its bricks fading
then brightening again as the clouds part,
as if some small god, reaching down from his bureau
had inked them on his pad and stamped them fresh

or Palmerston important with trees, long gardened, high
granite stepped — Expect! Expect! — or Belgrave Square or
narrow doored Holy Trinity right in the middle of Belgrave Road
itself a ship descended, signalling Come, Come quickly,

they're sleeping, they're sleepwalking. Not long now,
not long before we find a way, before we're holding hands
in the new worlds, trying for perfection, scouring the Classifieds
on Ranelagh, Rathgar, Rathmines

brick-red planets in the galactic suburbs
where the old retire and the young climb late
up granite steps, fumbling to open the promising doors,
searching for their rooms while the light lasts.

PETER SIRR (*b.* 1960)

Flatland

Take-away foods, small late-night stores,
record dealers, posters for Folk Mass.
Coke and fried chicken make an ideal meal here,
unpacked in a bedsitter and swallowed near a one-bar fire.

Down bicycle-cluttered corridor, by coinbox telephone,
special-offer leaflets, buff uncollected post,
weekends open optimistically beforehand
like sands of package holiday brochures.

Falling plaster bares ceiling laths, like piano keys
stripped of their ivory; fireplaces are blocked.
Revolving record wheels, slow music after pubs,
will transport lovers into a seagull-velvet dawn,

into stale cigarette smoke, lingering tastes of beer;
outside, ivy-bearded trees conceal the rubbish bins;
milk cartons roll through long-haired lawns;
the hall door buttoned with bells.

In neat gardens on the next street, wickerwork branches
will be baskets plump with fruit yet.
Couples yawn and part. Sunday now,
the heavy hours weigh down the watch's scales

to 4 o'clock, sports programmes on the radio,
as evening's cigarette-butt is stubbed out,
leaving an ash-grey sky
which only a working Monday will illuminate.

DENNIS O'DRISCOLL (1954–2012)

'One Night I'

One night I ended up in a flat in Rathmines
With a girl who told me she used to go out
With Paul Hewson. I sat on the bed and read
Her Beckett's verse.

It's rather fun, though not such fun as sex,
Reciting *Echo's Bones* to Bono's ex.

TOM MATHEWS (*b.* 1952)

An Ghrian i Ráth Maonais

sin siar thar scáilmhaidin
a ghrian sheaca shamhna seo
a chaith coincheap criostail
suas trí lár Ráth Maonais
a las foilt chatacha
i bhfuinneoga

is breá liom na scátháin
a mbíonn tú iontú
a bpáirtíocht lem thaibhrithe

neadaigh i gcrann dom tamall
go sciorrfad síos an chanáil dhuilleogach chugat
amach thar mo mheabhair

a chaoinghrian chaointeach
dall mé

MICHAEL DAVITT (1950–2005)

The Sun in Rathmines

spread yourself back over the shadowy morning
frosty November sun
that bowled a crystal concept
right up through Rathmines
and beamed on curly heads
in windows

i'm mad about the mirrors
you haunt
in company with my dreams

nestle awhile in a tree for me
so i can glide down the leafy canal to you
out beyond my senses

gentle, grieving sun
dazzle me

MICHAEL DAVITT (1950–2005)
Translated from the Irish by Paddy Bushe

Wet Morning, Clareville Road

Under morning greys of rain the roses
are washed, glowing faces, and in near gardens
the limp washing hangs with no hope

311

although all the slate roofs down Westfield Road
shine like polished chrome. Up early to make
a little door that opens out, a word passage
into the rain-filled air among the flowers
and the morning traffic — as if the words
themselves could offer light, could make
some sense of that muddle in which the heart
flutters. Dark green the over-arching
ascension of trees; walled gardens
where scarlet roses are exploding; yellow
the cylinders of chimney pots; luminous
and edgy the fretwork clouds: how things
fall into place from a window, as if the given
were a pattern with precise meanings
and could console us for the loss
of signs, and spires, and words like *Consecration,*
or could speak at least a little comfort
after sounding brass, and after
the manic world where men go on
killing as usual, bringing lovely cities down
to rubble, dust. The town of minarets and bells
becomes a cry in the snipered street, hunger
a dog that howls all night, and out
among the hills not too far north of here
the consonantal guns and drums keep beating
and repeating their one word. But here
in our apparent peace there's nothing
but a wet hiss of traffic on glistening road,
the stark green shock of a privet hedge,
that bloodthirsty nude sunburst of roses.
If I went under the rain to smell the roses,
I would inhale your arms, the warm breath
between your breasts, the whole heady
exhalation of you moving by me on the stairs.
Is it because we can't hold onto something
as evanescent as a smell that when it
finds us again it brings the whole body
back into our ready arms, the steady undoing

of straps and buttons, cotton and silk things
drifting from our hot skin, a white shirt
forgetting itself awhile and flying
beyond its own down-to-earth expectations?
Shaken by a slight breeze, lace curtains
let light filter through to the room
I only imagine, where a bowl of roses burns
on a low glass table by the window:
blue mutations agitate air; sea salt
stings the tip of the tongue;
and no ghosts but ourselves to stand
in that early play of light and its solutions
which may contain for the moment
time and all its grazing shades. The room
a flowering branch of details: this
brimming glass, this swimming mirror,
these peaches, this open book, this cracked
black and white Spode bowl, these trials of love.

When that space — with its shades of love
and its impossible colours — fades
to the wet morning outside my window,
I only see the tree in the back garden
bowed down as it is every summer
under a rich crop of bitter little apples.
But my brother makes the garden grow
once more, coaxing its flowers into the sun
like those unhappy patients he'll listen to
all day for their broken stories, crying out with joy
at the first start of the begonia
into pale pink blossom. *I thought it was dead,*
he says without thinking, *and now
just look at it!* He can talk of little else,
learning as he is not to grieve
but go on, and will — when he gets himself
out of bed this morning — fill the house
with his good will, looking forward
to whatever happens, ironing his shirts

to the sound of that soprano he loves
singing *Tosca:* when he thinks it's ready,
he'll test the hot iron as our mother would
with a spittled finger, then sing along as he listens
for the startled hiss that steams away
and, like a quick kiss, vanishes.

EAMON GRENNAN (*b.* 1941)

The Dartry Dye Works

I often walked past the Dartry Dye Works,
three storeys of dark limestone, known as calp,
the name spelled out in large capital letters
of blue and white enamel —

D
A
R
T
R
Y

D
Y
E

W
O
R
K
S

It was just to the right beyond the tram sheds
where the tarred road sloped down to the Dodder
(a river liable to flashy floods
from its heathery catchment in Glencree).

Ash and sycamores stood around it, breathing;
I never saw anyone leave or enter,
but steam often flowed from a rusty pipe
that stuck out sideways through the north wall,
so there was surely something going on.

I now believe they only dyed things black.
That would be for the aftermath of death
and to see people through their times of mourning.
Once black, of course, there was no reverting
to burgundy or beige or powder blue,
which explains all those sombre-looking people
hanging around the Lower Rathmines Road
after making their vows and intercessions.

There is never any shortage of blackness
among the stage props of revealed religions.
Blackness is something abstract, like an absence;
but on nights without stars or electricity
when the curtained sky is up to nothing,
the pupils of a dreamer's eyes can shrink
against the glare of sunlight on a hillside
across which he finds himself on the move.

Reaching a station is not the end, though,
only another beginning, from which
he sets off once more in the wrong direction.
There are no seats, no bulbs in the light-sockets
and the tunnel is tortuous and black.
Emerging into unprepared-for light
the world he finds himself in is the image
of the one he left with such a commotion.

Deep under his feet in dolomite caves
explored only by hearty speleologists
lives a creature, *Leucippus*, pale and blind,
the size of his little finger with legs,
whose life is lived as though in Indian ink.

Slithering gingerly through the lime water,
black is a word for which it has no use.
Nor is absence what it would call its lot.

In the abyssal trench it's much the same;
phosphorescence is merely self-advertisement,
not a lighting up of dismal surroundings;
while the drizzle of decomposing debris
from those that feed and spawn up there in daylight
is little more than fertilizing rain
falling in endless night. So black is best —
to which I'd add least seen, soonest forgotten.

Another just invented motto says
the sweetest songs come from the blackest birds.
In Palmerston Park they whistled their titles
over the heads of children, who were keener
on playing tig and hide-and-seek than listening
to the fowles' parliament; but when the bell
rang out for closing time, the darkness studied them
on their way home past the Dartry Dye Works.

FERGUS ALLEN (*b.* 1921)

Walking in Yellow Leaves

After the late October storm
Harold's Cross Green is calm:
its gardens all brown and yellow.
I walk through mulchy leaves
pasted to the pathway.
Such a quiet peaceful day
after strong gales and rain:
a broken branch a reminder
of the power of the squall.
Once again, all the colours

of the season touch my soul
with that strange autumnal sense
of aesthetic joy and sorrow
an exquisite melancholy.

How many years have passed
since I watched my children race
under the verdurous leaves?
Grown now out of childhood
their days lengthen, mine shorten:
it is the autumn of my span.
The season matches not alone
my mood, but also my years:
the September days have gone,
soon it will be Hallowe'en.
Leaving by the Mount Jerome gate
I return by Mount Argus:
the light in the West is pale
gold, as the sun prepares to set.

HUGH McFADDEN (*b.* 1942)

To the Oaks of Glencree

My arms are round you, and I lean
Against you, while the lark
Sings over us, and golden lights, and green
Shadows are on your bark.

There'll come a season when you'll stretch
Black boards to cover me;
Then in Mount Jerome I will lie, poor wretch,
With worms eternally.

JOHN MILLINGTON SYNGE (1871–1909)

317

Casimir Road

Ivy on the breeze wall resists arrest.
Scent of Old Spice in the bathroom.
The landing's dusty May altar:
The Blessed Virgin standing on a snake,
Plastic pink roses in a vase,
The drawers stuffed with mass cards,
A rosary coiled in its silk-lined box.

The pantry's red floor tiles. Lubricant oil.
A bulb wearing a dust toupée.
Traveller's Joy tobacco tins containing tacks,
Brass screws, and dust-furred curtain hooks.
The toolbox innards on display:
A family of screwdrivers, assorted pliers,
Claw hook hammers, fuses, measuring tape.
Rust-spotted saw and its hacksaw sibling.

I see him through tobacco haze,
Sitting on the storage heater,
Scorching his pipe bowl with his flame thrower.
He stoop-shuffles to the kitchen, punctures
Sausages with a fork and lays them on the grill.
The tap nozzle dangles its drop over the sink.
The fridge pontificates in the corner.

A tea towel trapezes on the washing line.
I chew my blackened toast.
"Have you given up mass altogether?" he says.
"It means nothing to me," I say.
He dons his overcoat and black beret,
Breathing like Darth Vader.
The letter-box flaps as the door closes.
I like his honesty.
The way his Cortina expectorates
In unison with him.

Mirage pools on Casimir Road.
Red armchairs beside the coal-effect fire.
The frigging mantel clock, the silver cigar box.
The brass urn on the grey doily.
Vulture jumper and purple corduroys.
She finishes her masters on *la Boétie*.
Her Gauloise butts in the ashtray,
A smouldering rail disaster...
Haunch hug on my growling Honda.
In the Greyhound, a Pacman gobbles up the dots.
A scrum of coats at the stairpost.
Ash lips on mine.

Grass clipping scent. It's almost noon.
Grandfather clock tuts to itself.
On the floor a red sock, a sweaty turquoise top.
Taps fill the bath with a gush of applause.
I listen to *Brain Damage* by Pink Floyd.
A froth of iridescent bubbles grows.
I settle myself in the cackling brew.
"You want me to join you?"

Ash sky. I gaze from the bedroom window.
Casimir Road under assault by snow.
The flakes descend erratically and merge
With others that control the lilac verge.
The cars are now white humps by the roadside.
It's famine for the gawking crows. They hide
In their nests high above snow-wigged gravestones:
Rows of freshly made beds for weary bones.
I trepanate my egg and drink my tea.
Grandad scans the death list, coughing hoarsely.

ALAN MOORE (*b.* 1960)

When I Think of You
for John Jordan

It will be verdant summer
with cloudless blue days
and star-dusted nights
of laughter, wine and music:
the chestnut trees on the Green
in full and glorious bloom.

Or it will be joyous Easter,
both of us in great form;
you singing the Easter Parade,
as we walk up the avenue.

Wild flowers growing out of stone:
and, always, we'll be going home.

HUGH McFADDEN (*b.* 1942)

Landmarks

Recalling childhood, houses are the most
Decisive landmarks; first, a red-brick house
Near the canal, where, giggling and afraid,
We went to see a classmate's father, dead
And dressed in brown; his mother pouring out
Weak lemonade in breakfast cups; a cat
Stealing the milk from an enormous jug.
Next, a slaughter-house in Harold's Cross,
Where two of us at lunch-time watched a man,
Red-faced, with rubber boots and bloody hands,
Kill with a spoke a lean bedraggled sheep,
Which bleated only once, but twitched long after.
Lastly, a white-washed house near Dolphin's Barn,
Where, it was rumoured, lived, alone, a witch.

I saw her once: a woman dressed in black,
With massive ankles; hobbling to the yard
Outside, she shook an apron-full of crumbs,
Or something, to her hens; then, seeing us,
Shouted "clear off, clear off, you little brats!"
Running away, I tripped and cut my knee,
And heard her mumble dreadful, dreadful things.

BASIL PAYNE (1923–2012)

Local Nightlight

Turning home into Clareville
from Larkfield, facing North,
the oval harvest moon glows —
shines brightly on Kenilworth —
newly-risen, pale yellow,
a pearl pendant, it hangs
low on the horizon,
as twilight's violet gleams.

HUGH McFADDEN (*b.* 1942)

Waking
in memory of my father, died November 1960

Someone is breathing in the room
apart from me. It is my father;
I recognise the hiss of his nostrils
closing, closing .... It is late;
he is doing Milltown work,
we can use the extra money.
That stub in his hand is a rent book
high as a bible, thin as his widow.

Below that, in the shadow, I imagine
the soft metal of his heart
(a gold cog, slipping) finally burred,
refusing to bite. The angle
of his nose, the slight furrow
of moustache escape me. All I have
is that sound fathered in darkness
carrying a reek of tobacco-y linen,
the taste of his lip.
                                He rustles
like a curtain. Outside it is six a.m.
A sudden fleet of cars passes
drowning my breath for about the length
of a funeral. This has gone on ten years.

HUGH MAXTON (*b.* 1947)

Milltown Road

Before the buses came we'd half a mile to walk
Down Milltown's country road, innocent of tar,
Its grassy banks dusted as if by white chalk,
The fine road dust. It almost was too far
This distance, once we'd gone beyond the fields,
Passing a terrace of six houses with balconies,
Narrow gateway leading to the garden that shields
Their privacy from passers' glance. Opposite rise
Twin flights of granite steps to Greenmount's door,
Then the pierced iron gates, the door in the wall
Of Grove House where some artist or illustrator
Built a third storey, a simple room, perched tall
Above the roof, an aircraft carrier's superstructure.
Next massive wooden gates, the farm of Milltown Park,
And the high granite-walled road's long curvature
Winds dully along its bend, gloomy and dark
Until the last open stretch, past St James's Drive

To the crossroads, where, on the last of the double lines,
An eleven tram, inert, waits for its fellow to arrive
Clattering down single line that led from twin sheds,
Where all the trams, I was told, had their beds,
Their trolleys wound down at night, the day's work done —
The eleven was a dull route, its only thrill,
After the rush along the narrow, leafy Appian Way,
Leeson Street bridge, where the lock might be ready to fill
For some turf barge pulled by a patient horse.

DERRY JEFFARES (1920–2005)

from **Clonskeagh Haiku**

The Little Sisters,
butterflies for just one day:
doorstep collection.

Islamic Centre
Shell-Al. Shurely shome mishtake:
two nuns pushing prams.

Heron on our roof,
stand-in postman for the stork.
Wrong delivery.

Thick brown urban fox
jumps over the lazy dog
barking all damn night.

Shading Roebuck House
(old and grey and full of sleep)
nouvelles maisonettes.

The Dodder River
betwixt mill and pleasure dome
takes my paper boat.

Ad hoc halting site:
boxing ring around the trees,
all going for gold.

IGGY MCGOVERN (*b*. 1948)

Mo Thaibhse

Mo thaibhse dá dtagadh an treo
Níos faide anonn san aimsir,
Is séarsa aonair a thabhairt
Bóthar an Dún Ghoirt is thairis
Go Bóthar Thí Mológ ar aistear,
Le neach de Chlann an Bhéarla
Mo chló níorbh ionadh,
Mo bhás dá mb'eol dóibh
An tásc níor chás leo:
Ní foláir nó is taibhse mé
I meabhair an tsóirt sin cheana:
Leo is neamhní mo bheo ná mo mharbh.

MÁIRTÍN Ó DIREÁIN (1910–1988)

My Ghost

Were my ghost to pass this way
At a future time
Hurrying down
Fortfield Road and
Travelling on to Templeogue Road
No English speaker would be surprised,

Even if they knew I was dead
It would not bother them.
I'm surely already a ghost
To those of that mind:
They are not concerned about me living or dead.

MÁIRTÍN Ó DIREÁIN (1910–1988)
Translated from the Irish by Declan Collinge

Language Lessons in a Churchtown Chipper

The door swings wide for him,
sixtyish and slight, green overalls,
a whiff of compost following
as he hands the fiver
to the man behind the counter.
"Una bella giornata, Luigi,"
pronounced in best Rathfarnhamese.

He states his order, then they chew
the fat and Luigi stirs. I catch
odd syllables, guess prospects
for a better day *domani*
and the season's flower crop,
nod tacit agreement
primavera's in the air.

One last *salute*
before he leaves. I meet
Luigi's eye. "You speak Italian?
Ah, that is a pity.
Mick the florist, he say
it is the language of love."

I spot him as I head back to the car.
He sorts the long-stem flowers,
mouthing the latest phrase:

La bella luna.
And all the while
Luigi ladles oil,
savouring the words:
Daphne, Dianthus, Centaurea.
Cleome, Muscari, Primula,
Rosa.

NESSA O'MAHONY (*b.* 1964)

Dublin Tramcars

I

A sailor sitting in a tram —
A face that winces in the wind —
That sees and knows me what I am,
That looks through courtesy and sham
And sees the good and bad behind —
He is not God to save or damn,
Thank God, I need not wish him blind!

II

Calvin and Chaucer I saw to-day
Come into the Terenure car:
Certain I am that it was they,
Though someone may know them here and say
What different men they are,
I know their pictures — and there they sat,
And passing the Catholic church at Rathgar
Calvin took off his hat
And blessed himself, and Chaucer at that
Chuckled and looked away.

THOMAS MACDONAGH (1878–1916)

from **Transformations**

What miracle was it that made this grey Rathgar
Seem holy earth, a leaping-place from star to star?
I know I strode along grey streets disconsolate,
Seeing nowhere a glimmer of the Glittering Gate,
My vision baffled amid many dreams, for still
The airy walls rose up in fabulous hill on hill.
The stars were fortresses upon the dizzy slope
And one and all were unassailable by hope.
And then I turned and looked beyond high Terenure
Where the last jewel breath of twilight floated pure,
As if god Angus there, with his enchanted lyre,
Sat swaying his bright body and hair of misty fire,
And smote the slumber-string within the heavenly house
That eve might lay upon the earth her tender brows,
Her moth-dim tresses, and lip's invisible bloom,
And eye's light shadowed under eyelids of the gloom,
Till all that dark divine pure being, breast to breast,
Lay cool upon the sleepy isle from east to west.

GEORGE WILLIAM RUSSELL, 'AE' (1867–1935)

Rathgar Pastoral

Half a century or more ago, a Rathgar woman kept a cow
which she stabled nightly on ground
we now call garden. What was then open country
is all but inner suburb; swallowed, too, the calp quarry
and its over-spilling lake. A lone windmill,
deployed to drain the lake, whirls again in a story told at bedtime
to set our children dreaming. The quarry cow
slips our minds. She wanders off to graze the spaces
between strewn boulders, where grass glistens.
The woman is unconcerned. She ambles into the setting sun,

just away from our sapling Victoria plum,
which is opening in blossom. Casually as my mother
might, she reaches for her milking bucket
and clasping it about the middle starts to rattle the handle.

PATRICK DEELEY (*b.* 1953)

Midnight in Templeogue

Young wives unzipple near our Bridge,
Suburbed, soon to be bigger again.
Cork, Kerry, gossip above their weanlings
With Moy, Claremorris. Little ones fidget,
Whimper at drop of skirt, slack, jean.
Villa by villa, condition makes friend.
All dress, remark that lunch is late, or
Tidy the pair in perambulator.

Here, after dark, is city-light,
Faint glow, advertisement in cloud,
Our frankincense, a grace reflected.
Forgetting their salaries at midnight,
Instalment, bank withdrawal, unreckoned,
Husbands enjoy what is allowed:
Obedience, unpyjama'd, receiving,
Receiving, quietly conceiving.

Templeogue House is without a lodge now.
Rooms have been blessed in which a pen scratched
Punch parties, elopements, chapterful
Diversion. Devil tries an old dodge
On Fathers O'Leary, O'Malley, wraps them
In warmer sleep. Hot jar is no match
For wily adept, young believer.
Few pledge the novels of Charles Lever.

Sky-light is bolted at Cypress Grove,
Where African students learn our meekness.
Beneath my window, garden is jungling.
Thrice, awful shriek of catkin or coven.
Tom-tomming in undergrowth has blundered.
I dream of Mumbo Jumbo seeking
His fled apostates, manhandling forest,
Wake, double. How can metaphor rest?

AUSTIN CLARKE (1896–1974)

The Quaker Graveyard in Blackrock
for Gerard and Bríd

From up in your sun-cage, your bibliotheca
and scriptorium, you look out on the Quaker cemetery
with its Spartan arrangement of balance and order;
its mercantile names in strict, straight lines.
This is where body leaves soul and goes where it must.
A Quaker graveyard, not in Nantucket
but under the old and mammoth oaks —
a row of them with their high branches
and bird-chorus hidden under cover.
No sign of any Gabriel blowing his horn —
only the caretaker keeping grass cropped
and the twilight visitor, a sudden fox just staring in,
reminding you that life is for the living.

GERARD SMYTH (*b.* 1951)

Willow Park Winter (*from* 'Watercut')

Sky pale as a child's coffin,
A token dimness denoting day.

Snow mauls the garden, driving
Its white tooth into the corners
Or, exhausted from falling, trails
Along branches like gunpowder.
The washing hanging like bones
Shifting with the odd wind.
From an albino skin protrudes
The grassy stubble of two days.

Young willows, winter novices,
Float like dead coral above
An avenue of deserted reef.
The usual lone streetlamp
Presides fanatic on the parade.
Down to their last skin, the
Trees consoled in mutual impotence;
Shrivelled berries tap their
Weighty republics against the
Antlers of paralysed beasts.

Tundra telephone lines bracket
The broken ice-rink park
Trampled to bits early
By some invisible stampede.
The road is meaty slush,
Yet still rejecting colour.
New snow lands on it warily,
Bracing itself fully for
The guttural indigestion
Of a car combing the corner.

In slow-motion a begrudging
Planet crawls into view.

JAMES MCCABE (*b.* 1966)

One Who Was Not Invited to the Opening of the Joyce Tower Complains Bitterly

They came:
Jesuits, judges, Telefís jokers,
Visiting firemen, Cork pipe-smokers,
Monumental patrons, UCD wives:
Time, O you beast you, despite your worst forgives.

They goggled:
Columnists, socialites, jolly old pals,
Round-the-clock drinkers, Trinity gals,
Play okay-ers, the Minister, haute couturières:
Time, O you pup you, has made you one of theirs.

They guzzled:
Doctors, lawyers, departmental bosses,
BBC balladmen, drawn by lucky horses,
Socialists, capitalists, Fianna and Fine:
Time, O you fiend you, has put you back in line.

They went:
Piling into taxis, limousines and growlers,
Titivating tipsily the afternoon's howlers:

'God, it must have cost
Scott a lot of lolly.
Tell me now boys,
Does he leave the key with Dolly?'

But, O you man you,
It was different in 'twenty-two
When few but Cons were pro
And most of the rest were anti.

Blanchardstown, 1962

JOHN JORDAN (1930–1988)

Tai Chi at Sandycove

Seaweed like arms outstretched
in the still high tide floats inland
as cars zip by the shrouded pier,
the grey-blue sky stacked beyond.

An old boy pauses on the stairs
to see what I see —
the lighthouse keeper's house,
the great granite rocks — before he

returns to his guests who are all
shadows of themselves,
like you at the water's edge,
like the heron that's about to strike.

GERALD DAWE (*b.* 1952)

Haiku

Amid red and green flashes
the moon enters
Dún Laoghaire Harbour

ANATOLY KUDRYAVITSKY (*b.* 1954)

Dip

Scuff down sandy steps,
arches stipple and sink
on crunchy damp stones;
shell rims.
Toes, naked pink
lead the wade,
skin gasping,

going down
into grey-green
thick of salt,
shiver of wave-tip
on thigh, belly,
breast,
up to the chin,
hair-ends
ribboning,
white arms
marked
with the cling
of magenta fronds.

Eyes rove
to whale hump
of mountain;
pink and yellow
of shore blossom;
the island
goldening up
out of the mirrorball bay.

My playbody
needs no virtual reality,
only this
late summer dip
in the sea.

KATIE DONOVAN (*b.* 1962)
(*Dalkey Island*)

Deansgrange Cemetery

My name in lettering
chiselled in crumbling marble
that stands like a hoarding

over my grandfather and -mother,
my father, advertises that this
is a family affair.

The neat rows laid out like flat streets
house other people's families.
The few carved words —
Baby John who lived for one year —
encode all the tears of parents
who will never see Baby John grow.

Over near a screen of hedge
my eye snags on an edge of black
marble, cut with another family name,
the same as my mother's mother's.
She lives under this swathe of lichen,
green pebbles, holding her own.

My day's visit over, I leave the quiet
streets for the screech of traffic outside
that could surely raise the dead.

JEAN O'BRIEN (*b*. 1952)

Dublin Roads

When you were a lad that lacked a trade,
Oh, many's the thing you'd see on the way
From Kill-o'-the-Grange to Ballybrack,
And from Cabinteely down into Bray,
When you walked these roads the whole of a day.

High walls there would be to the left and right,
With ivies growing across the top,
And a briary ditch on the other side,
And a place where a quiet goat might crop,
And a wayside bench where a man could stop.

A hen that had found a thing in her sleep,
One would think, the way she went craw-craw-cree,
You would hear as you sat on the bench was there,
And a cock that thought he crew mightily,
And all the stir of the world would be

A cart that went creaking along the road,
And another cart that kept coming a-near;
A man breaking stones; for bits of the day
One stroke and another would come to you clear,
And then no more from that stone-breaker.

And his day went by as the clouds went by,
As hammer in hand he sat alone,
Breaking the mendings of the road;
The dazzles up from the stones were thrown
When, after the rain, the sun down-shone.

And you'd leave him there, that stone-breaker,
And you'd wonder who came to see what was done
By him in a day, or a month, or a week:
He broke a stone and another one,
And you left him there and you travelled on.

A quiet road! You would get to know
The briars and stones along by the way;
A dozen times you'd see last year's nest;
A peacock's cry, a pigeon astray
Would be marks enough to set on a day;

Or the basket-carriers you would meet
A man and a woman they were a pair!
The woman going beside his heel:
A straight-walking man with a streak of him bare,
And eyes that would give you a crafty stare.

Coming down from the hills they'd have ferns to sell,
Going up from the strand they'd have cockles in stock:

Sand in their baskets from the sea,
Or clay that was stripped from a hillside rock
A pair that had often stood in the dock!

Or a man that played on a tin-whistle:
He looked as he'd taken a scarecrow's rig;
Playing and playing as though his mind
Could do nothing else but go to a jig,
And no one around him, little or big.

And you'd meet no man else until you came
Where you could look down upon the sedge,
And watch the Dargle water flow,
And men smoke pipes on the bridge's ledge,
While a robin sang by the haws in a hedge.

Or no bird sang, and the bird-catchers
Would have talk enough for a battle gained,
When they came from the field and stood by the bridge,
Taking shelter beside it while it rained,
While the bird new-caught huddled and strained

In this cage or that, a linnet or finch,
And the points it had were declared and surmised:
And this one's tail was spread out, and there
Two little half-moons, the marks that were prized;
And you looked well on the bird assized.

Then men would go by with a rick of hay
Piled on a cart; with them you would be
Walking beside the piled-up load:
It would seem as it left the horses free,
They went with such stride and so heartily —

And so you'll go back along the road.

PADRAIC COLUM (1881–1972)

The New Luas Bridge in Dundrum
for Eileen

Brobdingnagian construct
of clothes peg and shoelaces;
or spokes
on the surreal bicycle wheel
of local boy Stephen Roche;
or the taut strings
of the heavenly harp that ever
is plucked
by 'wee' Derek Bell;
or the scales of blind
justice in never-never
tribunal land;
or you and I, turning our faces
upwards, stretching our wings
as the strain
takes the first train.

IGGY McGOVERN (*b.* 1948)

The View from Dundrum

If I stand on the wash-hand basin
I can look out through the gates
of the Central Mental Hospital
(above, as we say, in Dundrum)
at the Chinese takeout place
inscrutably named *The Great Wall*.

When my time is finally up,
in a week or a month or a year
(or maybe a little longer),
I will open an Irish Pub

above in Tiananmen Square
inscrutably named *The Great Hunger.*

IGGY MCGOVERN (*b.* 1948)

Radharc ó Chában tSíle

Le hathrú an tsolais tosnaíonn na bruachbhailte ag geonaíl.
Searrann is tagann chucu féin tar éis lae eile a bhí folamh fuar.
Filleann leanaí ó scoileanna is daoine fásta ón obair sa chathair
le hoscailt fuinneoga is doirse ba dhóigh leat na tithe ag
meangadh athuair.

I measc na línte bana tithíochta foghraíonn fothram fo-chairr.
Gaibheann lucht rothar thar bráid i strillini mantacha dubha.
Éalaíonn ribíní deataigh ó gach simléir; i gcistiní
tá scáileanna laistiar des na cuirtiní lása ag ullmhú suipéir.

Éiríonn liathróidí caide idir chrainn ghiúise na gcúlghairdín.
Tá madra caorach breac is sotar gallda ar an bplásóg
mar a bhfuil *round*áil sliotar le clos is scata garsún ag
screachail.
Tá dhá snag breac go dícheallach i mbun cleatarála ar an díon.

Lasann fuinneoga móra na seomraí suite le loinnir ghorm
is tá teaghlaigh ag cruinniú timpeall ar scáileáin na dteilifíseán,
mar a bhfuil an nuacht ar siúl is iad ag rá go bhfuil buamaí is
diúracáin
ag titim ar bhruachbhailte mar seo i mBaghdad, Tel Aviv,
Dhathran.

Eanáir, 1991

NUALA NÍ DHOMHNAILL (*b.* 1952)

The View from Cabinteely

A swivel-wing of light. The suburban drone
kicking in after one more hopeless day.
Kids home from school. Grown-ups from the job.
Doors and windows flashing. Grimaces. Grins.

A car backfires in the next avenue.
The bicycle-brigade in headlong, straggling retreat.
Smoke rising from chimneys. Those shades
behind lace shades, cooking up a storm.

In back-yards footballs score direct hits
between pines. A collie and an English setter
dispute a bit of green. The thunk of a hurley-ball.
Two magpies on the roof, giving it their all.

The picture-windows now have a blue glow
where families huddle round their TV screens
for news of the missiles and smart bombs
falling on the suburbs of Baghdad, Tel Aviv, Dhahran.

January, 1991

NUALA NÍ DHOMHNAILL (*b.* 1952)
Translated from the Irish by Paul Muldoon

Bluebell

The factories were here even then,
the pylons fizzed above this same stretch
of sad canal. Juggernauts creamed
the asphalt hill. And sky might
be raddled with sunrise, or clouded grey,
but was traversed, either way,

with cables which I'm still in the habit
of counting, thirty years later,
from the vantage of a push-bike,
below the brow of Bluebell. Imagining
blackberry rambles, a country village
away on its own, with woods
enough to coax shade-loving flowers,
bluebells so profusely pooled
a child might pick one for a place-name,
and everybody else agree to wear it
afterwards. But all I can attest to
are the pylons and factories — and this
piebald horse, standing glum,
his paddock a patch of cutaway ground.
Once, I dreamed him the original
inhabitant, old man of the place,
the king dispossessed. It was a myth
to shorten my journey. But again today
it comes around, as a startling sound
assails me up by Bluebell hill:
the trouble-boast of a rooster, flung
from a hollow heaped full of tyres
and junk metal. There, with flames
blazoned on his breast, he raises himself,
rattles his wattles in defiance
of our convoyed progress. And for
a moment I credit the earth is breaking
at my heels afresh, as a horse,
a rooster, a capercaillie — all fabulous,
indefatigable creatures restored.
And that the child has picked the bluebell.

PATRICK DEELEY (*b.* 1953)

Thanksgiving
to May Sinclair

I thank God when I kneel to pray
That mine is still the middle way,

Set in a safe and sweet estate
Between the little and the great;

Not troubled with wealth's cares nor yet
Too poor where needs that cark and fret

Push out sweet leisure and green nooks,
And give no chance for talk and books.

I take my middle way between
The mansion and a lodging mean.

My cottage at the country's edge
Hath sweetbriar growing in its hedge,

Honesty, heartsease and sweet-peas,
Herb-bennet, love-in-idleness.

KATHARINE TYNAN (1859–1931)

Clondalkin Concrete

Late again! You know we keep regular hours
in Clondalkin Concrete

I was the Temp
The one who worked from five past nine till six
with no let-up
but they kept regular hours at Clondalkin Concrete

From Clondalkin Concrete I wrote a letter to Paul
I told him I was writing concrete verse
and very soon I would send them, block on clock
In Clondalkin Concrete we keep stanzas
numbered and counted carefully, cement and sand
We keep regular poems in Clondalkin Concrete

All the while I worked in Clondalkin Concrete
I must have sold a million tons of blocks
I was a bungalow blitz of a typist
invoice-neat in my work
But I wrote, Dear Paul, I dedicate to you
every block of a concrete stanza
every freezing grain of sand
for I'm up to my neck in Clondalkin Concrete

While directly gazing into my boss's watery studs
All that Fall, I shouted, All that Fall

LELAND BARDWELL (*b.* 1922)

Jesus of Clondalkin

Maybe Jesus is wandering these roads tonight,
Unrecognised, unacknowledged, utterly alone,

Passing half built apartment blocks investors own,
Passing burnt-out cars, glass shards, twisted chrome,

Threading a path through Neilstown and Quarryvale,
In Dunnes Stores white socks, with his jacket torn.

Maybe we are so adrift in our own cares that we fail
To see whip marks, collapsed veins, his crown of thorns.

DERMOT BOLGER (*b.* 1959)

In Memory of Veronica Guerin

> It matters what we journalists do.
> If I didn't think my work made a difference,
> I'd probably give it up.
> — Veronica Guerin

She must have known. As the junkies squirmed out
like grubs from the tower-blocks, shuffling their sun-shy bodies

in search of gear and Vienetta, she'd drive down through
the tenements at evening, past betting-offices, past bars,

to hold hushed truck with murderers in the buildings' shadows.
They were shabby entrepreneurs, almost children,

with their ridiculous Marvel-ian sobriquets, Zombie and the
    Vampire,
with their contested tyrannies like patches of school-yard.

She must have known they were stupid and callous as children
when she wrote them and herself into her story all that damp year

mortality became penetrable and forbidding as police-tape.
As she continued to file dispatches from the land of shattered
    windows,

to traffic gossip, to shape — in installments — a teasing penny-
    dreadful,
she must have known about the indicator's tick-tock trochees

at the traffic-light, about the black bird taking wing from the
    traffic-light,
about her glance into the rearview mirror at the motorbike

approaching through a grubby swirl of diesel fumes, into the sun,
into the shotgun's muzzle, its black-zero that was forever.

BILLY RAMSELL (*b.* 1977)

Common Ground

Through stable centuries
The Common stretched unbounded
Below the sheltering hills —
The hooves of racing horses resounded
Over its gentle sward,
From Greenhills to the glebe land
Around St Mary's —

Our interloping terraces
Cut swathes through its grass,
Overturned its topsoil
To strike our bedrock
On streets of song:
Percy French, Crotty,
Field, Bunting, Harty.

Young lords of muck
We jibed at Crumlin 'schemers'
Passing through our
Streets, scorning them as 'common' —
We knew the motley lure
Of field and builders' sand,
Of farms truncated by
Our gardens, and bramble lanes
Winding vaguely
Into uncharted country.

Neither fish nor fowl
We paddled in turbid waters,
Unsure of what was common:
The cadence of dialect,
The pitch of accent,
The ribald music of our street?
And we were surely commonplace
In our common-or-garden schemes,
Our lives common as

A million post-war children —
Crumlin common.

DECLAN COLLINGE (*b.* 1949)

The Globe on Captain's Road
for Brian McGovern

At the amphitheatre
in Waldron's back garden
we balanced on an old plank,
sipped juice from melted ice pops,
munched Marietta biscuits.
We could have been in the Abbey Theatre
watching a performance
of O'Casey or Brecht.
The puppets on Paul Hanna's hands
projected sagas onto a sheet
flapping on the line:
Captain Boyle stumbling home
from Mooney's in the village;
Mother Courage catching
the early bus to do
a bit of a cleaning job.

We screamed at Missus Punch —
tears blotting her papier-mâché face —
to hide the baby under the bed,
away from her husband's
unrelenting fists;
booed at the Garda
as he tried to stop two women
tousling over a ball that flattened
antirrhinums and dented
the symmetry of a privet hedge.

Warrior, magician, maid and hag,
all the archetypes were there;
impersonating the neighbours,
exposing the quirks in our society
at the amphitheatre
in Waldron's back garden.

TERRI MURRAY (*b.* 1956)

Father and Son 1966

In Dublin drawl
My grandfather holds forth
On Tolstoy and Joyce:
Autodidact, authoritative voice,
Resilient veteran
Of Salonica,
The Volta
And the Theatre Royal,
He has met them all
From Yeats to Behan.

Over pints in The Cherry Tree
My retiring father
Cringes at the bravado
Of his talk, turns impatiently,
Mindful of makeshift long ago
In the rover's absence,
The precarious childhood
In the inner city.

Undaunted, Lennie banters
In Dublin Italian
As Mrs Morelli drains
Sizzling chips, smiling
Gap-toothed, radiant

As the Mezzogiorno, winking
An eye under his spell,
Whispering to my father
"He's a very well,
Keeping a very well!"

On greasy plates
The white-boned ribs of ray
And smell of chips
Tell of the return
Of father and son,
Of guarded reconciliation:
Not quite at Ithaca
Ulysses does his clips
And heads for Inchicore —
At seventy-six, with a
Wiry frame and gimlet mind
He cannot ask for more.

DECLAN COLLINGE (*b.* 1949)

Funeral Games

Dommo didn't expect to see boss-man Acchi
At the NCT centre,
Testing wheels and hubs,
Eyes under thick eyebrows

Weighing up everything.
He nodded towards a red-haired guy
Holding two restless mares.
Dommo read ice in his eyes.

It will not be easy to score there, he thought.
But Acchi insisted, a race on the M50.
"In memory of the Westies".
To the roundabout and back.

347

Taunted, Menie from Inchicore
Stroked a windshield overlaid with gold.
Dommo agreed and they sped off
On the fast lane in a quiver of silver light

Disturbing rows of flowers on the edge
And rooks cawing overhead,
Menie, electric hair flowing,
Sped by on the West-Link.

But Dommo caught him at the Red Cow.
In a trail of dust both cars were locked
At speed on the return lap.
Reckless now nearing the finishing line

Zeus dared Menie to show his skills.
An unseen hand whipped the cars around
Locked in an embrace.
A haze grows as flames rise.

PADDY GLAVIN (*b.* 1934)

Them's Your Mammy's Pills
for Edward McLachlan

They'd scraped the top soil off the garden
and every step or two they'd hurled a concrete block
bolsters of mud like hippos from the hills
rolled on the planters plantings of the riff-raff of the city.

The schizophrenic planners had finished off their job
folded their papers, put away their pens —
the city clearances were well ahead.

And all day long a single child was crying
while his father shouted: Don't touch them,
them's your mammy's pills.

I set to work with zeal to play 'Doll's House',
'Doll's Life', 'Doll's Garden'
while my adolescent sons played 'Temporary Heat'
in the living room out front
and drowned the opera of admonitions:
Don't touch them, them's your mammy's pills.

Fragile as needles the women wander forth
laddered with kids, the unborn one ahead
to forge the mile through mud and rut
where mulish earth-removers rest, a crazy sculpture.

They are going back to the city for the day
this is all they live for —
going back to the city for the day.

The line of shops and solitary pub
are camouflaged like check-points on the border
the supermarket stretches emptily
a circus of sausages and time
the till-girl gossips in the veg department
Once in a while a woman might come in
to put another pound on
the electronic toy for Christmas.

From behind the curtains every night
the video lights are flickering, butcher blue
Don't touch them, them's your mammy's pills.

No one has a job in Killinarden
nowadays they say it is a no-go area
I wonder, then, who goes and does not go
in this strange forgotten world
of video and valium.

I visited my one-time neighbour
not so long ago. She was sitting
in the hangover position.

I knew she didn't want to see me
although she'd cried when we were leaving.

I went my way
through the quietly rusting motor cars and prams,
past the barricades of wire, the harmony of junk.
The babies that I knew are punk-size now
and soon children will have children
and new voices ring the *leitmotif*:

Don't touch them, them's your mammy's pills.

LELAND BARDWELL (*b.* 1922)

Warriors

The Grand Canal is silvery as a new coin.
I'm on the Luas thinking of nothing in particular
when a man, swift as an antelope,
runs from the houses towards Suir Road.
Legs, long as spears, gather speed —
this Luas is a wild one

broken free from the herd.

On the grass, thawing frost steams a mirage,
dust rises.
His winter coat, shirt and navy trousers
dissolve to gorgeous Maasai colours.
He gleams like the skin on these tracks,
each muscle and sinew
zig-zagging a perfect quarter arc
bearing down on the metal beast,

and I'm back on the Midland streets
side-stepping pools of greenish-
hued cow dung. Straw

straggles from trailers, haggling
wasps swarm around my ears.

A cow breaks from a loose bunch,
is chased by a farmer in breeches
held up with braces, his face berry-red,
legs akimbo; the stick in his hand
orchestrating a fair day.
Later, there'll be whiskey in the pubs,
chocolate for children of the tribe
creeping in to sit on the long benches.

My warrior comes on board
scarcely out of breath. Beyond
Rialto
Fatima
St James's
Heuston Station,

we journey towards the city.

EILEEN CASEY (*b*. 1956)

The Bingo Bus

In Killinarden there was nothing —
Nothing — but nearer town
There was the Bingo Bus

The Bingo Bus, the Bingo Bus
Nearer to Thee, my God, the Bingo Bus
And *Strip the Willow,* they played
With the driver, trussed the conductor —
Danced *Turkey in the Straw.*

Every Thursday without fail
The ladies rode on the Bingo Bus

And Booze before Bingo and after
And lots of Booze in between
Returning late from Bingo
They ate the conductor whole.

We in Killinarden, wanted, O so much
To have a Bingo Bus of our own.

We wrote to the Authorities,
Begged and begged on our knees.
TDs were hammered, we marched,
Made flags, went on hunger strike
Outside the Dáil.

You lot aren't ready for Bingo,
You've only been here a year,
You must have lots more babies
Before you deserve a Bingo Bus.

So every year to the clinic,
Three out, one in, four out, one in,
But still no Bingo Bus.

I had to leave Killinarden
Wearied from making flags,
Marching and lobbying and having kids.
So I moved right into a hotel.
St Brendan's is its name.

I make sanitary towels for Bingo players,
I do my bit for Bingo players,
I am on the ball for Bingo players,
I'm saving up for Bingo,
Saving up for Bingo.

LELAND BARDWELL (*b.* 1922)

In the Spring of My Forty-First Year

I was never young or always was —
and was forever on my way

to becoming someone
whom I could sit or be silent with

running through Marlay Park
or up into Glencullen

with the rain on my face
my heart thirsting for nothing

no clock to keep time
no finish line either

the ease of distance in my legs
the breath bringing me

to who I am
away from the country

across time
to where we are

and back again to rough terrain
where I am no one nowhere

a figure in the evening
passing

my footfall ringing silently
through Pearse's Park

or Pine Forest or farther still
wordless and weightless

moving like the sun-scattered light
at once and irrevocably

towards you

PAUL PERRY (*b.* 1972)

ACKNOWLEDGEMENTS

The poems in this anthology are reprinted from the following books and are reproduced here with the permission of the publishers, authors or estates who retain all rights and to whom requests for subsequent permissions should be addressed. Poems and song understood to be out of copyright are not listed. The editors and publisher are grateful to all of the copyright holders for their permission and support.

Fergus Allen: *Gas Light & Coke* (Dedalus Press, 2006), 'The Fall' by kind permission of the author; Leland Bardwell: *Dostoevsky's Grave: Selected Poems* (Dedalus Press, 1991) and *The Noise of Masonry Settling* (Dedalus Press, 2006); Sebastian Barry: *The Water-Colourist* (Dolmen Press, 1983), by kind permission of the author; Samuel Beckett: *Collected Poems* (Faber and Faber, 2012), by kind permission of Faber and Faber Ltd; John Berryman: 'Dream Song 321' by kind permission of Kate Donohue, executrix of the John Berryman Estate, (c) The Estate of John Berryman, 2014; Eavan Boland: *New Collected Poems* (Carcanet Press, 2005), by kind permission of Carcanet Press, 4th Floor, Alliance House, 30 Cross Street, Manchester M2 7AQ, UK; John Boland: *Brow Head* (Abbey Press, 1999), by kind permission of the author; Dermot Bolger: *Taking My Letters Back* (New Island, 1998), *The Chosen Moment* (New Island, 2004), *The Venice Suite: A Voyage Through Loss* (New Island, 2012), by kind permission of the author; Pat Boran: *New and Selected Poems* (Dedalus Press, 2007), *The Next Life* (Dedalus Press, 2012), additional poems by kind permission of the author; Rory Brennan: by kind permission of the author; Christy Brown: 'City Dweller' from *Collected Poems* (Secker & Warburg, 1982), by permission of The Random House Group Limited; Paddy Bushe: *To Ring in Silence: New and Selected Poems* (Dedalus Press, 2008); Kevin Byrne: by kind permission of the author; Mairéad Byrne: *You Have to Laugh: New + Selected Poems* (Barrow Street, 2013); Rosemary Canavan: 'Visiting the Book of Kells', *Trucker's Moll* (Salmon Poetry, 2009), by kind permission of Salmon Poetry; Moya Cannon: 'Isolde's Tower', *The Parchment Boat* (Gallery Press, 1997), by permission of The Gallery Press, Loughcrew Oldcastle, Co. Meath; Eileen Casey: *Drinking the Colour Blue* (New Island, 2008), by kind permission of the author; Philip Casey: *tried & sentenced: selected poems* (eMaker Editions, 2014); Austin Clarke: *Collected Poems,* ed. Dardis Clarke (Carcanet Press, 2008); Harry Clifton: 'Eccles Street, Bloomsday 1982' and 'Magazine Hill' from *The Desert Route: Poems 1973-1988* (Gallery Press, 1992), 'The Early Houses' and 'A Son! A Son!' from *The Winter Sleep of Captain Lemass* (Bloodaxe Books, 2012); Rhoda Coghill: *The Bright Hillside* (Hodges, Figgis & Co., 1948), no traceable copyright holder; Declan Collinge: *Common Ground* (Inisfail Press, 1996) and *The Lonely Hush of Eve/ Tost Uaigneach na hOíche: Selected and New Poems/Rogha Dánta agus Dánta Nua* (Mentor Books, 2012), by kind permission of the author and publisher; Padraic Colum: by kind permission of the Estate of Padraic Colum; Enda Coyle-Greene: *Snow Negatives* (Dedalus Press, 2006) and *Map of the Last* (Dedalus Press, 2013; Maurice Craig: *Poems* (Liberties Press, 2011), by kind permission of Michael Craig; Anthony Cronin: from 'The End of the Modern World', *Collected Poems* (New Island, 2004); Catherine Ann Cullen: *A Bone in My Throat* (Doghouse, 2007) and *Strange Familiar* (Doghouse, 2013); Tony Curtis: *Folk* (Arc Publications, 2011); Pádraig J. Daly: *This Day's Importance* (Raven Arts Press, 1981), by kind permission of the author, *Poems Selected and New* (Dedaus Press, 1988); Ailbhe Darcy: *Imaginary Menagerie* (Bloodaxe Books, 2011); Michael Davitt: 'Sráid an Amhrais' from *The Oomph of Quicksilver / Freacnairc Mhearcair: Selected Poems / Rogha Danta 1970–1998* (Cork University Press, 2000), by kind permission of Joe Davitt, translation by kind permission of Paul Muldoon; Gerald Dawe: by kind permission of the author; John F. Deane: 'The Dead and the Undead of St. Michan's' from *Manhandling the Deity* (Carcanet Press, 2003), 'Dublin, Dublin' by kind permission of the author; Patrick Deeley: *Groundswell: New and Selected Poems* (Dedalus Press, 2013); Damien Dempsey: by kind permission of the author and of Spirit Management; Francis Devine: *Red Star, Blue Moon* (Elo Publications, Dublin, 1997), by kind permission of the author; Denis Devlin: *Collected Poems* (Dedalus Press, 1989); Neil Donnelly: *Tullamore Train* (Arlen House, 2011); Katie Donovan: *Rootling: New & Selected Poems* (Bloodaxe Books, 2002); Theo Dorgan: *What This Earth Cost Us* (Dedalus Press, 2008), 'Croke Park' and 'Vigil'' by kind permission of the author; Katherine Duffy: *Sorrow's Egg* (Dedalus Press, 2011); Noel Duffy: *In the Library of Lost Objects* (Ward Wood Publishing, 2011); Séan Dunne: 'The Jewish Museum in Portobello', *Collected* (Gallery Press, 2005); Paul Durcan: poems copyright © Paul Durcan, reproduced by permission of the author c/o Rogers, Coleridge & White Ltd., 20 Powis Mews, London W11 1JN; John Ennis: *In a Green Shade* (Dedalus Press, 1991), by kind permission of the author; Kevin Faller: *Lament for the Bull Island and Other Poems* (Goldsmith Press, Newbridge, Co. Kildare, 1973); Gerard Fanning: *Hombre: New & Selected Poems* (Dedalus Press, 2011); Paddy Glavin: *Playground* (Lapwing Publications, 2011), by kind permission of the author; Oliver St John Gogarty: *The Poems & Plays* (Colin Smythe, 2004), by kind permission of Colin Smythe Ltd; Mark Granier: 'From Mount Street Bridge' from *The Sky Road* (Salmon Poetry, 2007) and 'Ringsend' from *Haunt* (forthcoming), by kind permission of Salmon Poetry, 'A Photograph of Fade Street' from *Fade Street* (Salt Publishing,

2010), by permission of the author; Robert Greacen: *Collected Poems, 1944-1994* (Lagan Press, 1995), by kind permission of the Estate of Robert Greacen; Eamon Grennan: 'Wet Morning, Clareville Road', *So It Goes* (Gallery Press, 1999); Vona Groarke: 'Imperial Measure' and 'Plane' from *Flight* (Gallery Press, 2002); Maurice Harmon: 'Undergraduate' parts 1 & 10 from *The Last Regatta* (Salmon Poetry, 2000), by kind permission of Salmon Poetry; Michael Hartnett: Haiku 1, 2, 73 and 78, from 'Inchicore Haiku', 'Fairview Park, 6 a.m.' and 'Charleville Mall Sestina' from *Collected Poems* (Gallery Press, 2001); Anne Haverty: *The Beauty of the Moon* (Chatto & Windus, 1999), by kind permission of the author; Seamus Heaney: 'Viking Dublin: Trial Pieces' and 'The Strand' from *Opened Ground* (Faber and Faber, 1998) by kind permission of Faber and Faber, 'Beacons at Bealtaine' and 'Dublin 4' by kind permission of the Estate of Seamus Heaney; FR Higgins: *Father and Son: Selected Poems* (Arlen House, 2013); Ben Howard: from 'Dublin in July', *Leaf, Sunlight, Asphalt* (Salmon Poetry, 2009) by kind permission of Salmon Poetry; Pearse Hutchinson: 'On the Crest of the Bridge at Portobello' from *At Least for a While* (Gallery Press, 2008), 'Refusals' from *Collected Poems* (Gallery Press, 2002); Valentin Iremonger: *Sandymount, Dublin* (Dedalus Press, 1988); Derry Jeffares: *Brought Up in Dublin* (Colin Smythe, 1987), by kind permission of Colin Smythe Ltd; Biddy Jenkinson: *Dán na hUidhre* (Coiscéim, 1991), by kind permission of the author; Fred Johnston: *The Oracle Room* (Cinnamon Press, 2007); John Jordan: *Selected Poems* (Dedalus Press, 2008) by kind permission of the Estate of John Jordan; Trevor Joyce: *with the first dream of fire they hunt the cold* (New Writers' Press, 2001); Patrick Kavanagh: *Collected Poems* (Allen Lane, 2004), edited by Antoinette Quinn, by kind permission of the Trustees of the Estate of the late Katherine B Kavanagh, through the Jonathan Williams Literary Agency; Colm Keegan, 'Stony, Grey, Soiled' from *Don't Go There* (Salmon Poetry, 2012), by kind permission of Salmon Poetry; Stephen Kennedy: 'Waiting in the Eye and Ear Hospital on Christmas Eve', by kind permission of the author; Brendan Kennelly: *Familiar Strangers: New & Selected Poems 1960-2004* (Bloodaxe Books, 2004); Thomas Kinsella: *Collected Poems* (Carcanet Press, 1999); Anatoly Kudryavitsky: by kind permission of the author; Winifred M. Letts: By kind permission of Mrs. Oriana Conner, great-niece of Winifred M. Letts; James Liddy: *Fest City* (Arlen House, 2010); Dave Lordan: 'Dublin Spire' from *Invitation to a Sacrifice* (Salmon Poetry, 2010), by kind permission of Salmon Poetry; Brian Lynch: *New and Renewed: Poems 1967-2004* (New Island Books, 2004); Phil Lynott: 'Dublin', by kind permission of Caroline and David Taraskevics, with thanks; Catherine Phil MacCarthy: *The Invisible Threshold* (Dedalus Press, 2012); Patrick MacDonogh: 'Feltrim Hill' from *Poems* (Gallery Press, 2001), by kind permission of the Estate of Patrick MacDonogh, c/o The Gallery Press; Sorley MacLean: *From Wood to Ridge/O Choille gu Bearradh: Collected Poems* (Carcanet Press, 1999); Louis MacNeice: *Collected Poems* (Faber and Faber, 2007), by kind permission of David Higham Associates; Derek Mahon: 'At the Shelbourne', 'At the Gate Theatre' and 'shiver in your tenement', *New Collected Poems* (Gallery Press, 2011); Gerald Mangan: *Waiting for the Storm* (Bloodaxe Books, 1990), by kind permission of the author; Tom Mathews: *The Owl & The Pussycat and Other Poems* (Dedalus Press, 2009) and *No Return Game* (Dedalus Press, 2013); Hugh Maxton: *The Engraved Passion: New and Selected Poems 1970-1991* (Dedalus Press, 1992), by kind permission of the author; James J. McAuley: *New & Selected Poems* (Dedalus Press, 2005), 'Ringsend Ferry' by kind permission of the author; John McAuliffe: 'North Brunswick Lullaby', *A Better Life* (Gallery Press, 2002); James McCabe: *The White Battlefield of Silence* (Dedalus Press, 1999); Thomas McCarthy: 'Dublin' from *The Last Geraldine Officer* (Anvil Press Poetry, 2009); Gerry McDonnell: by kind permission of the author; Hugh McFadden: 'Local Nightlight' from *Empire of Shadows* (Salmon Poetry, 2012), by kind permission of Salmon Poetry, other poems from *Pieces of Time* (Lapwing Publications, 2004), by kind permission of the author; Iggy McGovern: *The King of Suburbia* (Dedalus Press, 2005); Frank McGuinness: 'Booterstown', 'The Stillorgan Road' and 'Morehampton Road', from *Booterstown* (Gallery Press, 1994), 'The Stillorgan Road' from *In a Town of Five Thousand People* (Gallery Press, 2012); John McNamee: *A Station Called Heaven* (Weaver Publications, 2007), by kind permission of the author; Ted McNulty: 'St Teresa's – Clarendon Street' from *On the Block* (Salmon Poetry, 1995) and 'The Ring' from *Rough Landings* (Salmon Poetry, 1992) by kind permission of Salmon Poetry and the author's estate; Paula Meehan: *Mysteries of the Home* (Dedalus Press, 2013), 'Molly Malone' from *Dharmakaya* (Carcanet Press, 2000); Máire Mhac an tSaoi: *An Paróiste Míorúilteach: Rogha Dánta / The Miraculous Parish: Selected Poems* (Cló Iar-Chonnacht / O'Brien Press, 2011), translation by Louis de Paor; John Montague: 'Herbert Street Revisited', *Collected Poems* (Gallery Press, 2012); Alan Moore: 'Glasnevin North' and 'Casimir Road' from *How Now!* (Anvil Press Poetry, 2010); Alan Jude Moore, 'Perversion at the Winding Stair Bookshop & Café' from *Black State Cars* (Salmon Poetry, 2004) and '1941 (North Strand)' from *Lost Republics* (Salmon Poetry, 2008), by kind permission of Salmon Poetry; Aidan Murphy: *Stark Naked Blues* (New Island Books, 1997); Richard Murphy: *The Pleasure Ground: Poems 1952-2012* (Bloodaxe Books, 2013); Willa Murphy: by kind permission of the author; Paul Murray: *Paper Trails* (13th Door, 2010), by kind permission of the author; Terri Murray: *The Authority of Winter* (Stonebridge Publications, 2007), by kind permission of the author; Jordi Pujol Nadal: *Greatest Hits* (66 rpm,

Barcelona, 2013), translated from the Catalan by Ruth Murray, by permission of the author and the translator; Eileán Ní Chuilleanáin: 'Trinity New Library' from *Acts and Monuments* (Gallery Press, 1972), 'You never saw a bed-end in a Protestant fence' from *The Sun-fish* (Gallery Press, 2009); Nuala Ní Dhomhnaill: 'Radharc ó Chábán tSíle / The View from Cabinteely', translated by Paul Muldoon, from *The Astrakhan Cloak* (Gallery Press, 1992); Jean O'Brien: *Dangerous Dresses* (Bradshaw Books, 2005) and *The Shadow Keeper* (Salmon Poetry, 1997), by kind permission of the publishers; Peggy O'Brien: *Frogspotting* (Dedalus Press, 2009); Julie O'Callaghan: *Tell Me This is Normal: New & Selected Poems* (Bloodaxe Books, 2008); Clairr O'Connor: *Breast* (Astrolabe Press, 2004); Ulick O'Connor: *The Kiss: New & Selected Poems and Translations* (Salmon Poetry, 2008), by kind permission of Salmon Poetry; Máirtín Ó Direáin: *Na Dánta* (Cló Iar-Chonnacht), by kind permission of the publisher, translations by Declan Collinge by kind permission of the author; Hugh O'Donnell: *Planting a Mouth* (Doghouse, 2007); John O'Donnell: *On Water* (forthcoming, Dedalus Press, 2014); Mary O'Donnell: *September Elegies* (Lapwing, 2003), by kind permission of the author; Dennis O'Driscoll: 'Flatland' from *New and Selected Poems* (Anvil Press Poetry, 2004); Gréagóir Ó Dúill: *New Room Windows* (Doghouse, 2008); Sheila O'Hagan, 'Going to the Gaiety' from *The Peacock's Eye* (Salmon Poetry, 1992), by kind permission of Salmon Poetry, 'Hopkins in Newman House' from *The Living Stream: A Festschrift for Theo Dorgan* (Why Go Bald Books, 2000); Michael O'Loughlin: *In This Life* (New Island, 2011), and *Another Nation: New & Selected Poems* (Dublin, New Island Books, 1994/UK Arc Publications, 1996), by kind permission of the author; Nessa O'Mahony: by kind permission of the author; Liam Ó Muirthile: *An Fuíoll Feá: Rogha Dánta / Wood Cuttings: New and Selected Poems* (Cois Life, 2013), by kind permission of the publisher and author, translation by kind permission of Gabriel Rosenstock; Cathal Ó Searcaigh: *Out in the Open* (Cló Iar-Chonnacht, 1997), translation by Frank Sewell; Micheal O'Siadhail: *Collected Poems* (Bloodaxe Books, 2013); Pádraig Ó Snodaigh: by kind permission of the author, translation by kind permission of Paddy Bushe; Seumas O'Sullivan: by kind permission of Frances Sommerville / The Estate of Seumas O'Sullivan; Frank Ormsby: *Ripe for Company* (Ulsterman Publications, 1971), by kind permission of the author; Karl Parkinson: by kind permission of the author; Evangeline Paterson: *Lucifer, With Angels* (Dedalus Press, 1994), by kind permission of the Estate of Evangeline Paterson; Basil Payne: *Sunlight on a Square* (John Augustin, 1961), by kind permission of Norbert Payne; Keith Payne: by kind permission of the author; Paul Perry, from *Gunpowder Valentine: New and Selected Poems* (forthcoming, Dedalus Press, 2014); Billy

Ramsell: *Complicated Pleasures* (Dedalus Press, 2007); Padraig Rooney: *In the Bonsai Garden* (Raven Arts Press, 1988), by kind permission of the author; Liam Reilly: 'Summer in Dublin', written by Liam Reilly, as performed by Bagatelle, by kind permission of Bardis Music Co. Ltd; Gabriel Rosenstock: by kind permission of the author; Maurice Scully: *Love Poems and Others* (Raven Arts Press, 1981), by kind permission of the author; John Sheahan: by kind permission of the author; Peter Sirr: 'A Short Walk' from *The Ledger of Fruitful Exchange* (Gallery Press, 1995), 'Madly Singing in the City', 'Essex Street', 'The Hunt', 'Sráid na gCaorach' and 'Peter Street' from *Bring Everything* (Gallery Press, 2000); Michael Smith: *Collected Poems* (Shearsman Books, 2009) by kind permission of the author; Gerard Smyth: *The Fullness of Time: New and Selected Poems* (Dedalus Press, 2010), and new poems by permission of the author; Eithne Strong: *Spatial Nosing* (Salmon Poetry, 1993), by kind permission of Salmon Poetry and the author's estate; Francis Stuart: by kind permission of the Literary Executors of Francis Stuart; Betty Thompson: *Painting the Vestibule* (Scallta Media, 2009), by kind permission of Scallta Media; Daniel Tobin: *The Narrows* (Four Way Books, NY, 2005), by kind permission of the author; Jessica Traynor: *Liffey Swim* (forthcoming, Dedalus Press, 2014); Tomas Venclova: *The Junction: Selected Poems* (Bloodaxe Books, 2008), translated by Ellen Hinsey; Eugene R. Watters: *The Week-end of Dermot and Grace* (Allen Figgis, 1964), by kind permission of Rita Kelly; David Wheatley: Sonnets 1 and 12 from 'Sonnets to James Clarence Mangan', *Misery Hill* (Gallery Press, 2000); Joseph Woods: *Ocean Letters* (Dedalus Press, 2011); Macdara Woods: *Collected Poems* (Dedalus Press, 2012); Máiríde Woods: *The Lost Roundness of the World* (Astrolabe Press, 2006); Enda Wyley: *Poems for Breakfast* (Dedalus Press, 2004) and *To Wake to This* (Dedalus Press, 2009).

Every effort has been made to trace the copyright holders of the poems and songs included in this book. The editors and publisher apologise for any errors in or omissions from the above list and, upon receipt of written notice from the copyright holder, undertake to make good any such errors or omissions in future editions.

INDEX OF PLACE NAMES

Some place names appear more than once throughout this book (O'Connell Street, Grafton Street, the River Liffey, etc.) while many poems include mention of more than a single location. A small number do not make an explicit geographic or toponymic reference; in these instances we have taken the liberty of locating the poems in a part of the city where they might most readily come to mind: Yeats's 'Easter 1916', for instance, close to the GPO, Dennis O'Driscoll's 'Flatlands' in the general vicinity of Rathmines. For all of these reasons, this Index of Place Names should be taken as a general starting point rather than as a definitive guide to the places referenced in the book.

INDEX OF AUTHORS

Authors are listed alphabetically, with dates and place of birth included where known. Additional place names refer to the usual or long-term residence of authors born elsewhere. More extensive biographical notes may be found on the Dedalus Press website at *www.dedaluspress.com.*

A WORD OF THANKS

The editors and publisher would like to thank all those who have helped, in whatever way, over the past couple of years to make this anthology possible. We wish to thank The Arts Council / An Chomhairle Ealaíon for its support in this and other Dedalus Press projects; at Dublin City Libraries our thanks are due to Margaret Hayes, Dublin City Librarian; at Dublin UNESCO City of Literature our thanks and appreciation to Jane Alger, Jackie Lynam and Liz Cuddy, and to Michael Molloy and Hugh Comerford; at Poetry Ireland our thanks to Director Maureen Kennelly, and former Director Joseph Woods, for their enthusiastic support, also to Ayoma Bowe and in particular Paul Lenehan for his eagle-eyed proof-reading.

In securing permissions for this anthology we were fortunate to receive a great deal of support from the writing and publishing community: to publishers Neil Astley and all at Bloodaxe Books, Michael Schmidt and all at Carcanet Press, Peter Fallon and all at The Gallery Press, Jessie Lendennie and all at Salmon Poetry and Noel King at Doghouse Books, among others, our sincere thanks. Special thanks and acknowledgements are due to Dermot Bolger, both as poet and editor, for his generous help and expert advice.

Among the many others who have helped or advised along the way are Samantha Holman at the Irish Copyright Licensing Agency, writers (and readers) Seamus Heaney, Dennis O'Driscoll, Theo Dorgan, Paula Meehan, Paddy Bushe, Cathal Ó Searcaigh, Pádraig Ó Snodaigh, Liam Carson and Máire Nic Aodh. Thanks too to Lucy Collins, Andrew Carpenter, Philip Coleman, Jonathan Williams and Niall Stokes, for suggestions and bridge-building.

In terms of time and energy, a project as ambitious as this could never have been realised by a small press like Dedalus without the enthusiastic assistance of a number of part-time volunteers over recent months. To Aoife Byrne, Alanna Maxwell, Nicole Flattery and Laura King, heartfelt thanks and appreciation: if this is your first book to see into print, may it not be your last! *Go n-éirí an bóthar libh go léir.*

And, finally, sincere thanks to Raffaela Tranchino, General Manager at Dedalus Press, and to Lee and Luca Boran for their invaluable assistance with a variety of technological challenges!

ABOUT THE EDITORS

PAT BORAN was born in Portlaoise in 1963 and has lived in Dublin since the mid 1980s. He has been Writer-in-Residence in a number of city institutions, is a former editor of *Poetry Ireland Review,* former presenter of *The Enchanted Way* and *The Poetry Programme* on RTÉ Radio 1, and is currently editor at Dedalus Press. He has published five collections of poems, most recently *The Next Life* (2012), as well as *New and Selected Poems* (2007). His books have been translated into a number of languages. His prose works include *A Short History of Dublin* (1999), the writers' handbook *The Portable Creative Writing Workshop* (reissued, 2013) and the memoir *The Invisible Prison: Scenes from an Irish Childhood* (2009). He has published fiction for adults and children, and his children's book *All the Way from China* (1998) was a finalist for the Bisto Book of the Year. He has edited almost 100 books of poetry including half a dozen previous anthologies, among them, with co-editor Peter Sirr, the audio CD *Dublin 15: Poems of the City (Irish Writers' Centre, 1997)* and, in 2011, *Shine On,* in support of those affected by mental ill health. His awards include the Patrick Kavanagh Award and the Lawrence O'Shaughnessy Award for Poetry. He is a member of Aosdána.

GERARD SMYTH was born in Dublin in 1951. He is a poet, critic and journalist. His poetry has appeared in publications in Ireland, Britain and the United States, as well as in translation, since the late 1960s when his first poems were published by David Marcus in the New Irish Writing Page of *The Irish Press* and by James Simmons in *The Honest Ulsterman.* New Writers' Press published a limited edition small collection, *The Flags Are Quiet,* in 1969 and another limited, hand-printed edition, *Twenty Poems* in 1971, followed by *Orchestra of Silence,* a Tara Telephone publication, also in 1971. This early work also appeared in the Press's celebrated journal *The Lace Curtain.* Smyth is the author of seven poetry collections, most recently *The Mirror Tent* (2007) and his volume of new and selected poems, *The Fullness of Time,* with an introduction by Thomas McCarthy, was published by Dedalus Press in 2010. For many years he was Managing Editor at *The Irish Times* and continues to contribute to that publication in the role of Poetry Editor. He is the 2012 recipient of the Lawrence O'Shaughnessy Award for Poetry and a member of Aosdána.

Dedalus Press

Established in 1985, and named for James
Joyce's literary alter ego, the Dedalus Press
is one of Ireland's longest running and best-
known literary imprints, with a particular
interest in contemporary Irish poetry.

For more information, or to purchase
copies of this or other Dedalus Press titles,
visit **www.dedaluspress.com**.

*"One of the most outward-looking
poetry presses in Ireland and the UK"*
—UNESCO.org